Praise for
Chinese Calligraphy and Painting Studies in Postwar America: New Perspectives

"Historiographical studies, personal reminiscences, and autobiographical accounts by eight leading scholars of Chinese art history present a vivid picture of how formative figures in the field shaped American understanding of Chinese art. These accounts of what was accomplished in the decades after WWII, accompanied by suggestions for the future, are invaluable readings for students and scholars alike."
Julia F. Andrews, Professor of Art History at The Ohio State University; author of *Painters and Politics in the People's Republic of China* **and co-author (with Kuiyi Shen) of** *The Art of Modern China*

"This remarkable collection of essays by outstanding authorities celebrates some of the influential personalities who have shaped the field of Chinese art. They give a kaleidoscopic view of the diverse ways in which knowledge of Chinese art is acquired and transmitted."
Alfreda Murck, author of *Poetry and Painting in Song China: The Subtle Art of Dissent* **and co-editor (with Wen C. Fong) of** *Words and Images: Chinese Poetry, Calligraphy and Painting*

"*Chinese Calligraphy and Painting Studies in Postwar America: New Perspectives* presents a collection of eight unique essays by experts in the field. It examines the trajectory of academic research on Chinese art history in the United States, which in recent years has become the center of the field. The book offers an opportunity to engage with the latest scholarship on Chinese art and discover how it arrived at its current state. The wide-ranging and insightful essays include historiographies of art historical research, veteran art historians' vivid memories of firsthand research experiences, biographical and scholarly investigations of major players in the field, and the systematic analysis of path-breaking explorations conducted by

U.S. scholars. In reading, we are reminded how closely Chinese art history is connected to our own time and place. The book liberates the history of Chinese art from hackneyed narratives anchored solely in historical past and geographical confines, while providing a compelling account of how the history of art history has itself become a new avenue of academic pursuit."
J. P. Park is the June and Simon Li Associate Professor in the History of Art and Fellow of Lincoln College, University of Oxford; author of *Art by the Book: Painting Manuals and the Leisure Life in Late Ming China* **and** *A New Middle Kingdom: Painting and Cultural Politics in Late Chosŏn Korea (1700–1850)*

"This anthology reveals how the history of the collecting, study, and teaching of Chinese calligraphy and painting in Postwar America has been enhanced and stimulated by diverse cultural, historical, and institutional factors. The essays provide a spectrum of methodological perspectives and are certain to contribute to a better understanding of the historiography of art history in general and Chinese art history in particular."
Hanwei Wang, Professor of Art History and Director of the Jiangsu Research Center of Calligraphy and Painting, both at Nanjing Normal University; author of *Studies on the Calligraphy of Dunhuang Documents in the Southern Dynasties* **(in Chinese)**

"A groundbreaking collective endeavor, this anthology shall appeal to anyone who is interested in the journey that the study of Chinese calligraphy and painting has taken in the United States in the past seven decades. Chapters in this volume interweave stories of the teaching, mentorship, scholarship, and lives of giants, pioneers, and legendary figures in the field of Chinese art history, and offer multifaceted perspectives for understanding the historical, cultural, and institutional as well as personal factors that shape the practice of the field."
Meiqin Wang, Professor of Art History, California State University Northridge and author of *Socially Engaged Art in Contemporary China*

Chinese Calligraphy and Painting Studies in Postwar America

Chinese Calligraphy and Painting Studies in Postwar America

New Perspectives

Edited with an Introduction by Jason C. Kuo

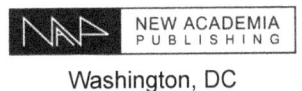

Washington, DC

Copyright © 2020 by Jason C. Kuo
New Academia Publishing, 2021

All rights reserved. No part of this book may be reproduced or transmitted in any form or by any means, electronic or mechanical, including photocopying, recording, or by any information storage and retrieval system.

Printed in the United States of America

Library of Congress Control Number: 2019920720
ISBN 978-1-7333980-7-7 paperback (alk. paper)

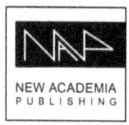

New Academia Publishing, 4401-A Connecticut Ave. NW, #236,
Washington, DC 20008
info@newacademia.com - www.newacademia.com

Contents

Acknowledgments and Note on Transcription	viii
Introduction, *Jason C. Kuo*	1
Chapter 1: Approaches to the History of Chinese Calligraphy in American Scholarship *Stephen J. Goldberg*	9
Chapter 2: Historiography of Liao and Jin Painting: The United States Contribution *Nancy S. Steinhardt*	33
Chapter 3: In Pursuit of Depth and Breadth: The Impact of C. C. Wang, Wai-kam Ho, and Wang Fangyu on Chinese Painting Studies *Arnold Chang*	55
Chapter 4: Collecting and Exhibiting Chinese Paintings in Postwar America: Sherman Lee and the 1954 *Chinese Landscape Painting* Exhibition *Noelle Giuffrida*	87
Chapter 5: Patrimony and Posterity: The "Confucian" Legacy of James F. Cahill (1926–2014) *Xiaoqing Zhu*	121
Chapter 6: Fault Lines: Notes toward a Memoir *Anne Burkus-Chasson*	153
Chapter 7: Michael Sullivan and His Study of Modern and Contemporary Chinese Painting *Jerome Silbergeld*	187
Chapter 8: Beyond the Seas: A Sojourn in Chinese Calligraphy and Painting *Jason C. Kuo*	209
About the Editor	235
About the Authors	236

Acknowledgments

This book has grown out of papers presented at a conference held in May 2018 at the University of Maryland, College Park with the support of a generous grant from the Henry Luce Foundation. I am most grateful to Helena Kolenda, Director of Asia Programs at the Luce Foundation, for her continued encouragement and support. I would like to express my gratitude to colleagues who came to present their research at the conference, and to graduate students who traveled from Harvard University, Columbia University, New York University, Princeton University, the University of Pennsylvania, Duke University, the Ohio State University, the University of Michigan, the University of Chicago, the University of California Los Angeles, the University of California Santa Barbara, and the University of California San Diego to participate in the conference and contribute a great deal to its success. Although both Aida Yuen Wong and Peggy Wang could not include their conference presentations in this book, their continued support is very much appreciated.

For their support and organizing special study sessions for the participants of the conference, I would like to express my gratitude to Stephen D. Allee, Associate Curator, Chinese Painting and Calligraphy, National Museum of Asian Art, The Freer Gallery of Art and Arthur M. Sackler Gallery, and Jan Stuart, Melvin R. Seiden Curator of Chinese Art, National Museum of Asian Art, The Freer Gallery of Art and Arthur M. Sackler Gallery.

I am grateful to Bonnie Thornton Dill, Dean, College of Arts and Humanities, University of Maryland, and Linda Aldoory, Associate Dean for Research and Programming in the College of Arts and Humanities, University of Maryland, for their encouragement and support.

I also would like to thank many other colleagues at the University of Maryland, especially Steven Mansbach, Meredith Gill, Anthony Colantuano, Minglang Zhou, Robert Ramsey, Michele Mason, and Janelle Wong for their support and encouragement. The technical support of Quint Gregory, Theresa Morse, Deborah Down, and Caroline Blevins in the Department of Art History and Archaeology is very much appreciated.

I thank Rebecca McGinnis for her patience, intelligence, and generosity; her organizational skills are simply remarkable. I would also like to thank Kacy Yang for her logistical support. I am most grateful to Frances Klapthor, Registrar and Associate Curator of Asian Art at the Baltimore Museum of Art, for her support over the years and her enthusiasm for this project. I would also like to acknowledge additional financial support from the Wang Fangyu Endowment for Calligraphy Education, the Center for East Asian Studies, and the Nathan and Jeanette Miller Center for Historical Studies, all at the University of Maryland, College Park, as well as from Mr. Shao-fang Wang in New Jersey and an anonymous donor in New York City.

On behalf of all of the contributors to this book, I would like to thank Joel Kalvesmaki, whose patience and editorial expertise have been indispensable.

Jason C. Kuo

Note on Transcription

In general, both the Wade-Giles and the pinyin systems of transcribing Chinese names and terms are used in this book. Exceptions include self-chosen names of modern Chinese scholars and artists (such as C. C. Wang, Wai-kam Ho, Chen Chi-kwan), names and terms in titles of publications using different systems of transcription, and a few names in Southern Chinese dialects. Japanese names and terms are transcribed according to the modified Hepburn system.

Introduction

Jason C. Kuo

The study of Chinese calligraphy and painting has, over the past seven decades, made tremendous progress in the United States. Increasing collaboration between American and Chinese institutions and scholars has contributed to better understanding of Chinese art history. Scholarship on Chinese calligraphy and painting in the United States has been shaped by a number of historical, cultural, and institutional factors. Knowing what those factors were and how they have shaped the academic discipline is critical if the field is to maintain its momentum. As the field of Chinese art history moves into postcolonial studies, institutional critique, and economic and social contextualization, it is especially important that studies focused on questions of the canon, value, historiography, and large-scale historical structures not be left behind.[1]

A number of exiles and émigré art collectors and scholars, migrating to the United States through the early part of the twentieth century, became the art historians who wove the fascinating and complex fabric of today's scholarship. Their language skills, their cultural awareness and understanding, and their private collections formed the rich and unique foundation on which scholars have built our complex field of art history. In recent years, we have mourned the deaths of many of the most prominent scholars in Chinese calligraphy and painting working in the United States. Many other scholars have retired. It is time for us to celebrate their scholarship and the American contribution to the study of Chinese calligraphy and painting. The present volume examines critically the historiography of the field of Chinese calligraphy and painting in Postwar America, to assess its achievements, and to explore how various practices in the field have been affected by the personal backgrounds of its scholars and by the constraints of its institutions (such as universities, museums, private and public funding bodies).

In "Approaches to the History of Chinese Calligraphy in American Scholarship," Stephen J. Goldberg has written a systematic account of the major contributions of American scholars to the historiography of Chinese calligraphy. This study is organized around six fundamental approaches to the study of Chinese calligraphy: the aesthetic reception of Chinese calligraphy; connoisseurship and the question of authenticity; formal analysis and the question of calligraphic style; periodization of calligraphic styles; calligraphic influence, emulation, and creative imitation; and reader reception and the genre of calligraphic texts. Each approach is introduced through a discussion of a representative work of art historical research and the methods employed for the specific topic. All the art historians discussed in this study have greatly contributed to the development of the history of Chinese calligraphy as an academic discipline.

In her essay, "Historiography of Liao and Jin Painting: The United States Contribution," Nancy S. Steinhardt offers a history of the study of Liao and Jin painting in the United States. The lack of research on the topic is due in part to the fact that the majority of Liao and Jin painting survives on walls, available for study mostly by way of archaeology, and its medium is generally regarded as inferior to painting on silk or paper. Also, traditional scholarship has tended to regard Liao and Jin painting as less rigorous, and less Chinese. Liao archaeological finds have been documented in Japanese publications and European scholarly literature since about the 1920s. Material was sometimes misidentified as Korean. Through the 1980s, Susan Bush and just a few other scholars were drawn to Liao or Jin. Ellen Laing studied Liao and Jin murals together with relief sculpture, and Linda Johnston and Robert Rorex turned to Liao murals, in attempts to authenticate paintings in U.S. collections. To date, only a handful of U.S. dissertations have focused on Liao and Jin paintings, murals, funerary drama, and sculpture. In her essay, Steinhardt calls our attention to several relevant questions: Should we distinguish Liao from Jin mural painting? Should Western Xia painting be considered in the discussion? Did Liao and Jin painting come to scholarly attention because of interest in Yuan murals? Why has adequate attention not been given to the two paintings on silk discovered in a Liao tomb at Yemaotai? What barriers steer scholars away from study of Liao and Jin? Why is Buddhist painting under Liao and Jin not well explored? Do challenging iconographic issues discourage scholars? The number of questions indicate how understudied this field is, despite the overwhelming quantity of visual material, as demonstrated in her essay.

Three giants in the field of Chinese painting studies in America are C. C. Wang (Wang Jiqian, 1907–2003), Wang Fangyu (1913–1997), and Wai-kam Ho (1924–2004). These individuals shared a love of Chinese culture and art, but approached the study of Chinese painting differently and transmitted their knowledge in distinctive ways. They represent a generation of Chinese *wenren*, or literati, who grew up in China but emigrated to the West after the Communist takeover in 1949 and lived out the rest of their lives in the United States. In "In Pursuit of Depth and Breadth: The Impact of C. C. Wang, Wai-kam Ho, and Wang Fangyu on Chinese Painting Studies," Arnold Chang informs us what he has learned from each of these experts: with C. C. Wang, through a twenty-five-year apprenticeship; with Wang Fang-yu, as a student taught at Columbia University and as a friend and occasional translator; with Wai-kam Ho, as a junior co-advisor to a private collector. He learned from each gentleman through comments overheard during viewing sessions, through personal conversations, and through auction strategy sessions. These three men bridged China and the West, and largely due to their influence the United States came to be established as a major center for Chinese painting studies. In his essay, he asks us to ponder the following important questions: How did their relationships to Chinese art change in the decades they worked in the United States? How did they engage with and share their passion for Chinese art with a Western audience? How did they not only survive but flourish in a culture that was so different from the one in which they were raised? How did they influence the way that Chinese paintings are studied, collected, and understood in the West?

In "Collecting and Exhibiting Chinese Paintings in Postwar America: Sherman Lee and the 1954 *Chinese Landscape Painting* Exhibition," Noelle Giuffrida uses the activities of American curator and museum director Sherman E. Lee (1918–2008) as a lens through which to investigate the factors that affected curators' choices of Chinese paintings to acquire and exhibit during the 1940s and 1950s. She also reveals the strategies that curators and scholars then used to present Chinese paintings in exhibitions and publications. During the immediate postwar decade (1946–1956), Lee served first as a monuments man in Occupied Japan, then as curator and assistant director at the Seattle Art Museum, and finally as curator of Asian art at the Cleveland Museum of Art. Giuffrida's essay demonstrates the largely unexplored significance of exhibitions held at American museums and of serious scholarly publications produced by experts living in the United States during this crucial period, when the field of Chinese art history was shaped.

James Cahill, in his tribute to his teacher Max Loehr for his seventieth birthday, in 1975, said that the occasion "signals that we must begin to stop regarding him as a fixed institution, and take some time to consider this extraordinary man and his effect on Chinese art studies."[2] Thirty years later, in 2005, invited to a graduate seminar centered on his scholarly contributions to Chinese painting studies at the University of Maryland, College Park, Cahill mused, "Now I feel like an institution." In "Patrimony and Posterity: The 'Confucian' Legacy of James F. Cahill (1926–2014)," Xiaoqing Zhu looks into Cahill's commitment to establishing a "style history" for Chinese painting from Yuan to Ming, following Loehr's legacy in the stylistic analysis model, derived from his studies of Anyang bronzes. Moving beyond the style-analysis model, Cahill diverged in his later works to alternative methods, especially socially contextualized art history. Both style-analysis and contextual methods are still largely employed in Chinese art history survey courses for undergraduates. Cahill's legacy is perhaps best carried forward by his many distinguished students active in art history departments in universities and museums across the country and abroad. The posterity of Chinese painting studies undoubtedly continues to bear his imprint. With this generation of scholars' proclivity to question "institutions," perhaps there is something to be learned from how

Cahill celebrated his teacher. Perhaps we should stop regarding him as "a fixed institution," and instead take time to consider him in the lineage of Chinese painting studies: his larger-than-life repertoire of publications; his filial piety to his teacher's scholarship; his digression from Loehr's focus on canonical studies of Chinese painting; and his impact as a "great teacher" on his successors in Chinese painting studies.[3]

Anne Burkus-Chasson's essay, "Fault Lines: Notes toward a Memoir," takes the vantage point of an intimate history of the author's experience learning Chinese painting in the United States with a brief interlude in Japan. It is also a meditation on the books the author encountered over the years and the ideas to which she was drawn. The essay comprises four parts. The first dwells on different approaches to close looking, which was the focus of her graduate studies with the late James Cahill. The second dwells on the author's learning how to use archival resources in Japan. The third and the fourth parts examine problems the author has encountered in striving to write a cultural history of Chinese painting, notably the friction between sinology and art history, and the hazards of practicing global art history.

It is important to contextualize the field of art history in general, and the subfield of modern and contemporary Chinese painting. The discipline of art history has undergone a deep transformation from an object-oriented and connoisseurship-motivated training program to a complex field of contesting research methods and approaches. It is also increasingly interdisciplinary. New types of art historical inquiries are interwoven with other fields, such as cultural studies, film studies, literature, sociology, intellectual history, and anthropology. Generally, "non-Western" art, particularly modern and contemporary art, has been marginalized. This is obvious not only in older, well-known college textbooks such as Horst W. Janson's *History of Art* (co-authored with Dora Jane Janson, first published in 1962),[4] but also in more recent ones such as Hal Foster et al., *Art Since 1900: Modernism, Antimodernism, Postmodernism* (third edition, 2016).[5] Often, instead of seeing modern and contemporary Chinese art as a dynamic, complex ebb and flow of transformations, led by artists searching for numerous diverse modernisms, many Eurocentric scholars have tended to see, uncritically, modern and contemporary Chinese painting as a single, static phenomenon. Jerome Silbergeld's essay, "Michael Sullivan and His Study of Modern and Contemporary Chinese Painting," on the pioneering career of Michael Sullivan in the study and teaching of modern and contemporary Chinese art, illuminates for readers the special contributions of Sullivan and should, as we enter the third decade of the twenty-first century, inspire more students to continue important work in this area.

My essay, "Beyond the Seas: A Sojourn in Chinese Calligraphy and Painting," reflects on how my personal background has contributed to my scholarly activities. I am, of course, fully aware of "the treacherous task of self-evaluation," as J. M. Coetzee put it.[6] But I hope to show that my combined experience in academia and museums have played important roles in my chosen research topics and approaches to scholarship and teaching over several decades of my career. Various institutional constraints, though not easily discernable, have contributed to my choices and emphases. As Linda Nochlin once put it, "Nothing, I think, is more interesting, more poignant and more difficult to seize, than the intersection of self and history."[7] Nochlin's words, on the relationship between scholarship and scholars' life experience, are echoes of what have been perceptively and sensitively expressed by poets such as Ezra Pound: "And even I can remember / A day when the historians left blanks in their writings, / I mean, for things they didn't know." (Ezra Pound, *Cantos*, XIII).[8]

There are clearly gaps in this modest collection of essays and reflections. The book is offered "to cast a brick to get a gem" (*p'ao chuan yin yu*). It is my hope that readers will continue to look for stories that will help us understand better how the field of Chinese calligraphy and painting studies has been shaped in postwar America.

Notes

1. I have adapted some of the comments here from my "Introduction" to Jason C. Kuo, ed., *Stones from Other Mountains: Chinese Painting Studies in Postwar America* (Washington, D.C.: New Academia Publishing, 2009). In many ways, the present volume can be regarded as a sequel to the 2009 publication.
2. Cahill, "Max Loehr at Seventy," *Ars Orientalis* 10 (1975): 1.
3. See also Kuo, *Stones from Other Mountains: Chinese Painting Studies in Postwar America* and Jason C. Kuo, ed., *Discovering Chinese Painting: Dialogues with American Art Historians* (Dubuque, Iowa: Kendall/Hunt Publishing, 2000); second edition as *Discovering Chinese Painting: Dialogues with Art Historians* (Dubuque, Iowa: Kendall/Hunt Publishing, 2006).
4. New York: Abrams, 2004.
5. London and New York: Thames & Hudson, 2016.
6. J. M. Coetzee, *Stranger Shores: Literary Essays, 1986–1999* (New York: Penguin Books, 2001), 113.
7. Quoted in Maria Roth, "Of Self and History: Exchanges with Linda Nochlin," *Art Journal* 59, no. 3 (autumn 2000), 18.
8. Ezra Pound, *The Cantos of Ezra Pound* (London: Faber and Faber, 1957), 64.

Chapter 1

Approaches to the History of Chinese Calligraphy in American Scholarship

Stephen J. Goldberg

> While Western scholarship has made significant contributions to the study of Chinese archaic bronzes, jades, and ceramics, it has had less success thus far with Chinese painting and calligraphy. The difficulties encountered in the latter field are not only linguistic and technical but also cultural and philosophical; they involve different artistic sensibilities and attitudes toward authentication, as well as different notions of creation.[1]
> —Wen C. Fong

In this statement, the late Wen C. Fong identifies some of the fundamental challenges encountered by Western art historians in the study of Chinese calligraphy. In the decades since 1973, when he expressed this view, there have been major advances in the historiography of Chinese calligraphy. While many difficulties still remain, much progress has been made in the development of highly sophisticated methods of art historical research. In this essay, we shall undertake a historiography of the different methods and approaches adopted in American scholarship on Chinese calligraphy.

The studies that populate such a historiography can be generally classified into six basic genres: the aesthetic reception of Chinese calligraphy; connoisseurship and the question of authenticity; formal analysis and the question of calligraphic style; periodization and the transmission and transformation of calligraphic styles; calligraphic influence, emulation, and creative imitation; and reader reception and the genre of calligraphic texts.

Each approach will be introduced through a discussion of a representative example of art historical scholarship. All of the art historians included in this study have made fundamental contributions to the development of the history of Chinese calligraphy as an academic discipline. A careful inspection of their writings may reveal some of the historical and conceptual presuppositions upon which they are based.

The Aesthetic Reception of Chinese Calligraphy

Chinese Calligraphy by Lucy Driscoll and Kenji Toda is the first systematic study in the United States of this traditional and most revered art-form.[2] In the foreword to their 1935 book, the reader is informed of the purpose of their study: "It is not historical and it does not consider individual works of calligraphy. Its sole aim is to understand what the Chinese themselves have said about calligraphy as art."[3] And this is precisely where the strength of this groundbreaking study lies, for it affords the reader a cultural insight into traditional Chinese discussions concerning the aesthetic appreciation of Chinese calligraphy. Some thirty years later, Richard M. Barnhart would critically examine this early literature with an eye to exposing "historical anachronisms" and "violations of actual historical sequence."[4]

Driscoll and Toda begin their discussion of the art of Chinese calligraphy with a quotation from an unnamed writer: "The essence of beauty in writing is not found in the written word but lies in response to unlimited change; line after line should have a way of giving life, character after character should seek for life-movement."[5] From this phenomenological perspective, our authors make the following observation: "Life is continuous energetic change; but life is also equilibrium, dynamic adjustment. And a well written character is a symbol of the life-process. Although it lies static upon the silk or paper, to the perceiving mind it is a dynamic experience. The brushstrokes rise and fall, they stretch and sweep, crouch and spring; ink tone swells and diminishes; shapes expand and contract. These modalities of movement have their differences in speed and intensity: they may be slow or swift, heavy or light."[6]

From the very beginning, Driscoll and Toda acknowledge the central importance of "life-movement," activated in the perceptual experience of a calligraphic inscription. They correctly observe that the most fundamental qualitative feature of Chinese calligraphy is *shi* 勢, which can best be translated as "configurational force." "Chinese writing on calligraphy," they note, "proceeds along three lines: the dynamic content, the form or organization of that content (two aspects, of course, of one whole), and the requisite technique."[7]

This is then followed by a discussion of the rise and development of the different calligraphic scripts, erroneously termed "styles," and the conditions of their emergence. Our attention is also drawn to the emotive use by Chinese critics of imagistic metaphors to describe or capture the aesthetic experience of calligraphic inscriptions. Most insightful is the recognition of the importance of the development of the different calligraphic scripts and their role in shaping artistic expression and values. Squaring the written record with archaeological evidence, the authors give particular pride of place to the famous Stone Drums inscriptions, recounting the vicissitudes of their preservation and transmission. This is then followed by a discussion of the written sources on the development of the material basis of calligraphic inscriptions: the pliable writing brush, ink, and paper, in the Qin and Han dynasties, and their implications for expressive effect.

The remainder of the text is devoted to a review of the literature on brushwork, beginning with *Jiu shi*, or *The Nine Forces*, by Cai Yong (second century) and *Yong zi bafa* or *Eight Laws of Yong*, interpreted by Chen Si (thirteenth century). This is then followed by a discussion of the fourth-century teacher of Wang Xizhi, Wei Shuo's or Wei Furen's (Lady Wei) *Bi zhen tu*, or *Diagram of the Battle Array of the Brush*, followed by the writings of Wang Xizhi and Ouyang Xun (557–641). The patterned structure of the character in these writings was taken as a natural outcome of the dynamic interaction of the brushstrokes.

The authors end with a discussion of the changes in later writings dating to the Yuan and Ming dynasties. The focus is now on analytical studies of the systematic organization of characters, as a "dynamic pattern and its pervading order."[8] The text they discuss is the fifteenth-century Ming calligrapher Li Shun's *Da zi jie gou bashisi fa*, or "Eighty-four Laws in Construction of Large Characters." At the end of the book, Chinese characters are usefully listed for names, places, and titles, as well as miscellaneous terms.

Lucy Driscoll and Kenji Toda's *Chinese Calligraphy*, precisely because it is grounded in traditional Chinese sources and based on what Chinese themselves have written about traditional calligraphic practice, still ranks, despite Barnhart's critique, as one of the best introductions to the aesthetic reception of Chinese calligraphy.

The study and collection of calligraphy in the United States began slowly in the decades after World War II. Exhibitions and the catalogues that accompanied them have been a principal means of cultivating an interest in the art of Chinese calligraphy among Americans.[9] They have also been a principal vehicle for the production and publication of scholarly research in this little-understood area of Chinese art history.

The first American exhibition devoted solely to the art of Chinese calligraphy was held at the Philadelphia Museum of Art in 1971. It was organized by Tseng Yu-ho Ecke, and the catalogue she wrote to accompany the exhibition, *Chinese Calligraphy*, is pathbreaking in its attempt to introduce a Western audience to the traditional art of Chinese calligraphy.[10] This was followed six years later by the major scholarly catalogue and exhibition *Traces of the Brush: Studies in Chinese Calligraphy*, held in conjunction with a symposium on Chinese calligraphy at Yale University Art Gallery, New Haven, Connecticut in 1977. This was authored by Fu Shen, in collaboration with Marilyn W. Fu (M. W. Gleysteen), Mary G. Neill, and Mary Jane Clark. Then in 1981, *Masterpieces of Sung and Yüan Dynasty Calligraphy from the John M. Crawford Jr. Collection* was held at China House Gallery, China Institute in New York City. The catalogue and exhibition were curated and authored by Kwan S. Wong, who was assisted by Stephen Addiss. Some five years later, the catalogue and exhibition *From Concept to Context: Approaches to Asian and Islamic Calligraphy*, by Shen Fu, Glenn D. Lowery, and Ann Yonemura was sponsored by the Freer Gallery of Art, Smithsonian Institute, Washington, D.C., in 1986. For the first time, Chinese and Japanese calligraphy were set in relation to calligraphy in the Islamic world. Perhaps most important for the study, understanding, and aesthetic appreciation of traditional Chinese calligraphy is the 1999 exhibition and catalogue *The Embodied Image: Chinese Calligraphy from the John B. Elliott Collection*, organized under the direction of Robert E. Harrist, Jr. and Wen C. Fong, for The Art Museum, Princeton University.[11]

Connoisseurship and the Question of Authenticity in Chinese Calligraphy

The basic aim of connoisseurship is to determine the authenticity and authorship of works of art. It addresses questions of attribution, dating, and provenance. Emphasis is given to an evaluation of the visual qualities of a work of art and of the medium and technical procedures in its production. This requires a sustained involvement and intimate familiarity with authentic works of art. Technologies such as infrared photography are often employed to assist the trained but naked eye.

The techniques and issues of connoisseurship in the study of Chinese calligraphy were anticipated in the exhibition catalogue *Studies in Connoisseurship: Chinese Paintings from the Arthur M. Sackler Collection in New York and Princeton*, by Marilyn Fu and Shen Fu, published in 1973. This represents the most thorough and sustained investigation into the issues of the identification and authentication of Chinese works of art.

In an essay published four years later, "Reproduction and Forgery in Chinese Calligraphy," which opened the catalogue *Traces of the Brush*, Shen C. Y. Fu introduced the subject of connoisseurship and the study of Chinese calligraphy.[12] He examines the special circumstances surrounding the tradition of copying and reproduction for calligraphy and its distinction from the question of forgeries, "that is, exact copies made with the intent to deceive and meant to be taken for originals,"[13] among connoisseurs and collectors in traditional China.

One of the distinctive features about the tradition of reproduction in Chinese painting and calligraphy is precisely its role as a learning tool. Thus the importance given to the different "techniques of copying and their relationship to reproduction and forgery, as well as questions of style and quality." Fu considers five basic terms used to discuss the methods of copying in China: *lin* 臨 ("to copy in a freehand manner"), *mo* 摩 ("to copy by tracing"), *fang* 仿 ("to imitate"), *zao* 造 ("to invent"), and *ketie* 刻帖 ("carved reproductions" or "lithographs"). This is followed by a brief historical summary of copying. The remainder of the essay is devoted to case studies in connoisseurship.

To give but one example, there are two versions of a scroll known as *Hanshan and Pangyun chushih shi*, a transcription of three poems by the Tang poets Hanshan and Pangyun. One is in the Palace Museum, Taipei, and the other in the collection of John M. Crawford, Jr., in The Metropolitan Museum of Art, in New York. As Fu initially observes, "The two are quite close—the number of characters per line, and the number of lines are the same—but one is not an exact duplicate of the other. A comparison of the style of the two scrolls leads to the conclusion that they are neither written by the same hand, nor come from the same period."[14] Important at this stage in the comparison is a close examination of the differences in the stylistic features, recognizing that the style of a work of art is a function of its relationship to other works of art.

Fu then proceeds to discuss the provenance of the scroll in the Palace Museum. In addition to bearing a seal by Southern Song emperor Gaozong (r. 1127–62), "early documentation indicates that, from the twelfth century onward, the scroll was considered a genuine work by Huang T'ing-chien."[15] He then presents the following assessment:

> When examined under strong light and magnified, there is absolutely no indication that the Taipei scroll is a traced copy. Where one would expect to find such indications—such as the ends of the strokes and the "flying white" places—all are smooth, vigorous, and natural. The rounded brushstrokes contain tense, tremulous energy. The organization of the component elements is purposely asymmetrical. The shifting balance of characters in a column combines with outstretched horizontals and elongated diagonals to convey a dense, tangled expression. In sum, the brush method, structure, and spirit of the writing are all consistent with what we know of Huang T'ing-chien's work before the onset of his fully developed "old-age" style.[16]

Fu offers additional evidence, which leads him to the opinion that, "Given the documentation, brush methods, internal consistency of techniques, and content of the inscription, there is no doubt that the Palace Museum's *Hanshan and Pangyun* scroll is a genuine work by Huang T'ing-chien."[17]

Fu then engages in a careful examination of the documentary evidence concerning the Crawford scroll, including seals and colophons, and most importantly, a stylistic analysis of the calligraphy. This leads him to the following judgment, "In sum, the cumulative evidence supports the conclusion that the Crawford *Han-shan* is a free-hand copy, done at the latest, before the genuine version entered the Ch'ing Imperial Collection, and most probably after the revival of Huang T'ing-chien's influence in the second half of the middle Ming."[18]

In each instance of the case studies in connoisseurship discussed in Fu's essay, he brings out the variety of productive comparative uses of copies, not only to establish the authenticity of original works of calligraphy, but also to heighten one's aesthetic appreciation of the formal features and technical procedures in the execution of these calligraphic works.

Formal Analysis and the Question of Calligraphic Style

Formal analysis is a specific type of visual description of a work of art. It is an explanation of the visual structure, of the ways in which certain visual elements, such as calligraphic brushstrokes, have been arranged and function within a character composition. It explains how the eye is led through the work, visually interacting with gesturally expressive brushstrokes, and provides a solid foundation for other types of analysis, such as calligraphic style.

Style refers to the visual appearance that relates a work of art to other works by the same artist or from the same period, school, art movement, or culture. Commenting on the history of stylistics, the linguist and literary scholar Yufang Ho has noted that many scholars have suggested "the notion of style should not be considered as an attribute but as an implicitly relational concept. That is, to state that a text has a certain style is equivalent to stating that it differs in some respects from other texts."[19]

Style is one of the principal modes of classifying works of art and tracking developmental changes over time. Major changes in style are often indices of changes in the society in which the art was made and was intended to be viewed or used. Chinese art has a marked tendency to revive "classical" styles from time to time. The identification of an individual's style is especially important for the attribution of works.

An early discussion of the formal features and style in Chinese calligraphy can be found in Wong and Addiss's *Masterpieces of Sung and Yuan Dynasty Calligraphy from the John M. Crawford Jr. Collection*. The focus of the catalogue is the calligraphy of Song and Yuan dynasty masters in the John M. Crawford Jr. Collection, now in The Metropolitan Museum of Art, in New York. In the introduction, Wong observes that in order to understand the position of the calligraphers in the collection, "it is important to review the background of their work as well as to study the main currents of their eras."[20] Beginning with a discussion of the tradition of Jin calligraphy and the Two Wangs, attention then turns to a discussion of the calligraphy of the Tang masters. This is followed by a consideration of the Northern Song individualist calligraphers Su Shi, Huang Tingjian, and Mi Fu, and the Southern Song masters, culminating in the Yuan revival of Jin and Tang methods.

In Wong's discussion of the individual pieces in the Crawford collection, one of the important contributions made to the study of Chinese calligraphy is the visual description of the formal qualities of the calligraphy, the way in which certain visual elements are arranged and function within the composition of the characters. This affords the reader new to this art form a deep insight into the technical and expressive features of each inscription. This impact is illustrated in the discussion of two inscriptions by the Southern Song emperor Lizong (r. 1225–64), written in regular script on round fans mounted as album leaves. The first is *A Poem on West Lake after Snow*.

This poem describes the scenery of the snow-covered West Lake at Hangchow, the capital of the Southern Sung dynasty. Written in four lines of seven characters each, it may be translated as follows.

Stephen J. Goldberg 17

> After the snow in sunshine and mist, the cold air hovers over the lake.
>
> I am reluctant to leave such beautiful scenery.
>
> Up by the pavilion, as I gaze at the peaks,
>
> The hazy atmosphere and the color of snow seem to float on my cup of wine.[21]

Here Wong addresses the formal and stylistic aspects of the inscription of the poem.

The calligraphy shows the spirit of purity in the artist, inspired by the poem of the beautiful snow-covered landscape. The brushwork is rapid and straight, with strong energy and full control. Angular and sharp strokes can be seen in the hooking of lines powerfully impressed upon the silk. This style echoes the tradition of Six dynasties steles from North China, but is not as rough and awkward as the writing in the Buddhist caves of the Northern Wei dynasty.[22]

Wong continues the discussion of Emperor Lizong's calligraphy with a description of his second inscription, *A Couplet from a Poem by Han Hung*, dated 1261. As in the previous inscription, it is written in regular script, on a round fan mounted as an album leaf, found in the John M. Crawford Jr. Collection.

> The voice of the tide arises at noon
>
> The green of the mountains is deepest facing south.[23]

Wong addresses the formal and stylistic aspects of the second inscription in light of his discussion of the first.

> Li-tsung [Lizong] inscribed the fan when he was fifty-six years old, and it may be his last extant work. Although the brushstrokes are still angular, the movement of the brush is slower than in his earlier works, showing excellent control and a masterly sense of composition. Comparing the final character of the first column, "*ch'i*" (arise), with the same character in another work dated 1256 in the Cleveland Museum of Art, one can see that the structure is similar, but the

brushwork of this piece shows more strength and control, especially in the lowest (final) stroke, which displays a slow natural movement in the line. We can see how the emperor has matured as an artist; the strong contrasts of straight and rounded lines within a single character is handled with a sure sense of balance and internal vitality. The large characters on this fan display a confidence and boldness that are attributes of Li-tsung's [Lizong's] late writing. There is little left of the influence of Kao-tsung [Gaozong]; instead, the powerful diagonals and forthright dynamics of the brush show the character of Li-tsung [Lizong].[24]

Masterpieces of Sung and Yuan Dynasty Calligraphy is an important catalogue, for it showed the way forward in discussing the interrelationships of the meaning, stylistic appreciation, and historical significance of Chinese calligraphy.

Periodization and the Transmission and Transformation of Calligraphic Styles

Periodization, a fundamental approach to the study of art history, entails a chronological or diachronic sequencing and synchronic grouping of works of art. It is premised on the principles that "visual appearance is an index of history, and that style marked historical periods in art (as well as the work of individual artists)."[25] Period groupings are defined by the perception of shared stylistic qualities among works of art and of meaningful connections between art and its historical context. The divisions between periods shed light on artistic developments, and illuminate moments of discontinuous change. Stylistic periodization also serves to foreground distinctive features deemed significant in the aesthetic reception of individual works. It enables relevant comparisons between works of art to be made over time, and meaningful developments to be observed in the history of art, such as periodic revivals of earlier or "classic" styles from the past.

Periodization as an approach to the history of calligraphic style is most richly developed and conceptually nuanced in Qianshen

Bai's *Fu Shan's World: The Transformation of Chinese Calligraphy in the Seventeenth Century*.[26] This study elucidates the work of the eminent scholar, calligrapher, and art theorist Fu Shan (1607–1684/85) within a general discussion of the complex developments and radical transformations of Chinese calligraphy and Chinese society in the seventeenth century—a period marked by the fall of the Ming and rise of the Manchu-Qing dynasty.[27] By taking this approach, Bai provides a sociopolitical and cultural context in which to situate a more focused discussion of Fu Shan and his calligraphy, and to undertake a comprehensive historical analysis and explanation of the transformations in seventeenth-century calligraphy. As Bai notes:

> Fu Shan's calligraphy belongs both to the late Ming and to the early Qing. On the one hand, he was the last great master of wild cursive calligraphy, the most advanced of the individualist artists. On the other, he was an eloquent advocate of epigraphical calligraphy as a source of innovation and change. Because his life of nearly eighty years corresponds with crucial transitions in three different but nonetheless interrelated spheres—the political, intellectual, and artistic—I have chosen in this book to divide Fu Shen's life into four periods and to analyze aspects of his art in the context of the political and intellectual issues dominating each period.[28]

In this study, Qianshen Bai describes in masterly prose the salient stylistic features of individual works by Fu Shan and their historical significance, rooted in keen observations of the formal qualities of his calligraphy, and the rapidly changing intellectual and cultural circumstances under which they were produced. This can be seen in his discussion of the second period (1644–1650s), the early years of the Qing, marked by Fu Shan's interest in Yan Zhenqing, especially his late phase, seen in *Yan Memorial Ode on the Resurgence of the Great Tang*, carved on a cliff in Wuxi, Hunan in 771, which possessed the quality of *zhili* 支離 (deformation or fragmentation). As Bai observes, "The large size of the characters and their bold strokes, with ragged edges caused by the roughness of the cliff and by damage of wind and rain, make the work compelling."[29]

Qianshen Bai then turns his attention to a "handscroll in various scripts written in the early 1650's, later entitled *Wonderful Calligraphy by Fu Shan (Selu miaohan)*," which he asserts, "manifests in radical fashion the aesthetic of *zhili* in calligraphy."[30]

> In a section of the handscroll written in regular script, disorder and chaos predominates…. Character structures are severely deformed, even dismantled: characters pile up, strokes are disjoined from one another, there are striking contrasts in character size. Rather than separating the columns clearly, Fu jumbled the characters in a disorganized mass, allowing large characters to protrude into neighboring columns. Lacking the discipline imposed by clearly defined columns, characters with particularly diffused structures have strokes that are easily read as parts of nearby characters creating a text that is graphically confusing and difficult to read.[31]

The early years of the Qing was a period marked not only by Fu Shan's innovative willful deformity in the displacement of elements in his character's configuration but also by his adoption of *zashu juan/ce*, handscroll or album texts that are usually unrelated, written in assorted scripts. Bai observes that the *zashu juan/ce* "corresponds with a change in reading habits in the late Ming."[32] This is indicative of a period of increasing interaction between high and low culture in China.

And finally, in an observation that speaks to the continuation in the early Qing of sensibilities and calligraphic practices from the previous period of Fu Shan's life, Bai states,

> Not only does Fu Shan's *Selu miaohan* scroll testify to the lingering of late Ming cultural influence in a drastically changed political context, but it also demonstrates that many late Ming calligraphic trends—the search for *qi*, experimentation with unusual character forms, manipulative use of ancient canons, and interest in random and heterogeneous *zashu juan/ce* format—reach new levels of development in the early Qing. In the 1660s and 1670s, however, an intellectual trend that was soon to form the basis of a new aesthetic in the art of calligraphy began to evolve.[33]

Qianshen Bai concludes his exhaustive study of Fu Shan's world with the following reflections on the continuation of calligraphic practices and cultural patterns across the lines of demarcation that define the period of dynastic divide in the seventeenth century.

> In many ways, then, Fu Shan's late work is the result of an intertwining of late Ming and early Qing cultures. It synthesizes two currents, the expressive cursive calligraphy of the individualist calligraphers in the late Ming and the plain, epigraphical taste emerging in the early Qing. This synthesis took place in a specific historical context: although the intellectual climate underwent a significant transformation after the collapse of the Ming, late Ming cultural patterns lingered for a time; and in the early Qing, empirical scholarship which was in general less concerned with the metaphysical thinking and critical social issues that had absorbed scholars in the late Ming had not triumphed as it would in the eighteenth century. Thus the sociocultural environment in the second half of the seventeenth century still tolerated the eccentric expressiveness of wild cursive calligraphy, even if it was not entirely at home with it.[34]

Bai's *Fu Shan's World* clearly demonstrates that discussions of "period style" continue to play a vital role in the mapping of art historical change.

Calligraphic Influence, Emulation, and Creative Imitation

In a discussion of the ancient canons of Chinese calligraphy, Qianshen Bai stated, "For centuries, copying the ancient masters had been an essential element of calligraphic learning and transmission of the calligraphic tradition."[35] The practice of writing in the style of former masters served two important cultural functions: it was a principal means of learning the art of calligraphy, and it assured the ritual transmission of the tradition of Chinese calligraphy. Emulating the style of a former master thus became a common calligraphic practice. This raises important questions for the study of the Chinese calligraphy. How do we assess the nature of stylistic influence in a calligrapher's art? What are the different ways such influence can manifest itself? These issues are sensitively dealt with in Marilyn Wong-Gleysteen's "Calligraphy and Painting: Some Sung and Post-Sung Parallels in North and South—A Reassessment of the Chiang-nan Tradition."[36]

In this study, Wong-Gleysteen offers a counter-perspective to the recent view in Western scholarship that there was a state of decline in calligraphy produced during the Jin and Southern Song, in the aftermath of the extreme individualism in the calligraphy of Huang Tingjian (1045–1105), Su Shi (1037–1101), and Mi Fu (1052–1107), in the Northern Song. To accomplish the counter-perspective required the adoption of a different point of view, "one which does not regard artistic activity in terms of ascendance and decline from a particular qualitative standard. To do this, we will certainly compare the 'followers' with the 'masters', but we will also try to comprehend what these next few generations were trying to achieve, and why it was so compelling for them to make the choices they did."[37]

In undertaking this task, Wong-Gleysteen acknowledges the unique and enormous challenges faced by the followers of the Northern Song masters, and the different ways stylistic influence and emulation manifests itself in their calligraphy.

> With the individuality of the Song firmly established by such creative giants, each of whom set a standard unto himself, any master would have difficulty measuring up. If we understand this point of view, then we can begin to understand the psychological challenge to subsequent calligraphers. The next generation resolved this problem in the time-honored manner: by emulation, both spiritual and formal. Through emulation and creative imitation (*fang* 倣), they hoped to achieve a measure of "spiritual communion" (*shen-hui* 神會) of "communion of form" (*hsing-hui* 形會) with the great masters.[38]

This approach requires not only a comparative calligraphic stylistics, but a description and historical analysis of the intentionality of stylistic emulation. To carry this out, Wong-Gleysteen focused on "the Mi-family tradition, which was the dominant influence in both the north and the south."[39] The prevailing aesthetic associated with the calligrapher-painter-critic Mi Fu is known as the Jiangnan 江南, or southern, tradition.

The study of the Mi-family tradition begins with the next generation: a comparison of works by father and son. It is here that the author goes to the very heart of the matter of calligraphic influence studies:

> What interests us about Mi Fu and Mi Yu-jen is not only the vital issue of the transmission of the Mi style and its accompanying aesthetic, but also the notion of one generation deriving its style from a previous one. If close emulation was the stated goal of a master, then how do we evaluate the younger master's artistic stature? What do we do with the concept of originality? And what becomes of the time-honored concept of reading a man's character in his art, the "heart print" or "image of the mind" (*hsin-yin* 心印)?[40]

In her analysis the southern and northern branches of followers of the Mi-family style, one of the major contributions Wong-Gleysteen makes to the study of Chinese calligraphy is her vivid and precise descriptive analyses of the different ways in which calligraphers manifest their indebtedness to other calligraphers, and her insightful evaluations of the significance of this influence on the calligrapher's style. This is exemplified in her discussion of two Southern Song calligraphers in the Mi tradition: Fan Chengda (1126–1193) and Lu Yu (1125–1210). Fan Chengda was a painter, calligrapher, and poet during the Southern Song, and served as ambassador to the Jin court. An example of his calligraphy appears as a colophon on his painting *Fishing Village at Mount Xisai* at the Metropolitan Museum of Art. Wong-Gleysteen informs us that "Fan's indebtedness to Mi Fu shows itself primarily in the way he forms his characters. His brushwork method…shows some Mi characteristics in its variation of pace and pressure, but it is predominantly a 'flat-brush' style, splaying openly in the diagonals, hooks, and verticals.... Fan cared little about perfection of individual stroke form. His work is marked by a consistent rhythm of similar-sized characters in a sweep of spacious columnar forms, often punctuated with textured 'flying white' characters."[41]

She then makes the following telling observation, "What could be criticized as looseness in brushwork and lack of variety in composition by comparison with Mi Fu can be appreciated on another level as generosity of character and consistency of temperament."[42] This observation addresses the question of "calligraphic influence" and the traditional practice of "emulation and creative imitation" that argues, at least in this particular case, for evaluating differences from the model on its own terms as an autonomous aesthetic expression.

Lu Yu was a major poet of the Southern Song. His *My Poems* (*Zishu shi* 自書詩), a long handscroll in the Liaoning Museum, was executed when he was in his eighties. Wong-Gleysteen describes it as follows: "An exuberant celebration, it starts with a bold opening character and proceeds with an ever-changing variety of brushwork, small and finer alternating with plump and full, punctuated by sudden bursts of energy.... Wet ink follows dry in natural succession, and large and small characters succeed each other in complexity of stroke and internal pulse. All is in keeping with Mi Fu's numerous injunctions about calligraphic method...."[43]

This touches on another dimension of artistic influence discussed by the scholar Yang Renkai. When addressing the possible influences of the Tang masters Yan Zhenqing and Liu Gongquan on Lu Yu, Yang points out that he emulated the methods, not form.[44] This takes us beyond the question of stylistic influence and alerts us to the possible indebtedness of one calligrapher to another at the level of technical procedures and methods.

One of the most important calligraphers in the north under the Jin was Wang Tingyun (1151–1202). Wang Tingyun and his son, Wang Qing, were seen as the true heirs of the Mi Fu tradition. As Wong-Gleysteen states, "An outstanding connoisseur and painter, and the leading poet of the time, Wang possessed all the natural abilities to qualify as the heir to the Mi tradition in the north."[45] Two of his calligraphic inscriptions exist in the form of colophons, one to his painting *Secluded Bamboo and Withered Tree*, in the Fujii

Yurinkan, Kyoto, the other to Li Shan's handscroll *Wind and Snow in the Fir-Pines*, in the Freer Gallery of Art, Smithsonian Institute, Washington, D.C. As Wong-Gleysteen states, "His own inscription to *Secluded Bamboo* is particularly powerful, as it combines all of the compositional features of Mi's tall structures with a crisp attack and a feeling for dense ink. His colophon to the Li Shan scroll gives evidence of remarkable tip work, the graceful turning and gliding of the brush, a feeling totally in keeping with Mi Fu's brush principles, plus an interest in contrasting the brush tip with both flattened and plumply rounded forms."[46]

Once again, a comparison with the model emulated, Mi Fu's calligraphic style, calls for an aesthetic evaluation. "Judging on the basis of these works, Wang's brush movements have a lower 'energy level' than Mi's, and his style has none of the protean sense of change in the work of the elder Mi."[47] Reflecting upon her analyses, Wong-Gleysteen draws a distinction between the emulation of a master's style in the Jin and Southern Song and the concept of "imitation" (*fang*) practiced in the late Ming, "when there was a distant past to look back upon and a large body of masters' works and styles upon which to draw. The cultural psychology in operation here—the close imitation of a major master by the generation or two immediately following—needs to be understood in this earlier historical context as a prelude to the later development of *fang* and not as a question of decline."[48]

She then asks the rhetorical question, "Why would so many masters choose to follow Su, Huang, and Mi if they knew history would judge them to be inferior?" In answering this question, Wong-Gleysteen touches on a culturally specific dimension to artistic influence and emulation, the different motivations for imitating a master's style, and the historical conditions under which this occurred.

> Why would so many masters choose to follow Su, Huang, and Mi if they knew history would judge them to be inferior? Because there was no greater homage that one could pay than to imitate, successfully a master's style. For the northern calligraphers, there were political and cultural gains to be had by perpetuating the art and acquiring the

admired cultural symbols of the conquered dynasty, thereby strengthening the Chin claim to political legitimacy and recognition as proper heirs to the Sung. For the southerners, perpetuation of Sung culture assuaged wounded pride, restored some of the glory lost in the north, and continued Sung interests in the revival of antiquity, especially the Tsin and T'ang.[49]

Wong-Gleysteen returns to a view she expressed at the beginning of this essay, "In a larger context, it becomes clear how the post-Sung artistic traditions in both the north and the south played a vital role in continuing the Northern Sung trend toward individualism, derived from the achievement of three of the Four Sung Masters, in particular Mi Fu, reinforcing the subjective, imaginative, and spontaneous in art."[50]

Reader Reception and the Genre of Calligraphic Texts

"Reading Chinese Calligraphy," by Robert E. Harrist, Jr. is one of two introductory essays in *The Embodied Image: Chinese Calligraphy from the John B. Elliott Collection*.[51] In this essay, Harrist addresses a most important, but generally neglected, issue in the study of Chinese calligraphy, the role of reading and the genre of texts in the production and aesthetic reception of calligraphic inscriptions. "Throughout the history of calligraphy, reading texts has been as much a part of the experience of this art as has savoring fine brushwork. But because of certain underlying assumptions that took shape as calligraphy came to be regarded as an art form, the experience of reading and the significance of texts never received the type of exhaustive analysis accorded to topics such as script types and brushwork in the vast and sophisticated body of traditional writings on calligraphy."[52]

Harrist traces this back to the early Six dynasties period (222–589), when calligraphy began to be thought of not only as writing but also as an art among aristocrats living in southern China. Because of the importance of this discussion to his argument, it merits extensive quotation.

This period witnessed the burgeoning of critical and theoretical texts on calligraphy, the emergence of an art market, and the formation of collections of works by Wang Hsi-chih (303–361), the most famous of all calligraphers, and other masters. Treatises categorizing script types, discussions of connoisseurship, notes on calligraphic techniques, and rankings of calligraphers that proliferated in the fifth and sixth centuries laid the foundations for all later writing on the arts. The Six Dynasties period also witnessed the development of a specialized language of appreciation and assessment that metaphorically equated effects of brushwork with forms in nature or the physiology of the human body. During the Six Dynasties it also became common to speak of a person's calligraphy as an externalization of the writer's mind and personality open to interpretation by an informed observer—a view that still endures in China today.[53]

Here Harrist draws our attention to an important lacuna in our understanding of this formative period in the history of Chinese calligraphy. "Missing in the early discourse of this art is any systematic discussion of the relationship between the textual content of a work of calligraphy and the script or style in which it appears. A manifestation of this disregard for the literary content of calligraphy as a subject of theoretical discussion is the practice of classifying works solely on the basis of script type in which they were written."[54]

What is to be gained by redressing this lacuna in the study of Chinese calligraphy? Harrist argues that "by thinking about the history of calligraphy not only as a progression of period styles and individual masters but as a history of producing and reading texts, we can discern patterns and cultural conventions easily overlooked in most available accounts of this complex art."[55]

In the remainder of the essay Harrist undertakes an exploration of "some of the ways through which the dynamic relationship between the processes of writing and reading calligraphy have shaped the history of this art."[56] This is accomplished through a discussion of six fundamental types of calligraphic texts and a reflection on the possible expectations imposed on their production and reception:

inscriptions of texts on stelae and Buddhist sutras; transcriptions of classical poems and essays in one's own style; transcriptions for purposes of reproduction and dissemination of canonical masterpieces; the inscription of a text that is an original composition, not a transcription; the inscription of personal letters; and the inscription of colophons.

To give but one example, we shall now consider Robert Harrist's approach to the study of reader reception and the genre of stele inscriptions and Buddhist sutras, which he titles "Problems of Content, Format, and Script in the Stele and Sutra." The stele, or stone inscription, is an early format that "for nearly two thousand years signified authority, permanence, and orthodoxy."[57] It "assumed its classic form in the Han dynasty: a large rectangular monolith, often capped by a decorative carved top and resting on a stone base carved in the form of a gigantic tortoise."[58] The format of the stele, "through its imposing physical form and its close association with the power of the state, religious institutions, and illustrious families, acquired a unique importance in China, as a bearer of engraved writing."[59]

A central concern in this discussion of the conventions of writing and reading fostered by the engraving of texts on stelae is the monumentality and nature of the materiality of the medium and format of the stele. Harrist offers the following phenomenological description of the reading experience of the stele inscription, commensurate with the formal and authoritative nature of the genre of the textual inscriptions. "The physical dimensions and orientation of the stele impose protocols of reading on those who approach its polished and engraved surface. Looming vertically, the stone echoes but dwarfs the body of the reader, who normally is standing up, with head raised, to decipher the writing. Although the stele is a type of monument, not a genre of writing, it has generally been reserved for certain types of texts.... These texts intended for public readership asserted orthodox visions of history, religious doctrine, and self-generated records of genealogy and ancestral achievement."[60]

"Inscriptions on stelae," it is then noted, "demonstrate some of the ways through which the formal, nonsemantic properties of calligraphy structure the way a text is read. The most basic of these include the scale of writing and the organization of the characters on the stone surface."⁶¹

> The overall design of a stele inscription is orderly and balanced, and the script types normally used for these texts create complementary effects…. Stone inscriptions of the Han dynasty were written almost exclusively in clerical script (*li-shu*), which features blocky characters accentuated by flaring diagonals strokes. The gradual transformation of this script type into standard script can be traced through monumental inscriptions that were transferred from the brushwritten originals on silk or paper and engraved on the surfaces of stelae. In the classical stele inscriptions of the Tang dynasty (618–906), such as those of Liu Kung-ch'uan, which still serve as models of standard script, each character is a stable, architectonic unit.⁶²

Commenting on the almost exclusive preference for standard script for commemorative stelae ever since the Tang dynasty, Harrist observes, "Although the easy legibility of standard script made it popular for use in many other contexts…the intimate connection between the stele and standard-script calligraphy greatly enhanced the prestige of this form of writing, preferred for almost all formal contexts."⁶³

The second genre considered by Harrist, the transcription of Buddhist sutras, is governed by even more rigorous conventions of writing and reading than stele inscriptions. Typically written by professional scribes, the act of transcribing a sutra was understood as an act of religious piety. And, importantly, "the religious efficacy of a scripture was believed to reside in the physical artifact of the transcription itself."⁶⁴

As Robert Harrist notes, "By the seventh century a form of small standard script loosely called 'sutra writing style' (*hsieh-ching t'i*) became all but universal for the transcription of sutras in China."⁶⁵ This can be seen in the *Mahaprajñaparamita Sutra*, dated 674, in the Elliott Collection, "a classic example of sutra transcription from the golden age of Buddhism in China." Harrist succinctly describes it as follows: "Divided into neat columns, most of seventeen characters each, the layout of the text, like that of a stele inscription, promotes orderly, regularly paced reading."[66] In this respect, it perfectly exemplifies the "old decorum of sutra transcription."

Reflecting back on his discussions, Harrist comes to the following conclusion, "The texts of stele inscriptions and Buddhist sutras imposed on calligraphers and readers expectations shaped by religious, political, and social conventions and the variations of script within these genres were relatively limited and predictable. Only a narrow range of calligraphic forms were acceptable."[67]

In conclusion, this account of the fundamental contributions of American scholars to the development of the history of Chinese calligraphy makes us aware of some of the important approaches and methods that have been devised to address an array of historical and aesthetic issues. It is hoped that this modest study will inspire new and innovative research on this most noble contribution to world culture, the art of Chinese calligraphy.

Notes

I wish to dedicate this essay to the memory of Wen Fong, who is principally responsible for creating conditions and opportunities for students and scholars to conduct research in the field of Chinese calligraphy.

1   Wen Fong, preface to the exhibition catalogue *Studies in Connoisseurship: Chinese Paintings from the Arthur M. Sackler Collection in New York and Princeton*, by Marilyn and Shen Fu (Princeton: Princeton University Press, 1973), xiii.
2   Lucy Driscoll and Kenji Toda, *Chinese Calligraphy* (Chicago: University of Chicago Press, 1935). Another excellent early text is Chiang Yee, *Chinese Calligraphy: An Introduction to Its Aesthetic and Technique* (Cambridge, Mass.: Harvard University Press, 1973), first published in 1938.
3   Driscoll and Toda, *Chinese Calligraphy*, v.
4   Richard M. Barnhart, "Wei Fu-jen's Pi Chen T'u and the Early Texts on Calligraphy," *Archives of the Chinese Art Society of America* 18 (1964).
5   Driscoll and Toda, *Chinese Calligraphy*, 1.
6   Ibid.
7   Ibid., 2.
8   Ibid., 50.

9   For a discussion of the history of collection and scholarship of Chinese calligraphy in the United States, see Qianshen Bai, Craig Shaw, and Uta Lauer, "Chinese Calligraphy Meets the West," in *Chinese Calligraphy*, ed. Ouyang Zhongshi and Wen C. Fong (New Haven: Yale University Press, 2008), 339–454.
10 Philadelphia: Philadelphia Museum of Art, 1971.
11 That same year *Character & Context in Chinese Calligraphy*, an international symposium organized by The Art Museum, Princeton University, was organized, and the papers were published in conjunction with the exhibition.
12 Shen C. Y. Fu. "Reproduction and Forgery in Chinese Calligraphy," in *Traces of the Brush: Studies in Chinese Calligraphy*, by Shen C. Y. Fu in collaboration with Marilyn W. Fu, Mary G. Neill, and Mary Jane Clark (New Haven: Yale University Press, 1977), 3–39.
13 Ibid., 3.
14 Ibid., 10.
15 Ibid.
16 Ibid., 10–11.
17 Ibid.
18 Ibid.
19 Yufang Ho, *Corpus Stylistics in Principles and Practice: A Stylistic Exploration of John Fowles' The Magus* (London: Bloomsbury Academic, 2011), 5.
20 *Masterpieces of Sung and Yuan Dynasty Calligraphy from the John M. Crawford Jr. Collection*, by Kwan S. Wong, with the assistance of Stephen Addiss (New York: China House Gallery, China Institute in America, 1981), 11.
21 Ibid., 47.
22 Ibid.
23 Ibid., 50.
24 Ibid.
25 Thomas DaCosta Kaufmann, "Periodization and Its Discontents," *Journal of Art Historiography* 2 (June 2010): 3. In this essay, Thomas DaCosta Kaufmann discusses the reevaluation of stylistic periodization in recent decades by art historians employing criteria other than visual appearance in order to account for formal variation.
26 Cambridge, Mass.: Harvard University Asia Center, 2003.
27 Another excellent example of stylistic periodization is Peter Charles Sturman's *Mi Fu: Style and the Art of Calligraphy in Northern Sung China* (New Haven: Yale University Press, 1997).
28 Bai, *Fu Shan's World*, 4.
29 Ibid., 118.
30 Ibid., 120.

31 Ibid.
32 Ibid., 149.
33 Ibid., 151–52.
34 Ibid., 256.
35 Ibid., 34.
36 In *Words and Images: Chinese Poetry, Calligraphy, and Painting*, ed. Alfreda Murck and Wen C. Fong (New York and Princeton: The Metropolitan Museum of Art and Princeton University Press, 1991), 141–72.
37 Ibid., 152.
38 Ibid., 153.
39 Ibid., 152.
40 Ibid., 155.
41 Ibid., 157.
42 Ibid.
43 Ibid.
44 Ibid., citing Yang Renkai, "Shu-yuan ts'ung-tan," *I-yuan To-ying* 22 (1983): 36–43.
45 Ibid., 160.
46 Ibid., 160–62.
47 Ibid.
48 Ibid., 166.
49 Ibid.
50 Ibid., 141.
51 Robert E. Harrist, Jr. and Wen C. Fong (Princeton: The Art Museum, Princeton University, 2000), 3–27.
52 Ibid., 6–8.
53 Ibid., 3–4.
54 Ibid., 4.
55 Ibid., 3.
56 Ibid., 9.
57 Ibid.
58 Ibid.
59 Ibid.
60 Ibid.
61 Ibid.
62 Ibid., 11.
63 Ibid.
64 Ibid.
65 Ibid.
66 Ibid.
67 Ibid., 12.

Chapter 2

Historiography of Liao and Jin Painting: The United States Contribution

Nancy S. Steinhardt

Through more than half of the twentieth century, the dynasties Liao (907–1125), Jin (1115–1234), and Yuan (1267–1368) were often referred to by the unfortunate name "barbarian dynasties," barbarian being a translation of the Chinese character *hu*.[1] During this period, *hu* ruled increasingly large parts of China, culminating in Mongol rule from 1267 through 1368. The development of the study of painting of the first part of this period, during Liao and Jin, outside China and primarily in the United States, is the subject here. The Liao and Jin dynasties rose in China's northeastern provinces, Liaoning, Jilin, and Heilongjiang. The territories ruled by them extended into North Korea, eastern Inner and Outer Mongolia, and Russia. Centered in Liaoning and eastern Mongolia, the Khitan people, from which the Liao founder rose, are sometimes referred to as people of the grasslands. The Jurchen, based in Jilin, Heilongjiang, and Russia, are sometimes known as people of the forests. These locations, so far from China's major cities and their research centers, fueled the label barbarian, for until the last third of the twentieth century, research on Liao and Jin was rare in China. When it did occur, it happened mainly through Japanese research institutes, which published discoveries made during the Occupation of Manchuria, and through Russian and other European scholars, who published discoveries in Russia and Mongolia. These publications, especially the Japanese ones, often have not been available in China, and the Japanese research, in particular, has been ignored because it was conducted during occupation. The

United States was a latecomer to research on both Liao and Jin, including their painting.

It was primarily the Japanese publications, however, that brought attention in the United States to the material remains of Liao and Jin. Together with reports of expeditions at sites on the western side of China, in today's Xinjiang, undertaken by European and Japanese teams, these oversized tomes filled the folio sections of libraries at universities with programs in Chinese art, at museums with Chinese collections, and at a few research institutes. Any graduate student of Chinese art from as early as the 1920s through the 1970s could not but be aware of the publications by Torii Ryūzō, Takeshima Takuichi, or Tamura Jitsuzō: if one were to remove all books added to research libraries in the last fifty years, the Japanese publications would command an impressively large percentage of what remains.[2]

In general, only a few publications by Europeans, all on Liao, were read as widely. Ordained in Belgium, Father Jozef Mullie (1886–1976) arrived in the vicariate of Eastern Mongolia in 1909. He is believed to have been the first European to see and publish the architecture of the Liao ancestral precinct, today known as Liao

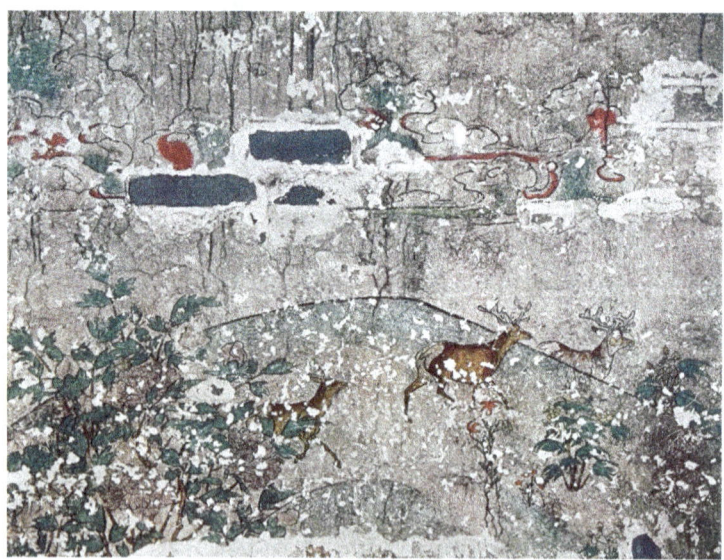

2.1. "Summer Landscape." Central chamber, Eastern Mausoleum, Qingzhou. Tamura Jitsuzō and Kobayashi Yokio, *Keiryō* [Qingling], 2 vols. (Kyoto: Kyoto Daigaku bungakubu, 1953), 2: pl. 55

Zuzhou, and the tombs of three Liao emperors at the site then—and in later publications—called Ch'ing-ling, today Qingzhou in Inner Mongolia (fig. 2.1).³ *T'oung Pao*, the major European journal for Chinese studies since 1890, published today as then by Brill, also included a partial translation of the Liao standard history by Rolf Stein (1911–1999).⁴ In 1949, Columbia professors Karl Wittfogel (1896–1988) and Feng Chia-sheng's 753-page *History of Chinese Society: Liao* was published.⁵ The paucity of English-language material about Liao through the 1960s was such that scholars of painting used this book widely, even if they did not read it cover-to-cover. The figure opposite the title page, titled "Landscape with Deer," was from one of the Qingzhou tombs. It was one of several that introduced readers to Khitan inscriptions and pagodas as well to paintings. The objects that would lead to blockbuster exhibitions, discussed below, were still unknown. Only one other painting in United States at that time was considered a possible Liao painting, or at least relevant to things Liao. It was "Tartars Traveling on Horseback," attributed to the son of the founder of the Liao dynasty, Yelü Bei (899–937), who had fled south and taken the Chinese name Li Zanhua when he became a court painter (fig. 2.2).⁶

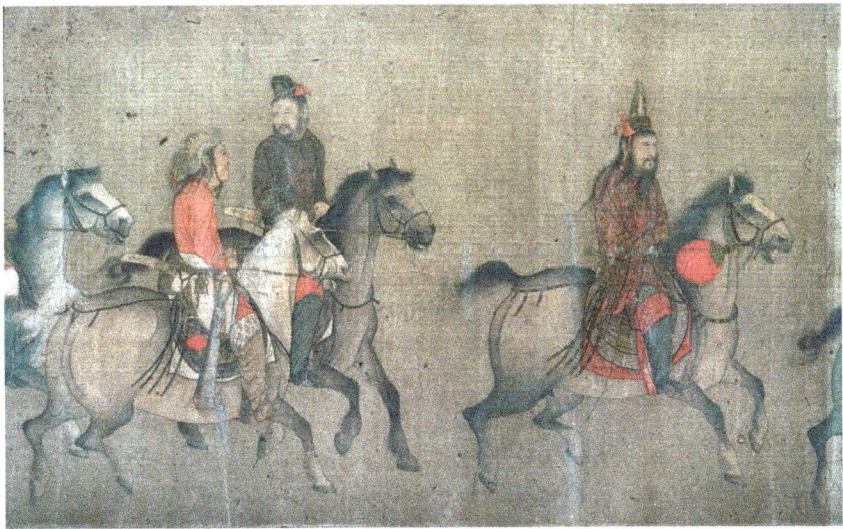

2.2. Detail of Li Zanhua (attr.), "Tartars Traveling on Horseback," Museum of Fine Arts, Boston. Courtesy of Museum of Fine Arts, Boston

Indeed, through the 1970s, Liao and Jin were largely ignored in art historical discourse in the United States. Yuan, on the other hand, the third so-called "barbarian dynasty," received a surge of interest beginning in 1968. Sherman Lee (1918–2008) and Wai-kam Ho's (1924–2004) landmark exhibition and catalogue, *Chinese Art under the Mongols*, published in that year, was a major turning point.[7] This focus on Yuan, it is suggested here, coincided with the realization that it was unlikely that many paintings of the Song dynasty (960–1279) beyond those that had been studied for the last several decades were available for study, but that there were abundant research topics offered by art in the century following Song.[8] Two scholars of Chinese painting who would dominate the discipline for the next four decades, James Cahill at the Freer Gallery and then Berkeley, and Li Chu-tsing (1920–2014) at the University of Kansas, embarked on this uncharted field. Li would produce dozens of scholarly publications.[9] James Cahill (1926–2014) would begin his anticipated five-volume series on Chinese painting with a book on Yuan with the premise that he would write about only authentic works.[10] The surge in focus on Yuan led to seminars in Kansas, Berkeley, and Princeton, and dozens of dissertations on Yuan painters, those directed by Wen Fong (1930–2018) at Princeton benefitting from twenty-five paintings from the collection of C. C. Wang that came to the Metropolitan Museum in 1971.[11] Further, the Palace Museum in Taipei had opened in 1965; access to paintings in Taiwan had become much easier than previously, when the collection was in T'ai-chung. Dissertation writers of the late 1960s through 1970s studied the Taipei Palace Museum collection firsthand. Paintings in Taipei and Japan, as well as the Metropolitan Museum, the Cleveland Museum of Art, the Nelson Gallery in Kansas City, the Museum of Fine Arts, Boston, and a few others would be the core subject material for courses taught by these dissertation writers and their teachers well beyond the 1980s.

Still, as late as 1994, the year *The Cambridge History of China*, volume six, was published, Liao, Jin, Yuan, and Western Xia were in the same volume, subtitled *Alien Regimes and Border States*.[12] Herbert Franke (1914–2011), one of the editors of this volume, spent his career in Germany but was highly influential in the study of Liao, Jin, and Yuan in the United States. His paper at the 1975 American

Council of Learned Societies conference in Monterey, California, Conference on the Legitimation of Chinese Regimes, was published as the monograph *From Tribal Chieftain to Universal Emperor and God* in 1978.[13] Although his focus was history, art historians followed his thesis something like this: one sought to prove how something painted or sculpted or built under the sponsorship of a Northeast or North Asian ruler or state became Chinese.

It is perhaps justifiable to say that publications about Liao and Jin painting, all of them articles, snuck into art historical discourse on the back of Yuan. This was not true of architecture: Japanese research teams had published pagodas and other freestanding monuments in the above-mentioned folios of the 1930s and 1940s, and it was widely known that the Yuan capital Dadu and before it the Jin capital Zhongdu and before it the Liao capital Yanjing were worthy of research because they were beneath the Ming-Qing city of Beijing. Uncovering the locations of the earlier cities' walls, however, was the work of archaeologists, and the wide separation between early Chinse art and archaeology, which included Neolithic pots and bronze vessels and lacquerware, and Chinese painting was very much upheld in the 1970s.

The most widely used textbook on Chinese painting, James Cahill's *Chinese Painting*, first published in 1960,[14] included only one painting that some believed to be Liao. The anonymous painting "Deer among Red-leafed Maples" was published as tenth century.[15] Around the year 2000, I asked Michael Sullivan (1916–2013) if he knew how that painting came to be attributed. He said that so little was known about Liao in the 1960s and 1970s, but everyone knew that the deer were in all four paintings of the seasons in the tomb at Qingzhou, so the possibility of Liao was floated.

Sullivan also wrote a textbook in 1960, *An Introduction to Chinese Art*. It was one of the first books to merge painting, excavated material, and architecture into a single narrative, and it influenced the teaching of Chinese art in the United States.[16] In general, however, in the United States all Chinese painting was on silk or paper. Beginning in 1950, the research libraries that housed the above-mentioned folios also received periodical literature from the People's Republic. *Kaogu* (*Archaeology*) and *Wenwu* (*Cultural Relics*) were widely received in the United States. Major research libraries subscribed to between five and ten periodicals; graduate students wrote papers based on reports in them. No one doubted that excavated material would rewrite China's art history. Yet whereas the early Chinese art field had turned to these references, as well as to monographs that were emerging from the People's Republic almost as rapidly, their articles on painting did not attract much attention among those who were by the late 1970s able to study authentic paintings in collections in the People's Republic of China. In the late 1990s I asked Jim Cahill why he had not included the landscape mural in the tomb of Feng Daozhen, with a dated inscription of 1265 and published in *Wenwu* in 1962, in *Hills beyond a River* (fig. 2.3).[17] He said without hesitation, "It's wall painting." I continued, "How about Yonglegong?" This Daoist monastery in southern Shanxi province, with nearly 700 square meters of dated and signed murals, offered a scholar the opportunity not only to write about authentic fourteenth-century paintings, but also to tell the story of the dramatic move of every building and reinstallation of every mural. Cahill said that perhaps in the future he might, and went on to say that the survey of Chinese art I taught was no doubt very different from his.

Except for ceramics, Liao and Jin art were the subject of neither dissertations nor monographs even through the 1980s.[18] The first scholarly writing about painting of these periods concerned Jin, and scholars seem to have backed into the subject when unattributed works or works that were not verifiably Song or Yuan presented research problems. In 1965, Susan Bush wrote about "Clearing

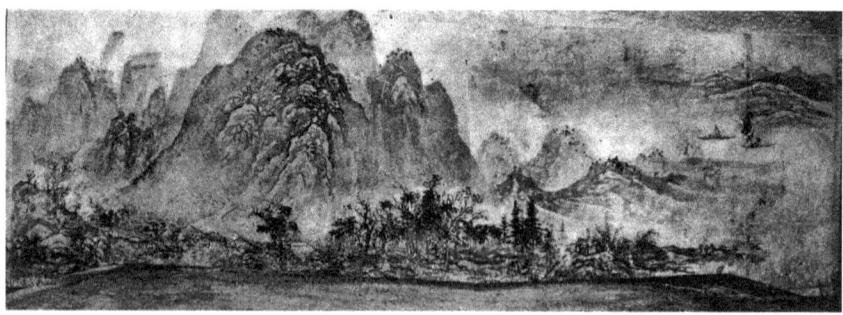

2.3. Landscape, wall of tomb of Feng Daozhen, Datong, Shanxi, 1265. *Wenwu*, no. 10 (1962): 45

after Snow in the Min Mountains" (fig. 2.4), and she tried to define criteria for identifying Jin painting in part through Li Shan, a painter who held a position at the Jin court.[19] The subject did not come up again for fourteen years. In 1979, Stephen Little wrote "Travelers among Valleys and Peaks: A Reconsideration of Jin Landscape Painting."[20] Susan Bush returned to the subject in 1986 and 1987.[21]

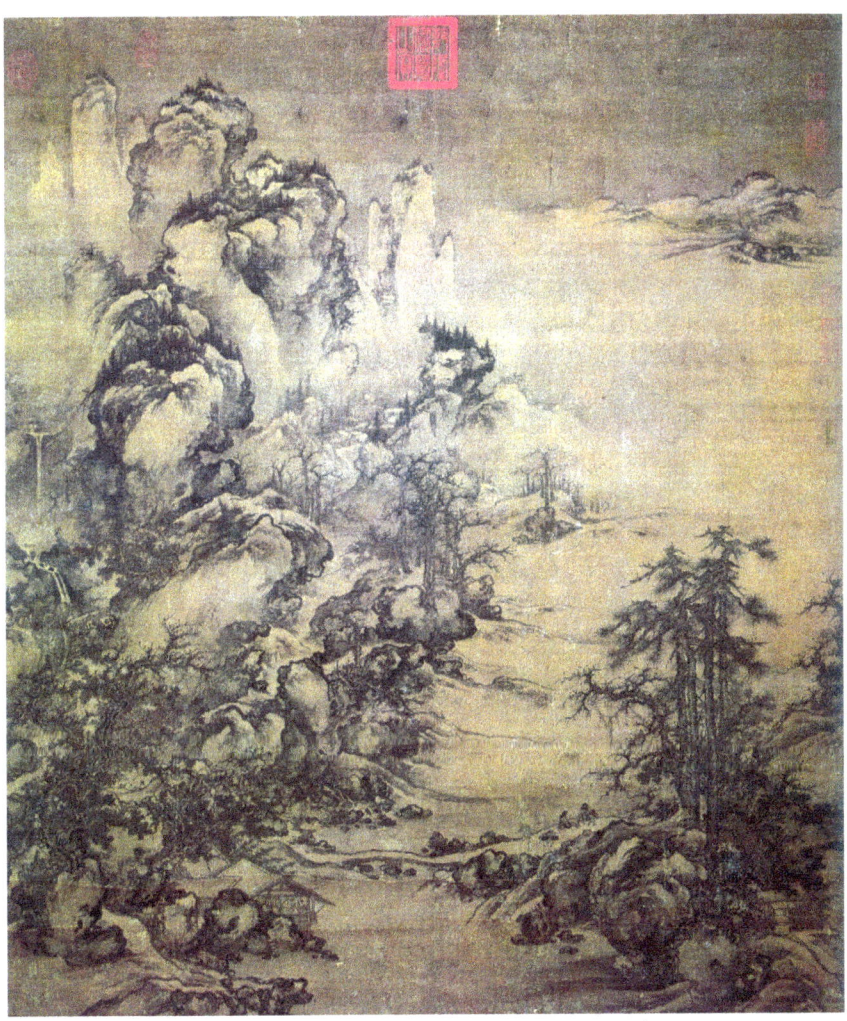

2.4. Anonymous, "Clearing after Snow in the Min Mountains," Jin. Photo courtesy National Palace Museum, Taipei

The need to study Jin and the potential to reveal something new in a field that by the 1980s included research opportunities in the People's Republic led to a conference at the University of Arizona in 1983 organized by Hoyt Tillman and Stephen West. Tillman was an emerging scholar of Jin and West and the majority of other participants scholars were trained in Song or Yuan. Herbert Franke wrote the forward and Susan Bush wrote the only article on painting or any other aspect of art. The book was not published until 1995.[22] Bush and Little would remain the main voices on Jin scroll painting, with an occasional contribution by Ellen Laing on Jin art,[23] until the 1990s, when Janet Carpenter wrote a dissertation on "Traveling among Mountains and Streams" at the University of Kansas.[24]

Wai-kam Ho, the Chinese art historian often and not incorrectly described as the man who knew everything, was consulted by Susan Bush and others doing research on paintings of the Song through Yuan period. In addition to co-curating the above-mentioned *Chinese Art under the Mongols* exhibition and editing its catalogue, Ho was a chief researcher, curator, and author of the landmark exhibition and catalogue of the major Chinese painting collections of the Nelson Gallery–Atkins Museum, Kansas City and the Cleveland Museum of Art.[25] "Chao Yü's Pacification of the Barbarians South of Lü," with the subtitle "by a Song artist," and Taigu Yimin's "Traveling among Streams and Mountains" were the paintings in the exhibition with Jin attributions. In 2018, Gabrielle Niu concluded that no more than fifteen paintings on silk or paper may be correctly attributed to the Jin period.[26]

Perhaps because the attributions were not irrefutable, or perhaps because the senior scholars in the Chinese art field still were uncertain about how Jin fit into the narrative, Jin painting did not join the Chinese art canon in the 1980s. Max Loehr's textbook *Great Painters of China*, for instance, mentions "Chin Tartars" six times to fill in historical facts, but no paintings are illustrated.[27] Jin was gaining attention in Chinese literature in a field that already by the 1980s was known to have a visual component. Stephen H. West's *Vaudeville and Narrative: Aspects of Chin Theater*, was an early monograph on the subject, to which he and Wilt Idema continue to make major contributions more than forty years later.[28] Already in the 1970s, scholars were asking whether illustrations of performance in murals and reliefs in Chinese tombs could be linked to specific plays. So far, the answer is no. Themes such as the four or five performers in *zaju* are generic. Jeehee Hong in 2008 and Zhang Fan in 2010 wrote dissertations on this subject, and both subsequently published on it.[29] China Institute had an exhibition on representations of drama and other aspects of popular culture in Jin tombs in 2012.[30]

Even into the twenty-first century, no aspect of Jin art except representations of drama has made enough of an impression to generate a monograph.[31] It is suggested here that, as for the Yuan dynasty, exhibitions rather than scholarly research or university teaching are the reason the United States gets interested in a Chinese art subject; and after exhibitions come graduate courses and articles and dissertations. By the twenty-first century, U.S. museum-goers were excited about Liao. Despite the China Institute exhibition, Jin is still largely ignored.

For Liao, and to a much lesser extent for Jin, the first turn of interest began, it is believed here, as part of an excitement about the opening of China and the resultant 1974 exhibition "Major Archaeological Discoveries from the People's Republic." This exhibition did not specifically stimulate interest in Liao. Rather it gave way to a shift in focus of Chinese art studies to excavated material. And indeed, post-1970s revised editions of Michael Sullivan's above-mentioned book and of Sherman Lee's *A History of Far Eastern Art* had newly excavated material.[32]

However, it is believed here that Liao and Jin lagged behind in attention in the United States for other reasons. They were not Yellow River or Yangzi River civilizations and Liao and Jin treasures could not be seen in the early 1980s by the flood of tourists to China, who went primarily to Beijing, Xi'an, Shanghai, Guangzhou, Suzhou, and Hangzhou and their museums. Even in the late 1980s, only occasionally did a tour group or even a researcher go to Liaoning or inner Mongolia, whose museums in Shenyang, Chifeng, and Hohhot at that time were small buildings that often shared commercial space or had very limited exhibition space.[33]

So much was coming out of the ground and was being published so fast in China in 1972, the year *Wenwu* resumed publication after a hiatus of a few years, that scholars had little incentive to turn to Liao, much less to Jin. In 1974, the year of the exhibition "Major Archaeological Discoveries from the People's Republic," the Han-dynasty tomb in Helinge'er, Inner Mongolia; Mawangdui tombs 2 and 3; a Nanjing tomb with Seven Worthies of the Bamboo Grove imagery; tiles from Jiayuguan in Gansu of the third–fourth century; the tomb of Tang prince Li Shou; and the star map from the sixth-century tomb of Yuan Yi in Luoyang were published in *Wenwu*. Murals in the Tang tombs of Princes Li Chongrun and Li Xian and the initial Mawangdui announcement had come in 1972/73. Mid-career scholars were quickly retooling so they could read excavation reports in simplified characters about these subjects. 1975 brought out yet more information about Mawangdui, new bronze vessels, new Neolithic sites, and important Tang-period finds from the Astana cemetery in Turfan. Published that year was a tomb with murals in Hebei, about an hour west of Beijing, that had painting with symbols of the Western zodiac and contained a long funerary inscription about a man in the service of Liao who read Buddhist sutras and had them painted on his walls. Finally, attention turned to Liao. Before the end of the year, excavators published a Liao tomb in Yemaotai, Liaoning, that contained two silk paintings that should have been all that was necessary for Liao to take its deserved place in United States academia. Beginning in 1974, however, scholarly and popular literature from China was flooded with perhaps the greatest discovery in the history of excavation in the People's Republic, certainly one that is universally known: the terra cotta soldiers in pits near the tomb of the First Emperor of China. Thus even though the potential of Liao painting, at least to help understand Song, if not in and of itself, may have been realized through finds in Hebei and at Yemaotai, graduate seminars, dissertations, and books about Chinese art, and of course exhibitions, turned to Mawangdui and other Han material such as jade suits, murals from the famous dynasties Han and Tang, and of course to the First Emperor. Except for the occasional publication in *Wenwu* or *Kaogu,* Liao material, like that of the still largely unknown Jin, was most often found in journals like *Liaohai wenwu* [Cultural Relics near the Liao Sea] or *Nei Menggu wenwu kaogu* [Cultural Relics and Archaeology of Inner Mongolia] or books and journals with the word *dongbei* (northeast) in the title. So much information was coming out of China by the late 1970s, much of it based on earlier research that did not get published during the Cultural Revolution (1966–1976), that even fewer research libraries than those that had acquired Japanese folio volumes in the 1920s and 1930s were able to acquire all of it.

It would be another eight years before Liao painting was the subject of scholarly articles with wide readership in the United States. Linda C. Johnson and Robert A. Rorex independently published articles in *Artibus Asiae* that relied on material from what by then was known either as Xiabali tomb 1 or Xuanhua tomb 1, the town and county, respectively, in Hebei where the tomb with the zodiac signs had been found (fig. 2.5).[34] By 1983, several more

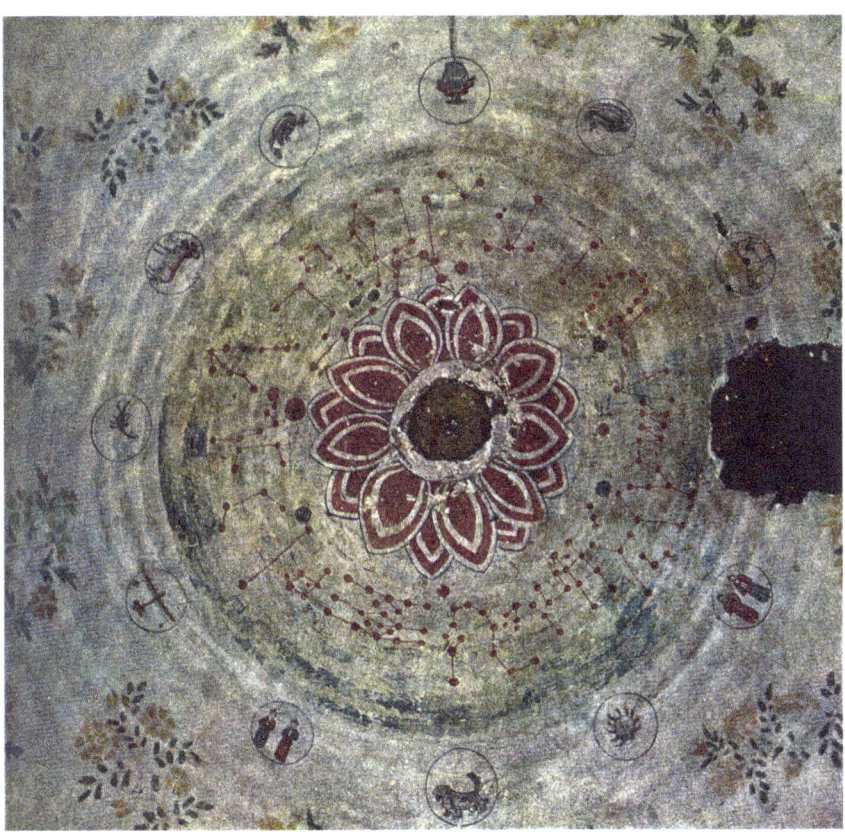

2.5. Ceiling of tomb of Zhang Shiqing, Xiabali tomb 1, Hebei. From *Wenwu*, no. 8 (1975): color pl. 1

tombs with murals had been excavated in the same cemetery, and tombs with murals from a Liao cemetery in Kulunqi, Inner Mongolia, also had been found.³⁵ Before then, in 1980, Patricia Karetzky had published an article on Jin murals in a hall at Yanshan Monastery in northern Shanxi.³⁶ Ellen Laing, who had included some material from Liao in her above-mentioned article of 1978 on "later" Chinese tombs, included some Liao material and in 1992 gave a paper on Liao bird-and-flower painting which became an article in *Journal of Sung-Yuan Studies*.³⁷

By the end of the 1980s, the metal wire suits, death masks, mannequins, and the two silk paintings from Yemaotai were all published in Chinese scholarly literature that was read by scholars and students in the United States. Still, Liao had at best made a ripple, certainly not a splash, and Jin was as obscure as ever.

Even the silk paintings in the Yemaotai tomb did not attract immediate or widespread attention from scholars of Chinese painting, despite their being authentic, done no later than the end of the Liao dynasty, earlier if the late-tenth century date proposed for the tomb was correct (figs. 2.6–7). The wooden outer sarcophagus on whose interior sides they hung had received its due attention from architectural historians. It was of the structural type *jiuji xiaozhang* (nine-ridge-roof-covered structure), described in the twelfth-century architectural manual *Yingzao fashi*. The architectural study of the sarcophagus was published in the same issue of *Wenwu* as the report on the tomb that included discussion of the paintings. Painting scholar Yang Renkai, who wrote the article in *Wenwu*, had published a monograph on the tomb in 1984.³⁸ His work was known to scholars of Chinese painting in the United States. In 1980, James Cahill talked about the Yemaotai paintings in a paper at a conference commemorating the seventieth year of the Republic of China in which he compared the painting with architecture to a work attributed to the tenth-century painter Wei Xian.³⁹ Richard Vinograd talked about the two paintings in a paper on tenth-century precedents for Yuan painting at a conference honoring the sixtieth birthday of Suzuki Kei.⁴⁰ Neither paper is known beyond the small circle of scholars who do research on Chinese painting of the "middle period" (ca. 9th–13th centuries). Marilyn Gridley, whose research focuses on Buddhist art of the Liao-Yuan period,

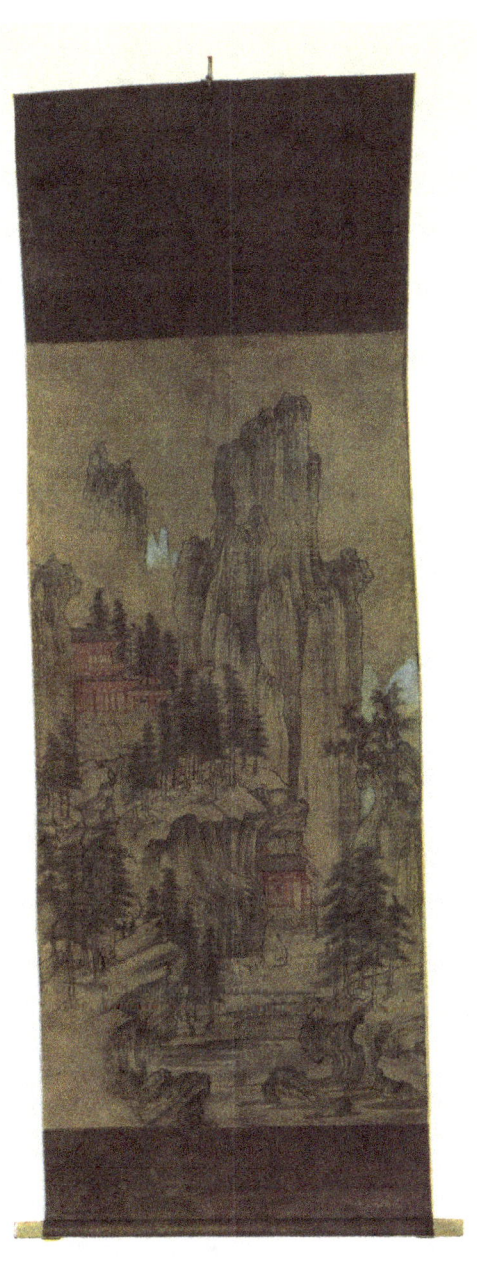

2.6. "Landscape," hanging scroll, Yemaotai tomb 7, Liao. From *Wenwu*, no. 12 (1975): color pl. 1

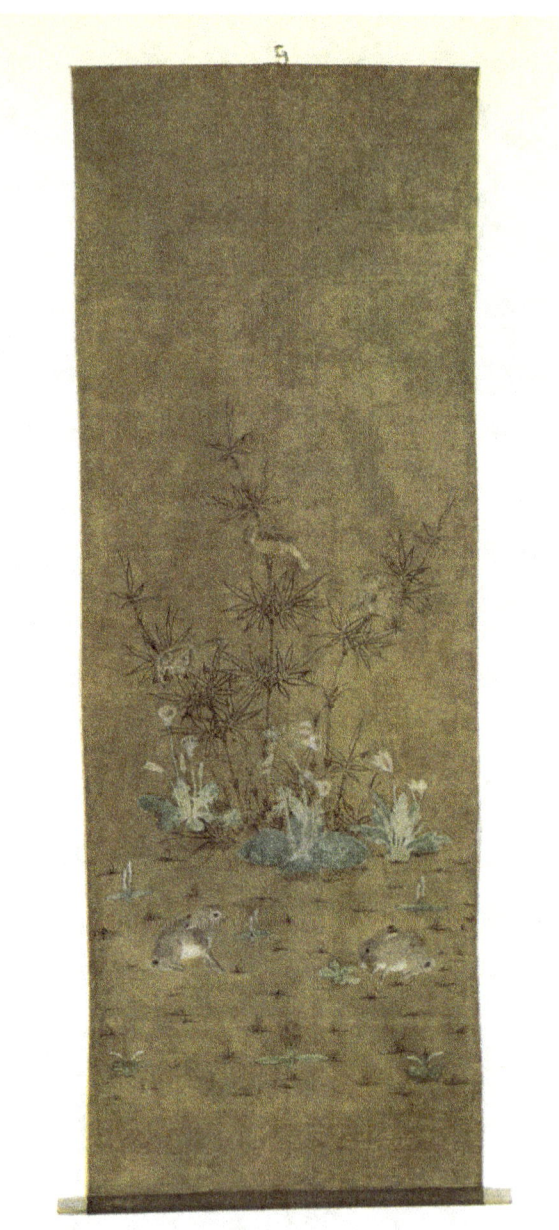

2.7. "Rabbits amid Flowers," hanging scroll, Yemaotai tomb 7, Liao. From *Wenwu*, no. 12 (1975): color pl. 2

wrote an article in a Festschrift for Li Chu-tsing on paintings of the Grasslands School, a group named to include the works of painters like Hu Gui, Hu Qian, and Yelü Bei.[41] Danielle Elisseeff wrote an article in *Arts Asiatiques* in 1996 in which she compared the Xuanhua murals to Song tomb painting.[42] The paucity of scholarly work on Liao rendered it, like several other articles by Europeans cited here, widely read by those doing research on Liao painting.

By this time, Hsing-yuan Tsao had completed her dissertation on Liao painting.[43] In the same year, 1996, she published "Deer for the Palace: A Reconsideration of the 'Deer in an Autumn Forest' Painting," in conference proceedings for an exhibition at the Metropolitan Museum of Art.[44] In 2000, Tsao organized an exhibition titled "Differences Preserved: Reconstructed Tombs from the Liao and Song Dynasties." Even though material from one of the Xiabali tombs was on exhibition, the catalogue and its material received little attention beyond the venues of the show.[45]

Exhibitions and archaeology, however, would be the forces that brought Liao and its painting to more national attention in the United States. *Gilded Splendor*, at Asia Society in 2006, was largely responsible, even though paintings were not displayed.[46] The focus on Liao brought attention back to murals from Qingzhou and Xiabali, and Kulunqi, and other places in Inner Mongolia and Liaoning, and to two tombs that had been excavated in Baoshan, Inner Mongolia, more than ten years earlier.[47] Those two tombs have paintings and inscriptions: we know they belong to a woman and a young man; that the earlier, male tomb is dated 923 and the woman's a little later; that a painting illustrates the Queen Mother of the West coming to greet the soul of Han emperor Wudi (156–87 BCE); that another painting is likely to be Yang Guifei (719–756), concubine of eighth-century emperor Tang Minghuang (685–762), teaching a parrot to recite the heart sutra; and that another painting may be a female poetess who sent her husband a palindrome while he was away at war. Wu Hung's article and lectures on the Baoshan tombs, as well as a conference on tenth-century art in China at the University of Chicago in 2009 and 2010, brought attention to the Baoshan tomb murals and Liao, more generally.[48] The Baoshan paintings, more than even the paintings from Xiabali, and in the decade after the exhibition "Gilded Splendor," seem to have finally captured the attention of scholars.

In the last ten years, few others have turned to Liao or Jin painting. The only dissertation of which I am aware, in addition to those already mentioned, was by Minkyung Ji in 2014.[49]

If there are conclusions, or at least take-away thoughts, about the historiography of Liao and Jin painting in the United States through 2018, they are to try to understand why so little attention has been given to material that is dated, authentic, and contains evidence of little-known civilizations that once were labeled barbarian. Perhaps it is because, easy as it is to travel in China, it is nearly impossible to see tombs and often nearly impossible to see temples with in situ murals or wall paintings even after they have been removed from tombs or temples. Or because before one comes to a Liao or Jin topic, one must commit to conducting research on works by anonymous painters that have little contextual material in standard histories, literary complications, or local records. Even Buddhist murals that survive in great numbers in Shanxi, including paintings in Ying County Timber Pagoda, Manjusri Hall at Foguang Monastery on Mount Wutai, Amitabha Hall at Chongfu Monastery in Shuo county, the south hall at Yanshan Monastery, on which there is the article by Karetzky, remain primarily the research of scholars in China. Perhaps the decrease in scholarly work on Buddhist art, including painting, in the United States in the last several decades has also affected the study of Liao and Jin. The increased interest in nomadic and semi-nomadic empires in the United States might lead to greater interest in the painting of Liao and Jin, and the lack of scholarship and resulting exotic aspects of the material might as well. For now, however, Liao and Jin painting are understudied subjects with tremendous research potential.

Notes

1. Luo Feng *Hu Han zhi jian: Sichou zhi lu yu xibei lishi kaogu* [Between *Hu* and Han: Archaeology of the History of the Silk Road and Northwestern China] (Beijing: Wenwu chubanshe, 2004).
2. Publications included excavation reports of every period from the Neolithic onward. The three listed here focus on Liao: Torii Ryūzō, *Kōkogakuō yori mitaru Ryō no bunka: Zufu* [Liao Culture Seen from Archaeology: Illustrations] 4 vols. (Tokyo: Tohobunka gakuin, Tokyo kenkyusho, 1936); Takeshima Takuichi, *Ryō-Kin jidai no kenchiku to sono Butsuzō* [Liao-Jin Architecture and Its Buddhist Sculpture], 3 vols. (Tokyo: Ryūbun shokyoku, 1934–44); and Tamura Jitsuzō and Kobayashi Yokio, *Keiryō* [Qingling], 2 vols. (Kyoto: Kyoto Daigaku bungakubu, 1953).
3. Mullie, "Les anciennes Villes de l'empire des grands Leao au royaume Mongol de Bārin," *T'oung Pao* 21 (1922): 105–231 and "Les sepulchres de K'ing des Leao," *T'oung Pao* 30 (1932): 1–25.
4. Stein, "Leao-tche," *T'oung Pao* 35 (1940): 1–154.
5. By the American Philosophical Society in Philadelphia.
6. Little is published about this painting. It is generally considered a copy painted four hundred to six hundred years later than the Liao period.
7. *Chinese Art under the Mongols* (Cleveland: Cleveland Museum of Art, 1968).
8. Masterworks known to scholars in the United States were published in: Chi-ch'ien Wang, *Album Leaves from the Sung and Yuan Dynasties* (New York: China House Gallery, 1970); Sherman Lee and Wen Fong, *Streams and Mountains without End: A Northern Song Handscroll and Its Significance in the History of Early Chinese Painting* (Ascona: Artibus Asiae, 1967); James Cahill, *Chinese Album Leaves in the Freer Gallery of Art* (Washington, D.C.: Smithsonian Institution, 1961); Zheng Zhenduo et al., *Songren huace* [Song Album Paintings] (Beijing: Zhongguo gudian yishu chubanshe, 1957), with an English edition; Tian Laige, *Tian Laige jiucang Songren huace* [Song Paintings in the Former Collection of Tian Laige] (Shanghai: Shangwu yinshuguan, 1957); and publications from major museums such as *Songren huace: Gongyuan 960–1279* [Song Paintings: 960–1279] (Beijing: Gugong Bowuyuan, 1955) or broader surveys from the Palace Museum, Beijing, and the Palace Museum in Taiwan.
9. Among Li's publications are: "The Freer 'Sheep and Goat'," *Artibus Asiae* 39, nos. 3–4 (1960): 279–346; "*Rocks and Trees* in the Art of Ts'ao Chih-po," *Artibus Asiae* 23, nos. 3–4 (1960): 153–208; Li Chu-tsing,

The Autumn Colors on the Ch'iao and Hua Mountains (Ascona: Artibus Asiae, 1965); "Stages of Development in Yuan Landscape Painting," pts. 1 and 2, *National Palace Museum Bulletin* 4, nos. 2 (1969): 1–10 and 3 (1969): 1–12; "The Development of Painting in Soochow during the Yuan Dynasty," in *Proceedings of the International Symposium on Chinese Painting* (Taipei: National Palace Museum, 1972), 483–500; "Uses of the Past in Yuan Landscape," in *Artists and Traditions*, ed. Christian Murck (Princeton: Princeton University Art Museum, 1976), 73–88; "The Role of Wu-hsing in Early Yuan Artistic Development under Mongol Rule," in *China under Mongol Rule*, ed. John Langlois, Jr. (Princeton: Princeton University Press, 1981), 331–70 and "*Grooms and Horses* by Three Members of the Chao Family," in *Words and Images*, ed. Alfreda Murck and Wen Fong (New York: Metropolitan Museum of Art, 1991), 199–220.

10 *Hills beyond a River: Chinese Painting of the Yuan Dynasty, 1279–1368* (New York and Tokyo, Weatherhill, 1976).

11 Song paintings were also included. See Wen Fong with Marilynn Fu, *Sung and Yuan Paintings* (New York: Metropolitan Museum of Art, 1973).

12 Herbert Franke and Denis Twitchett edited this volume. Franke also wrote about painting. He edited the painters volume for *Song Biographies* and he wrote two articles on Yuan painting, "Dschau Mong-fu," *Sinica* 15 (1940): 25–48 and "Two Yuan Treatises on the Technique of Portrait Painting," *Oriental Art* 3, no. 1 (1950): 27–32.

13 München: Bayerische Akademie der Wissenschaften, 1978.

14 Geneva: Skira, with many later editions.

15 Cahill, *Chinese Painting*, 68.

16 Sullivan was British, but received his Ph.D. in the United States, at Harvard in 1952. He taught at the School of Oriental and African Studies in London and at Stanford. The book went through many versions, all published by the University of California Press, the most recent the posthumous 2018 version adapted by Sheila Vainker. Sullivan had spent six years in China with the Red Cross in the 1940s and thus unlike those teaching Chinese art in the United States in the 1960s and 1970s, including Li, Cahill, Fong, and Alexander Soper, he had seen a lot of China. Sullivan was committed to the study of sculpture, architecture, and ceramics, as well as painting, including contemporary art, through his career.

17 Datongshi Wenwu Chenlieguan and Shanxi Yungang Wenwu Guanlisuo, "Shanxisheng Datongshi Yuandai Feng Daozhen, Wang Qing mu qingli jianbao" [Brief Report on the Tombs of Feng Daozhen and Wang Qing in Datong, Shanxi] *Wenwu*, no. 10 (1962): 34–46.

18 For example, Mino Yutaka, *Ceramics in the Liao Dynasty, North and South of the Great Wall* (New York: China House Gallery, 1973). In England, William Watson wrote *Tang and Liao Ceramics* (London: Thames and Hudson, 1984).
19 "'Clearing after Snow in the Min Mountains' and Chin Landscape Painting," *Oriental Art* 11 (Autumn 1965): 103–12.
20 *Artibus Asiae* 41 (1979): 285–308.
21 "Chin Literati Painting and Landscape Traditions," *National Palace Museum Bulletin* 21 (September–December 1986): 1–26 and "Yet Again Streams and Mountains without End," *Artibus Asiae* 48 (1987): 197–223. By then Bush had become engaged in the study of Jin more generally. In 1981 she wrote "Archaeological Remains of the Chin Dynasty (1115–1234)" in *Bulletin of Sung and Yüan Studies* 17 (1981): 6–31.
22 Bush's article is "Five Paintings of Animal Subjects of Narrative Themes and Their Relevance to Chin Culture," 183–215; two of the paintings today are usually dated to the Yuan period. The book is *China under Jurchen Rule* (Albany: SUNY Press).
23 Ellen Laing's articles include: "Problems and Patterns in Later Chinese Tombs," *Journal of Oriental Studies* 16 (1978): 73–126; "Chin 'Tartar' Dynasty (1115–1234) Material Culture," *Artibus Asiae* 49, nos. 1–2 (1988): 73–126; and "Auspicious Motifs in Ninth- to Thirteenth-Century Chinese Tombs," *Ars Orientalis* 33 (2003): 32–75.
24 Janet L. Carpenter's dissertation was completed in 1994. She wrote about another painting often dated to the Jin period in "A Landscape Painting and Its Literary Sources: Taigu Yimin's 'Traveling among Streams and Mountains'," in *Tradition and Transformation: Studies in Chinese Art in Honor of Chu-Tsing Li*, ed. Judith Smith, 136–61 (Seattle and Lawrence, Ks.: University of Washington Press, Spencer Museum of Art, and University of Kansas, 2005).
25 Wai-kam Ho, Sherman E. Lee, Laurence Sickman, and Mark F. Wilson, *Eight Dynasties of Chinese Painting* (Cleveland: Cleveland Museum of Art, 1980).
26 For the list and discussion, see Gabrielle Niu, "Beyond Silk: A Reevaluation of Jin Painting (1115–1234)" (Ph.D. dissertation, University of Pennsylvania, 2018), 20–59. Besides the three paintings mentioned so far in Cleveland and Kansas City, Li Shan's "Wind and Snow among Fir Pines," "Travelers among Fir Pines" in the Freer Gallery, "Travelers among Valleys and Peaks" in the Asian Art Museum, "Winter Landscape" in the Yale Art Gallery, "Flock of Birds Returning to Wintry Woods," "Clear Weather in the Valley," "Red Cliff" in the Museum of Fine Arts, Boston, "A Diplomatic Mission to the Jin" in the Metropolitan Museum of Art, and "Wangchuan Villa" in the Chicago

Art Institute are the subjects of notes or short publications by their respective museums.

27 Max Loehr, *The Great Painters of China* (Oxford: Phaidon, 1980).
28 The bibliography on Jin and Yuan drama is too long to list here.
29 Jeehee Hong, "Theatricalizing Death in Performance Images of Mid-imperial China" (Ph.D. diss., University of Chicago, 2008); "Virtual Theater of the Dead: Actor Figurines and Their Stage in Houma Tomb No. 1, Shanxi Province," *Artibus Asiae* 71, no. 1 (2011): 75–114; "Changing Roles of the Tomb Portrait: Burial Practices and Ancestral Worship of the Non-Literati Elite in North China (1000–1400)," *Journal of Sung-Yuan Studies* 44 (2014): 203–64; and *Theater of the Dead: A Social Turn in Chinese Funerary Art 1000–1400* (Honolulu: University of Hawai'i Press, 2016); and Zhang Fan Jeremy, "Drama Sustains the Spirit: Art, Ritual, and Theater in Jin and Yuan Period Pingyang 1150–1350" (Ph.D. diss., Brown University, 2011); "Jin Dynasty Pingyang and the Rise of Theatrical Pictures," *Artibus Asiae* 74, no. 2 (2014): 337–76; "Dreams, Spirits, and Romantic Encounters in Jin and Yuan Theatrical Pictures," in *Visual and Material Cultures in Middle Period China*, ed. Shih-shan Susan Huang and Patricia Ebrey (Leiden and Boston: Brill, 2017), 115–50.
30 *Theater, Life, and the Afterlife: Tomb Décor of the Jin Dynasty from Shanxi*, ed. Shi Jinming and Willow W. Chang (New York: China Institute, 2012).
31 The title of this author's "A Jin Hall at Jingtusi: Architecture in Search of Identity," *Ars Orientalis* 33 (2003): 77–119 was chosen to emphasize the lack of attention to Jin art and architecture.
32 New York: Abrams, first edition 1964; most recent edition, 2003.
33 Again I write from personal experience. In 1992, I visited the Chifeng Museum in a building in which furniture was sold. In the same year, the museum where I first saw the wooden sarcophagus from Yemaotai tomb 7, whose silk paintings are discussed below, was two rooms with one guard and no curator.
34 Linda C. Johnson's M.A. thesis at San Jose State in 1974 was titled "Jurchen Revival." Her article is "Wedding Ceremony for an Imperial Liao Princess: Wall Paintings from a Liao Dynasty Tomb in Jilin," *Artibus Asiae* 44, nos. 2–3 (1983): 107–36. Rorex's article is "Some Liao Tomb Murals and Images of Nomads in Chinese Paintings of the Wen-chi Story," *Artibus Asiae* 45, nos. 2–3 (1984): 174–98.
35 Murals from the Kulunqi tombs are published in Wang Jianchun and Chen Xiangwei, *Kulun Liaodai bihuamu* [Liao Tombs with Murals in Kulun] (Beijing: Wenwu chubanshe, 1989).

36 "Two Recently Discovered Chin Dynasty Murals Illustrating the Life of the Buddha at Yen-shang-ssu, Shansi," *Artibus Asiae* 42, no. 4 (1980): 245–60.
37 "A Survey of Liao Dynasty Bird-and-Flower Painting," *Journal of Sung-Yuan Studies* 24 (1994): 57–99.
38 Yang Renkai, "Yemaotai Liaomu chutu guhua de shidai ji qita" [On the Date and Other Aspects of Paintings Excavated in a Liao Tomb in Yemaotai], *Wenwu*, no. 12 (1975): 37–39. The article on the architecture of the sarcophagus is on 49–62. Yang's book is *Yemaotai diqihao Liaomu chutu guhua kao* [Research on Old Paintings Excavated in Tomb 7 of the Liao Period in Yemaotai] (Shanghai: Shanghai Renmin meishu chubanshe, 1984).
39 James Cahill, "Some Aspects of Tenth-Century Painting as Seen in Three Recently Published Works," *Zhongyang Yanjiuyuan Guoji Hanxue huiyi lunwenji* [Proceedings of the International Conference on Sinology, Academic Sinica] (Taipei: Zhongyang yanjiuyuan, 1980), 1–34.
40 Richard Vinograd, "New Light on Tenth-Century Sources for Landscape Painting Styles of the Late Yüan Period," in *Suzuki Kei sensei kanreki kinen: Chugoku kaigashi ronshū* [Commemoration of the Sixtieth Birthday of Professor Suzuki Kei] (Tokyo: Yoshikawa Kōbunkan, 1981), 3–30.
41 Marilyn Gridley, "Liao Painting and the Northern Grasslands School," in *Tradition and Transformation: Studies in Chinese Art in Honor of Chu-Tsing Li*, ed. Judith Smith (Seattle and Lawrence, Ks.: University of Washington Press, Spencer Museum of Art, and University of Kansas, 2005), 27–51.
42 Danielle Elisseeff, "À propos d'un cimitière Liao: Les belles dames de Xiabali," *Arts Asiatiques* 49 (1996): 70–81.
43 Hsing-yuan Tsao, "From Appropriation to Possession: A Study of the Cultural Identity of the Liao through Their Pictorial Art" (Ph.D. diss., Stanford University, 1996).
44 The article is published in *Arts of the Sung and Yuan*, ed. Maxwell Hearn and Judith Smith (New York, Metropolitan Museum of Art, 1996), 199–211.
45 "Differences Preserved: Reconstructed Tombs from the Liao and Song Dynasties" opened at Reed College Art Museum in February 2000. It traveled to Boston University, Boise, Idaho, and Middlebury College through June 2001.
46 Hsüeh-man Shen, *Gilded Splendor: Treasures of China's Liao Empire (907–1125)* (New York: Asia Society, 2006) is the name of the catalogue. The exhibition traveled to Cologne and Zurich the following year.

47 The report was published as Qi Xiaoguang et al., "Nei Menggu Chifeng Baoshan Liao bihuamu fajue jianbao" [Brief Report on the Excavation of Liao Tombs with Murals in Baoshan, Chifeng, Inner Mongolia], *Wenwu*, no. 1 (1998): 73–95.
48 Wu Hung's paper is "Two Royal Tombs from the Early Liao: Architecture, Pictorial Program, Authorship, Subjectivity," in *Tenth-Century China and Beyond: Art and Visual Culture in a Multi-centered Age*, ed. Wu Hung (Chicago: Center for the Art of East Asia, University of Chicago, 2012), 100–125.
49 "Commoditizing Tombs: Materialism in the Funerary Art of Middle Imperial China and Korea" (Ph.D. diss., University of Pennsylvania), includes material from Song, Jin, and Koryŏ tombs.

Chapter 3

In Pursuit of Depth and Breadth: The Impact of C. C. Wang, Wai-kam Ho, and Wang Fangyu on Chinese Painting Studies

Arnold Chang

I have been assigned the impossible task of summarizing, in thirty minutes, the contributions to the field of Chinese painting of three titans of the second half of the twentieth century, Wang Jiqian, Wang Fangyu, and Wai-kam Ho. I will not even attempt to list all of their accomplishments. Each of these three men deserves his own separate lecture, if not an entire conference. In the limited time allotted I will talk a bit about my personal relationships with each of them, to give a feel for how they approached the study of Chinese painting and a bit of what I learned from them. I will not talk about Wang Jiqian as a painter or Wang Fangyu as a calligrapher but bear in mind that they were both creative artists and how they practiced art was fundamental to their understanding of the art of the old masters.

A word on names: I will refer to Wang Jiqian as C. C. Wang, the name he is best known by in the western world. I always referred to him as *Wang laoshi*, and would never call him C. C. to his face, but in talking about him most people refer to him as C. C. Wang Fangyu also went by the name Fred Wang, but I could never see him as a Fred and he was always *Wang jiaoshou* (Professor Wang) to me. So I will continue refer to him as Professor Wang. Everybody seemed to refer to Wai-kam Ho as Wai-kam and he wasn't offended, so I will continue in that tradition.

Wang Fangyu

I first met Wang Fangyu (figs. 3.1–3) way back in the summer of 1973. I was attending a ten-week summer intensive first year Chinese language program at Columbia University. Although not a total immersion program like the one offered at Middlebury—where students lived in isolation and were not allowed to communicate in English at all—in some ways the Columbia method was more difficult because in addition to hours of class and language lab, you had to devote many more hours each day just to keep up, while still living your life in your normal English-speaking environment. My teacher was a wonderful woman named Irene Liu, who had been trained as a language instructor by Professor Wang Fangyu, who was at the time teaching Chinese at Seton Hall University. At some point that summer, toward the end of our ten-week course, Ms. Liu invited Professor Wang to pay us a visit. An elegant, scholarly gentleman sauntered in and proceeded to address the class. He began telling us a story in perfect Beijing-accented Mandarin. He spoke very clearly and slowly without pause for several minutes. I don't recall the content of his talk, but the amazing thing about the experience was that he was able to tell a whole story off the top of his head using only the vocabulary and sentence patterns that we had learned in first year Chinese! He made us all feel like we actually could understand Chinese and that our summer of torture was worthwhile. It gave us all confidence to continue our studies.

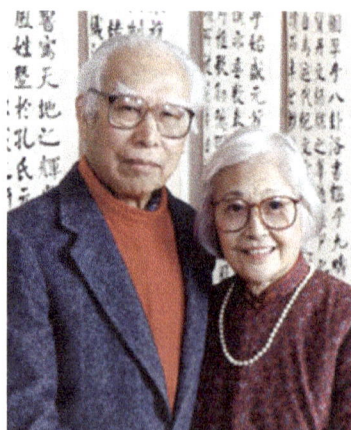

3.1. Wang Fangyu (1913–1997) and his wife Sum Wai (1918–1996)

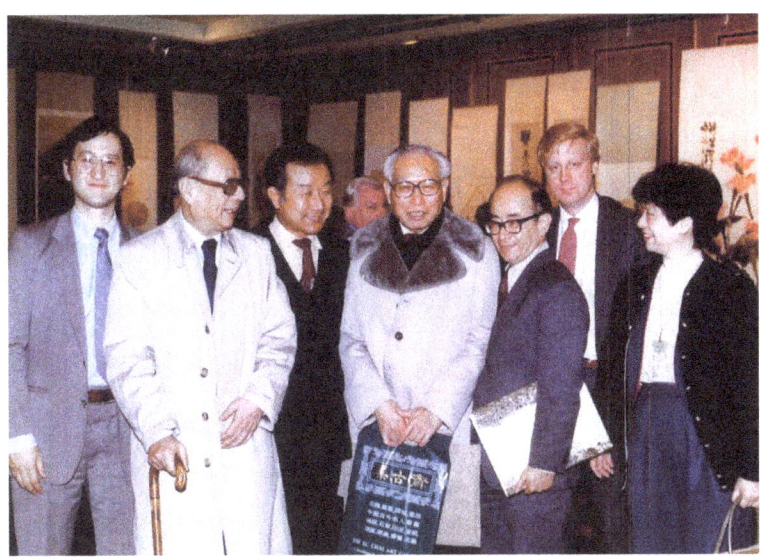

3.2. Left to Right: Arnold Chang, Wang Jiqian, Liu Guosong, Wang Fangyu, Chen Qikuan, Yien-koo King at Sotheby's Hong Kong exhibition, 1984. Photo by Jr-jye Chang

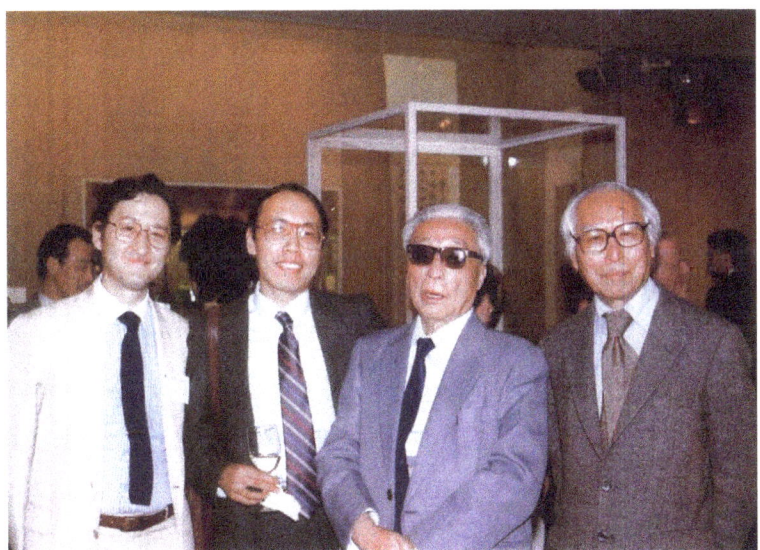

3.3. Left to Right: Arnold Chang, Xu Yunshu, Xie Zhiliu, Wang Fangyu at Sotheby's New York exhibition, 1985. Photo by Jr-jye Chang

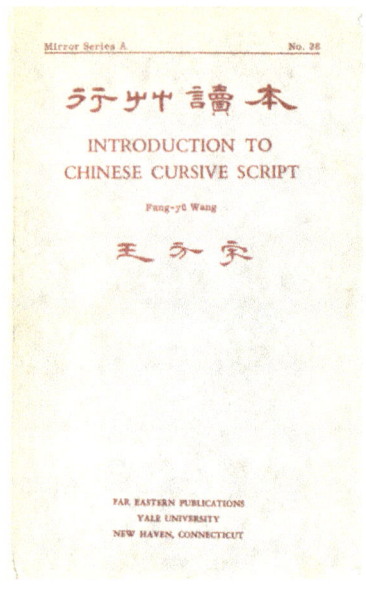

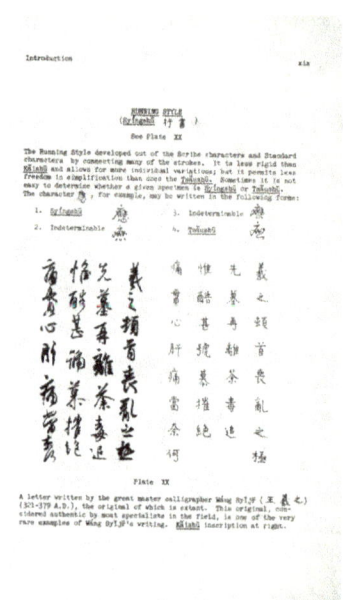

3.4. Wang Fangyu, *Introduction to Chinese Cursive Script* (New Haven, 1958). Top: book cover; bottom: "Running Style."

Wang Fangyu was above all else an educator. He wrote Chinese-English dictionaries and textbooks. I found one of these books to be particularly useful: *Introduction to Chinese Cursive Script* (fig. 3.4).[1] This book is still available on Amazon. The last line of the Amazon description reads: "This book teaches students to recognize the cursive versions of 300 basic, frequently-used characters in Chinese, radical by radical. In doing so, it fills a crucial gap in the bridge between academic learning and real-life competence."

I love that last line because it captures Wang Fangyu's overlapping roles as an educator, scholar, and collector. Despite his incredible erudition he was a humble man. He never presented himself as an extraordinary talent with a natural gift for connoisseurship, even though we all know him as the world's leading authority on the art of Bada Sharen. Through hard work and a methodical approach he was able to sift through all the available evidence, including visual and textual, to learn as much as he could about this seventeenth-century artist. I think Professor Wang wanted to take the mystery out of connoisseurship, and other areas of Chinese studies as well. He was interested in developing methodologies for simplifying the learning process and organizing the results. *Chinese Cursive Script* is a great example of this. Beginning with the three hundred most basic characters, he was able to identify and categorize the most commonly used simplified or abbreviated cursive forms and organize them by radical. This may not help too much when you are trying to decipher Huaisu's *caoshu*, but with a little effort even a first-year Chinese student could begin to recognize some handwritten Chinese.

Years later, in 1980 I believe, after I had already started working at Sotheby's, Professor Wang offered a non-credit course at Columbia University in reading seal script (fig. 3.5). I still have my materials from that class, including nearly one hundred pages of notes, exercises, quizzes, and articles, all prepared by Wang Fangyu for a class he wasn't being paid to teach. I don't think he ever taught this course again, but it couldn't have come at a better time for me. More than any other of the handful of students, I used the knowledge and practice gained from this course in my everyday work cataloguing Chinese paintings for Sotheby's auctions. For me at least it helped "fill the gap between academic learning and real-life competence."

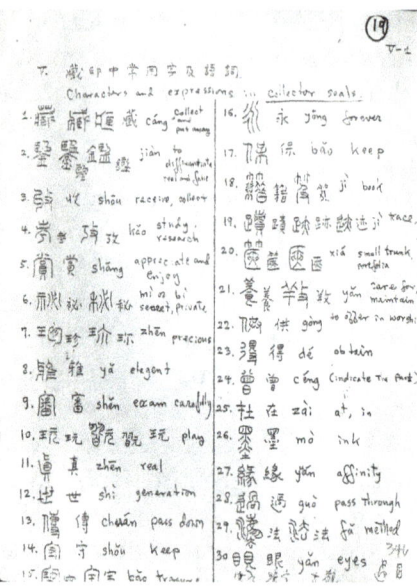

3.5. Wang Fangyu, Handouts for seal script class at Columbia University

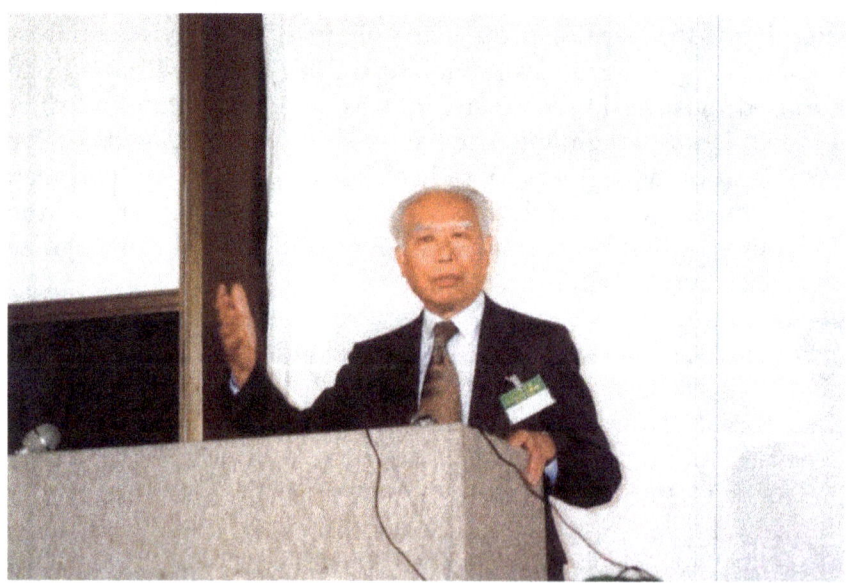

3.6. Wang Fangyu lecturing at "Four Monk Painters from the Early Qing International Symposium" at Shanghai Museum, 1987. Photo by Arnold Chang

In his study of the Chinese language Wang Fangyu searched for patterns in usage that he culled from his examination of the data. In teaching beginning Chinese he identified basic patterns of speech and sentence structure that could be used as models upon which to develop proficiency by adding vocabulary. In reading cursive and seal scripts he sought out visual elements that could likewise serve as basic patterns that could be recognized though repetition and built upon through the addition of new elements.

Identifying the hand of an individual painter or calligrapher required similar skills of pattern recognition. In examining the body of a specific artist's work, what were the underlying patterns of form, composition, brushwork, and subject matter?

Bada Shanren was the perfect choice of artist for this type of analysis (fig. 3.6). Over the course of his lifetime Bada signed his works using a variety of different names written in several different script styles, and after the age of sixty he employed obscure characters and ancient dating systems to inscribe his works. He also used a large number of seals, some of which were difficult to decipher (fig. 3.7). Professor Wang unlocked the mysteries of the

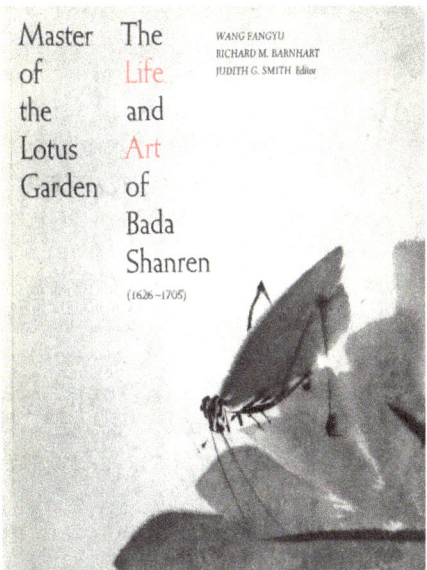

3.7A. *Master of the Lotus Garden: The Life and Art of Bada Shanren* by Wang Fangyu and Richard Barnhart, edited by Judith Smith, cover.

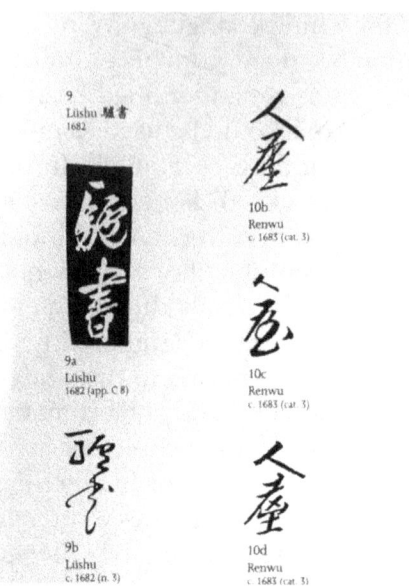

3.7.B *Master of the Lotus Garden: The Life and Art of Bada Shanren* by Wang Fangyu and Richard Barnhart, edited by Judith Smith, comparative material for signatures and dates by Bada Shanren

obscure dating systems that Bada used, and was then able to group and order the works based on date in order to identify broader patterns. He demonstrated that this enigmatic artist used certain signatures and combinations of seals at certain times in his life. Wang published his results in a number of articles and essays that have been crucial to the study of Bada Shanren's life and work, and have established Wang Fangyu as one of the leading authorities on Bada.

I remember hearing a lecture by Professor Wang at China Institute in which he discussed the issue of connoisseurship in Chinese paintings. He made a point of distinguishing between quality and authenticity. He said that in general a given work should fall into one of four categories:

1. Genuine and good (meaning good quality).
2. Genuine and not good.
3. Fake and good.
4. Fake and not good.

Category 1 and category 4 shouldn't be a problem—we should all be able to recognize a fine work by a great artist, and we should all be able to quickly dispense with a poor quality imitation by a lesser artist. But the two middle categories give us trouble. How do we distinguish between a painting that is authentic but not the best example of an artist's work and a really good painting that was done by somebody else? The question of course is rhetorical. Professor Wang was warning us to always keep in mind that not every work by even a great artist will be a masterpiece, and that some very fine paintings may be fakes. Authenticity and quality are both important, but we should never confuse the two. He made it sound so easy and logical.

Wai-kam Ho

All the stories you have heard about Wai-kam Ho are true (fig. 3.8). He was a brilliant scholar, a fabulous raconteur, and a true gourmand. He was also eccentric, absent-minded, and often oblivious to the mundane concerns of time and place, such as appointments, deadlines, and due dates for the return of library books.

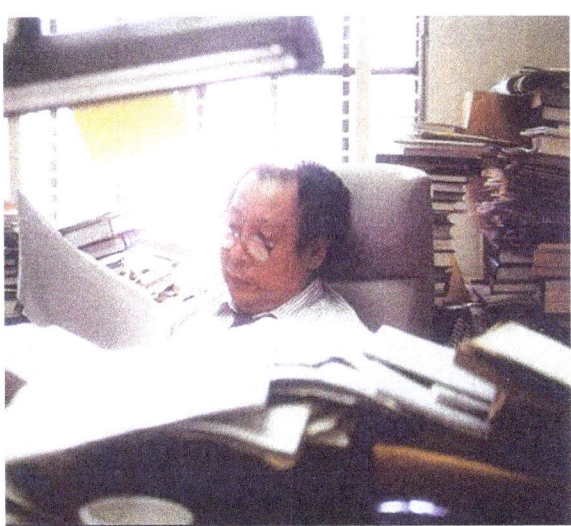

3.8. Wai-kam Ho, date unknown. Photo courtesy of Kaikodo

I got to know him late in his life but his reputation certainly preceded him, so I was forewarned about his quirky brilliance.

His crowning achievement was the 1991–1992 exhibition "The Century of Tung Ch'i-ch'ang, 1555–1636," which was accompanied by a hefty two-volume catalogue of unprecedented depth and breadth, as well as a star-studded symposium, in which nearly all of the major names in the field of Chinese painting participated (fig. 3.9).[2]

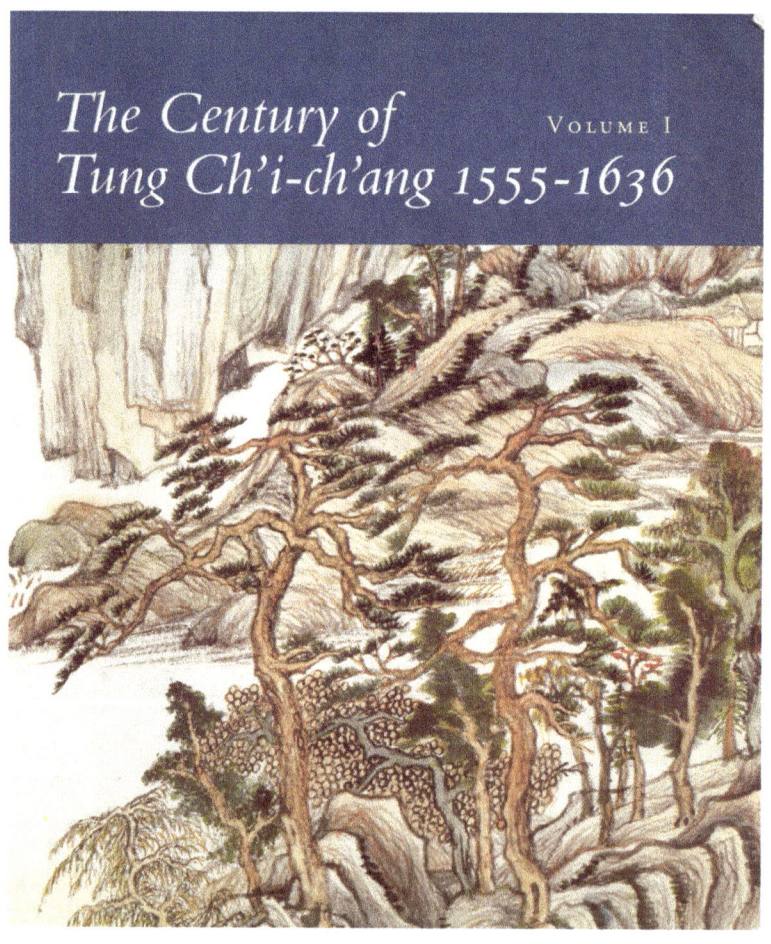

3.9. Cover of the first of two volumes of *The Century of Tung Ch'i-ch'ang, 1555–1636*

Shortly after the Dong Qichang exhibition, Wai-kam began advising an East coast collector of Chinese paintings and calligraphy whom I knew very well from my Sotheby's days. I got to know Wai-kam better through this connection. I left Sotheby's in 1994, about the same time Wai-kam left the Nelson, so we both began to devote more time and energy helping to build up this private collection. We frequently went together to preview the offerings at Sotheby's and Christie's in both New York and Hong Kong, exchanged views about authenticity and quality and huddled with the collector to devise our bidding strategy. In these discussions Wai-kam of course provided the intellectual firepower, breezing through inscriptions and colophons like they were children's comic books—which, by the way, he also loved—effortlessly drawing on his deep knowledge of history, literature, religion, and philosophy to assess the relative importance of each work. My primary contribution to the team was my experience with the market. This was the one area that I knew better than Wai-kam, who didn't value art in terms of dollars and cents. Of course I had my own ideas about quality, as did the collector, and it was through the spirited discussions that preceded each potential purchase over the next decade that I came to fully appreciate Wai-kam's genius.

Wai-kam Ho was generous with his knowledge and he loved sharing his insights. This could be a problem when we went to the auction previews. I guess he was not much of a poker player because he made it so obvious whether or not he liked the painting he was looking at. If he began unrolling a handscroll and after a few inches felt that it was of dubious attribution he would immediately roll it back up. If he noticed something interesting about a work, an obscure reference in an inscription, or a rare collector's seal, he would blurt out this valuable tidbit in a voice loud enough for everyone around him to hear. Naturally Wai-kam's appearance in the gallery would attract crowds who would look over his shoulder and note which pieces he spent the most time looking at. Part of my responsibility was to make sure that he didn't telegraph to our competitors which pieces we were going to bid on! In at least one instance we lost out on a very rare Song painting because Wai-kam had deciphered a small signature that nobody else had been able to read. Unfortunately he told this to the head of the Chinese painting department at Christie's, who proceeded to tell his best clients, because of course his job was to create competition in order to attain the best price for the consignor. We didn't let Wai-kam attend the actual auctions since he might tip our hand. I did all of the bidding.

I got to travel with Wai-kam to China a couple of times (fig. 3.10). It was great to tag along with him to the mainland museums because he was so well respected in China, where he got the VIP treatment and we were able to view whatever paintings he requested. On one occasion, in 1999, I found myself in the fortunate position of going with him to the fifty-year anniversary celebration of the Palace Museum in Beijing. In honor of this occasion the museum had mounted a special exhibition showcasing cultural relics

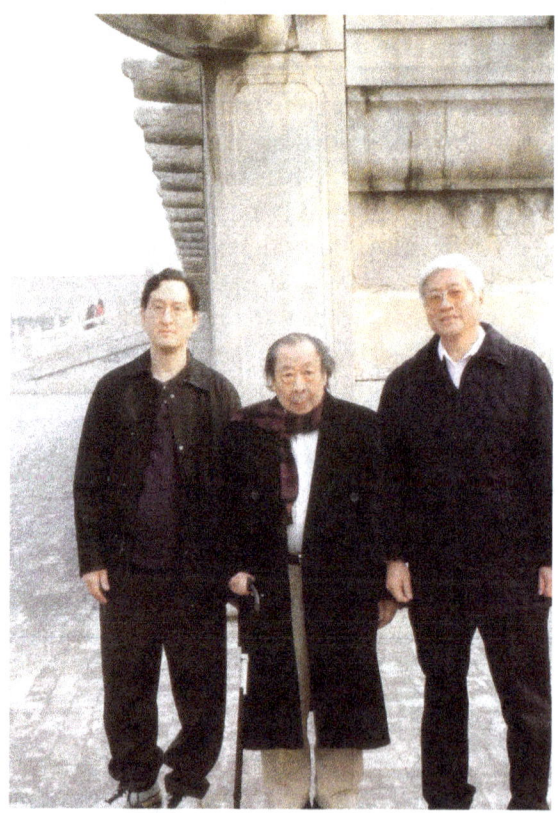

3.10. Arnold Chang, Wai-kam Ho, Shau Wai Lam. Photo by Steven Owyang.

collected since 1949, and published an illustrated catalogue (fig. 3.11). The museum also organized a Chinese-style symposium, by which I mean the participants all sat around a large table and made polite comments about the works in the exhibition. They divided the participants, experts from all across China—plus me and Wai-kam—into two groups, one for paintings and calligraphy, and the other for other works of art (ceramics, bronzes, jades, and other objects). We were directed to the paintings room. Wai-kam sat down at the table and I found an unobtrusive chair against the wall in the back of the room. Because he was a foreign visitor of such stature, they asked Wai-kam to speak first. I think they expected him to congratulate the museum on their new acquisitions, but instead he

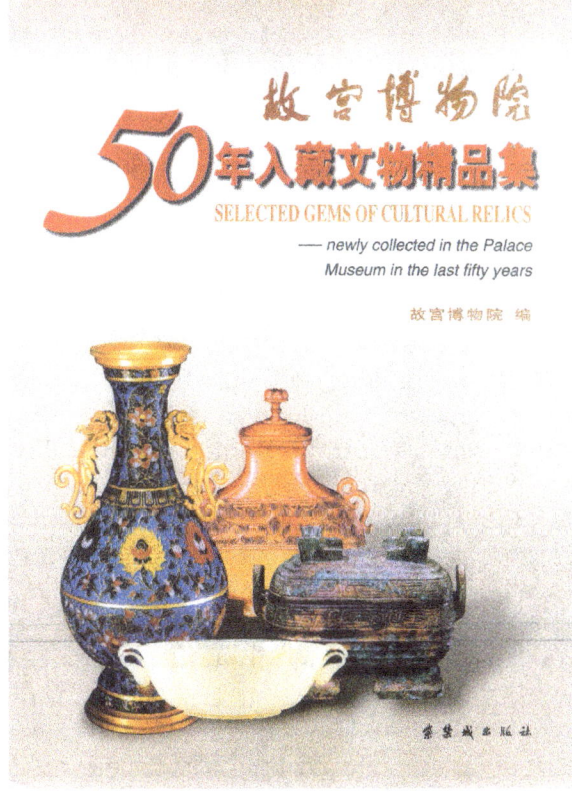

3.11. Cover of *Selected Gems of Cultural Relics: Newly Collected in the Palace Museum in the Last Fifty Years*

started flipping through the catalogue, page by page, pointing out all the mistakes. "This lacquer piece is not Chinese, it was made in Okinawa. This sculpture is dated incorrectly. This bronze is fake," so forth, and so on. Remember we were in the paintings section! This was typical Wai-kam Ho. He had a deep knowledge of all aspects of Chinese art. I learned a great deal from him about Chinese Buddhist sculpture just by accompanying him to exhibitions of recent finds from Qingzhou, held in Hong Kong and Beijing.

I should note that in my experience, and from what I've heard from others, Wai-kam was not a snob. He never talked down to people and he was happy to engage with nonspecialists. But if you were supposed to be an expert and you said something that was inaccurate he would call you out on it. He had no tolerance for posturing.

On that same trip, in 1999, we were leaving China for Hong Kong to attend a Christie's auction. Upon receipt of the catalogue, before departure, we were both struck by the image of a handscroll attributed to the Song artist Xiao Zhao (ca. 1130–1160) titled 中興瑞應圖 [In the Midst of Happiness and Auspicious Omens], depicting a series of Auspicious Omens that supported Emperor Gaozong's rise to the throne (fig. 3.12). This painting was a type of propaganda so several versions were made and distributed throughout the empire. There are several extant versions and many copies as well. This scroll is incomplete, with only five of the original twelve scenes, and two sections of calligraphy. Christie's illustrated only three of the five scenes and did not illustrate the calligraphy, and they believed that they were selling a sixteenth-century copy. Even based on the poor catalogue illustrations Wai-kam thought that the Christie's version looked earlier. Before going to Hong Kong for the auction we booked a car and traveled from Beijing to Tianjin to study a version of the composition in the Tianjin Museum (fig. 3.13). When we got back to Hong Kong we decided immediately that the Christie's version was far superior to the Tianjin version. Wai-kam thought that it was definitely Song and I saw no reason to disagree with his assessment. We bought it for our collector friend.

I relate this story for three reasons: 1. The auction houses make mistakes. Often they are too generous in their attributions but at other times they are too conservative. 2. You have to study the origi-

Arnold Chang 69

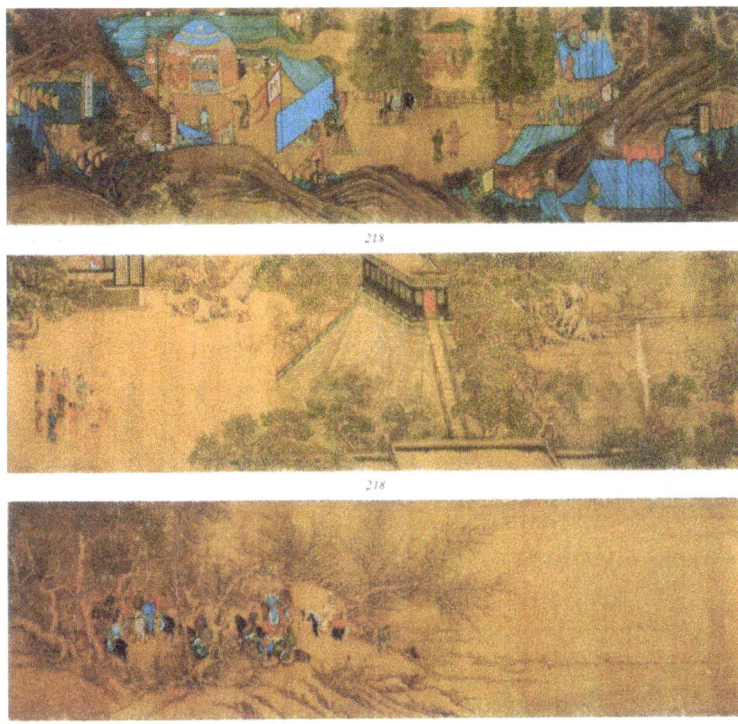

3.12. Anonymous, *In the Midst of Happiness and Auspicious Omens*, 16th century. Photo courtesy of Sotheby's

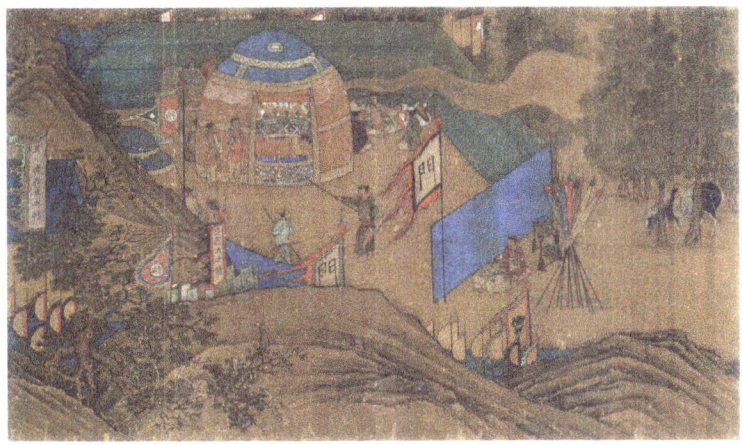

3.13. Anonymous, *In the Midst of Happiness and Auspicious Omens*, 16th century, Tianjin Art Museum. Photo courtesy Tianjin Art Museum

nals, not just photographs. 3. Most important, I got to spend several hours alone with Wai-kam Ho in a car. I just let him ramble about whatever he was thinking. It was an honor to be in the presence of genius.

Whereas Wang Fangyu chose to specialize and focus primarily on the works of one artist, Bada Shanren, and one of his goals as a professional educator was to inspire confidence in his students' abilities, Wai-kam Ho, on the other hand, intentionally or not, engendered humility. He seemed to know everything about a broad range of subjects. He was happy to educate, but he did not cut you any slack if you were not willing to do the work.

C. C. Wang

I was introduced to C. C. Wang (Wang Jiqian, fig. 3.14) in 1977, by Professor James Cahill. I was a graduate student at U.C. Berkeley, in the interdisciplinary department of Asian Studies, but focusing on Chinese art. C. C. was staying in the Bay Area for the summer and offered two classes at the Chinese Culture Center in San Francisco, one on techniques of landscape painting and the other titled "Appreciating Chinese Painting." I signed up for both. For C. C. the practice of painting was essential to developing a real understanding and appreciation of the art form. He couldn't understand why Western scholars of Chinese painting did not themselves learn how to paint, since it was certainly the quickest, if not the best way, to learn to appreciate the subtle nuances of the medium of brush and ink. Although C. C. had prepared slides to show in his "Appreciation" course, he showed only details, never a whole painting. For him, the devil was literally in the details. Composition, subject matter, and the content of the artist's inscription were important, but for C. C. the essence of the work was in the drawing, the *bimo* (brushwork), which was the most direct expression of the artist's soul.

My original plan was to enter the Ph.D. program in art history to continue my studies with James Cahill, but after spending a summer with C. C. Wang I decided that the way that he combined the practice of painting with connoisseurship made sense to me. I

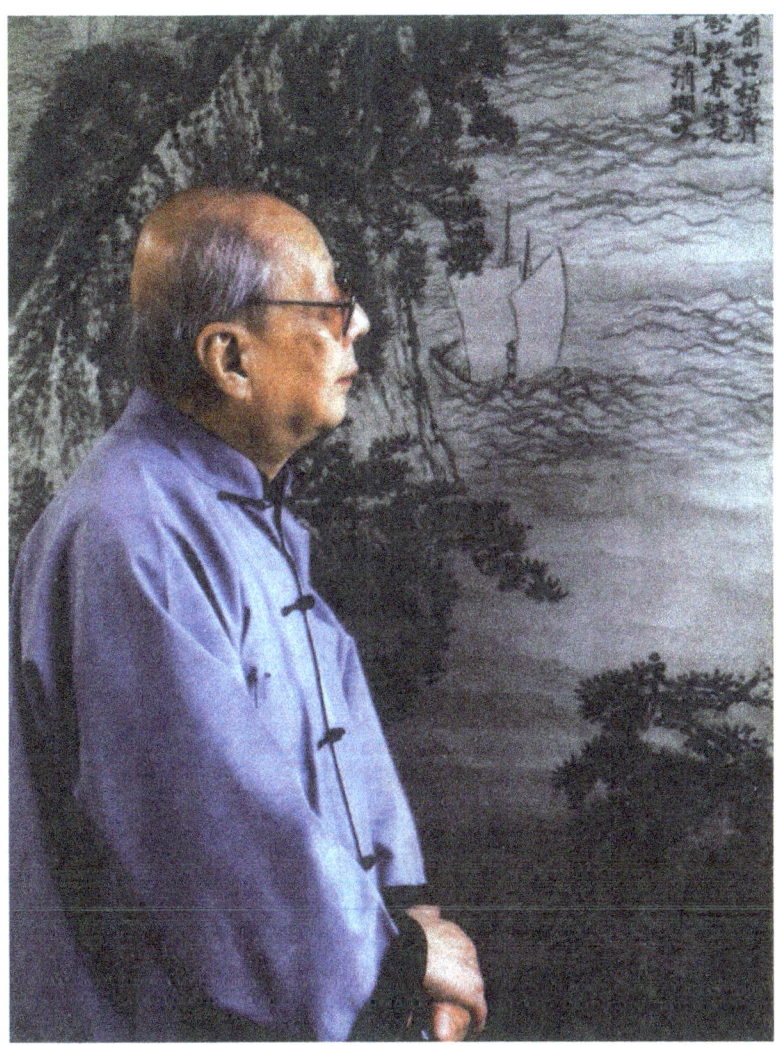

3.14. C. C. Wang, 1997. Photo courtesy of Sotheby's

decided to postpone my application to the Ph.D. program in order to spend some time learning from C. C., and so I moved back to New York. I had expected that after about six months or a year I would return to Berkeley to continue with Cahill. Well, I ended up studying with C. C. Wang for the next twenty-five years and I never went back to get my doctorate.

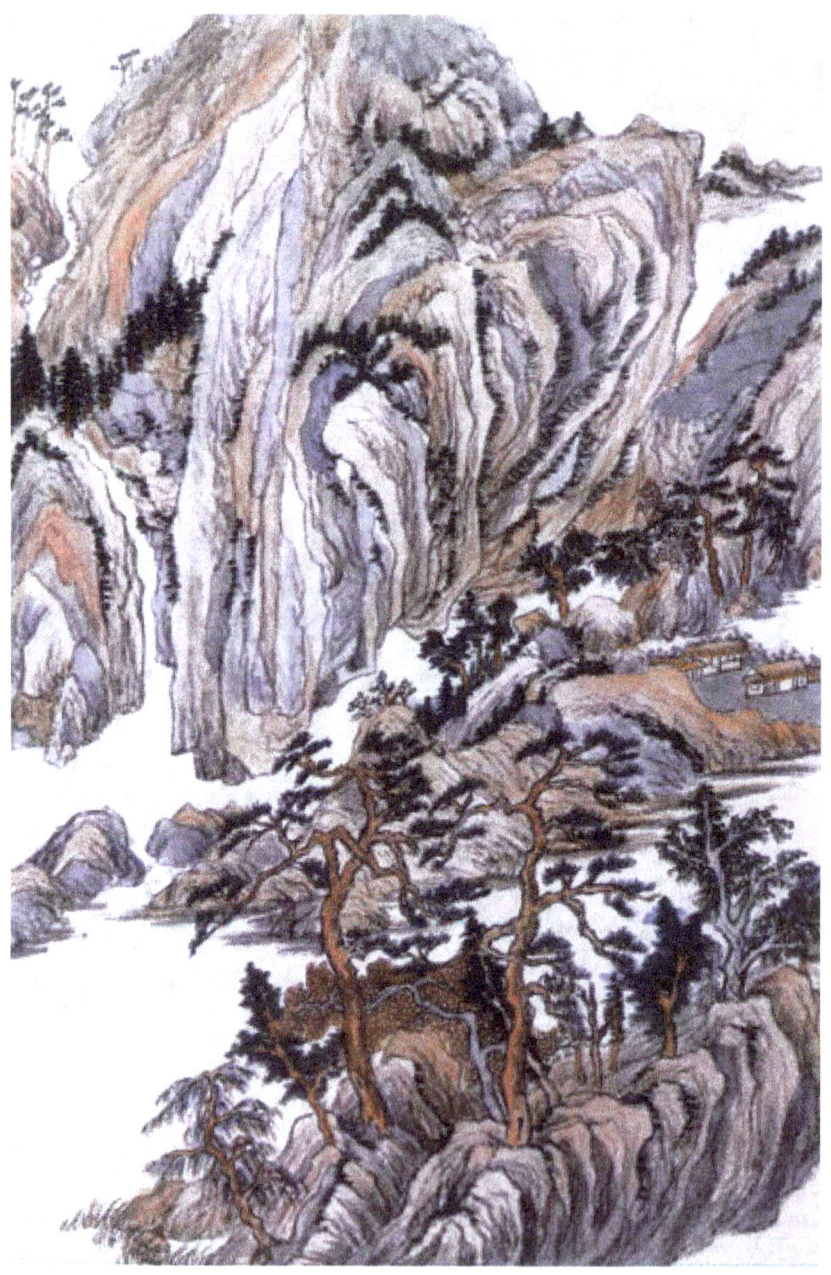

3.15A. Arnold Chang's copy of Tung Ch'i-ch'ang album leaf.

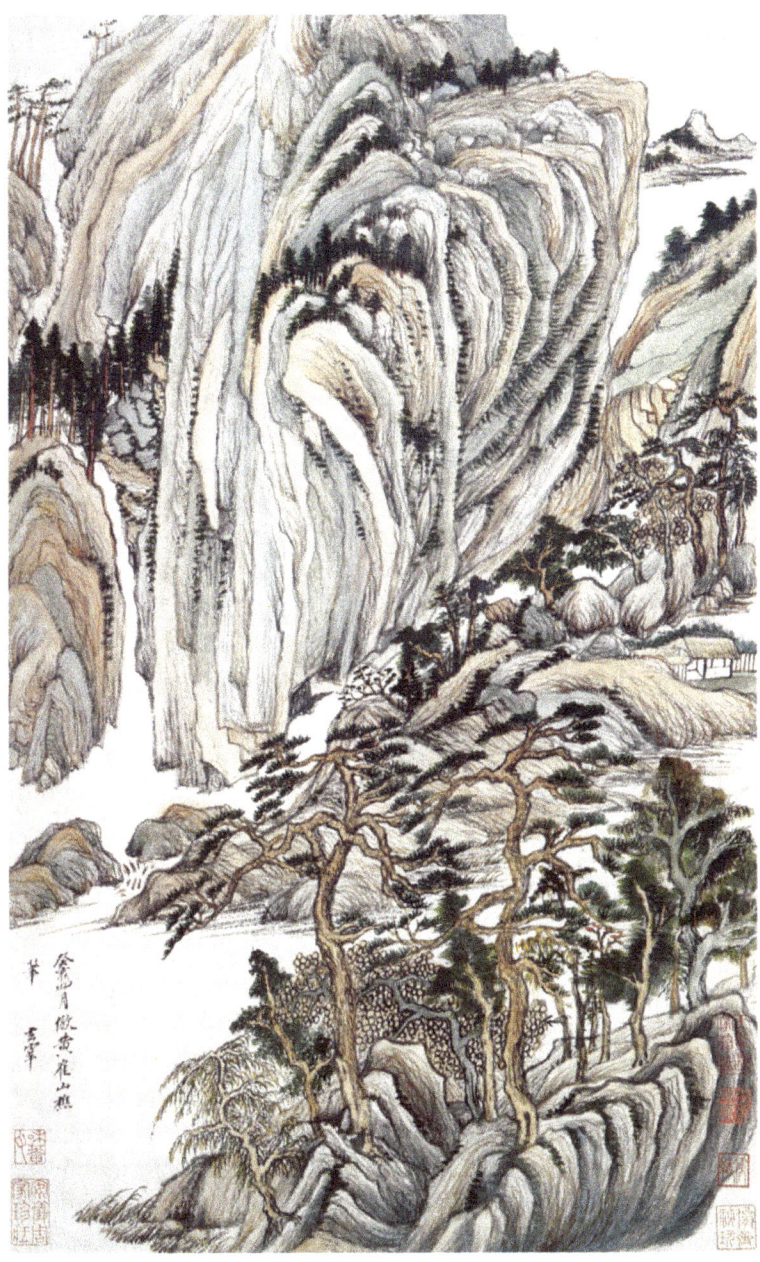

3.15B. Tung Ch'i-ch'ang album leaf. Photo courtesy Nelson-Atkins Museum of Art.

But I have no regrets. In 1978, I managed to get a job at Sotheby's (then Sotheby Parke-Bernet), where it turns out C. C. Wang was already employed as a consultant for Chinese paintings and calligraphy. For the next fifteen years Sotheby's paid me to learn from C. C. and paid him to teach me. A fifteen-year paid apprenticeship program! I traveled all over the world looking for Chinese paintings to sell and then for collectors to buy them. I did the initial vetting and brought the best ones back to New York to review with C. C. prior to selling them at auction. The job itself was an incredible amount of work and extremely stressful, but the reward was the opportunity to work closely with C. C. Wang. In addition to our Sotheby's work, I spent two days a week, from morning until night, in his studio (fig. 3.15A–B). My previous Chinese painting teachers had instructed me to copy their own works. C. C. alone insisted that I copy original paintings by Song, Yuan, Ming, and Qing masters. In a real sense I was learning directly from the Old Masters, with the guidance of a modern master.

I stopped working at Sotheby's full time in 1994, but I continued learning from him and looking at paintings with him (fig. 3.16). In all my years with C. C. I can't really remember any conversations that didn't revolve around Chinese paintings or art in general. We basically had one long conversation that lasted twenty-five years. Each time we got together we would pick up where we had left off. Invariably the subject of *bimo*, brushwork (literally "brush and ink") would come up. *Bimo* refers to any marks made by the artist, including lines, dots, smudges, washes, and so forth, but it is also a measure of quality, one that can be analyzed and judged independently of its descriptive function. The quality of one's *bimo* defines an artist's personal style, identifies his artistic lineage, and establishes his place in the historical hierarchy of past masters. *Bimo* therefore is also the key to connoisseurship.[3] An artist's *bimo* is like his fingerprint. Virtually all Chinese connoisseurs throughout history have talked and written about *bimo*. The problem is that they all use the same terminology but are not necessarily talking about the same thing. When C. C. Wang talked about *bimo* he was describing something very specific that was observable, but he also implicitly embraced subjective notions of quality. In other words, artistic lineages were defined not so much by what we think of in the West

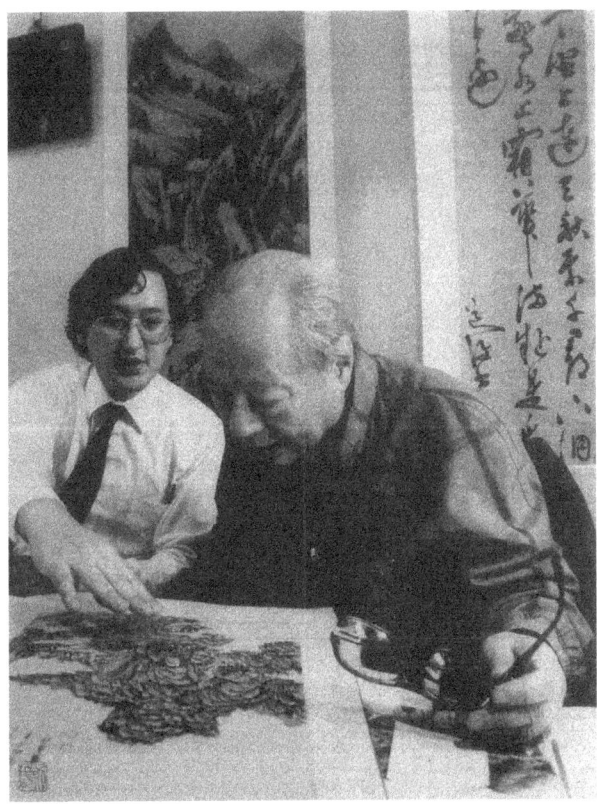

3.16. Arnold Chang and C. C. Wang, at Sotheby's New York, mid-1980s. Photo by Soobin Cha

as "style" but by shared notions of the relative artistic/expressive value of different modes of brushwork. C. C. learned this definition of *bimo* from the painter-connoisseur Wu Hufan. You might say that Wu imparted or transmitted this knowledge to Wang, because it was not something that could be taught simply through words or written down in a textbook. It involves both technical skill and visual acumen. C. C. learned by watching Wu Hufan paint and by looking at old paintings together with him. This is the same way that C. C. Wang taught me.

It was truly phenomenal to have this kind of opportunity in America, something that could never happen prior to the late twentieth century. It was also amazing to me that virtually nobody else took advantage of this opportunity because C. C. Wang was extremely generous with his knowledge and was more than willing to train anyone who was seriously interested in learning.

Whereas Wai-kam Ho surrounded himself with hundreds of books, Wang Jiqian surrounded himself with hundreds of paintings. When I would go to his studio to paint he would ask me: 張洪你今天要畫什麼? What do you want to paint today? I was like a child in a candy store: Wen Zhengming, Wang Yuanqi, Ni Zan, Wang Meng—whatever I wanted!

I have many, many other C. C. Wang anecdotes I could share, but you will have to wait for my memoirs. Today I will relate just one story that involves connoisseurship. In 1984, I discovered a painting in Europe (fig. 3.17). It is ascribed to the Yuan master Huang Gongwang. It is a strange work because the painting itself is on paper, but there is a piece of silk attached to the top. Huang Gongwang's inscription is written mostly on the silk but it extends onto the paper. Above this is a beautiful Dong Qichang colophon on the mounting. When I took this painting in for study, I showed it to many Chinese painting experts, including Cahill, Wen Fong, K. S. Wong, and others. Everyone dismissed it out of hand; nobody took it seriously. Only C. C. Wang told me he thought it could be genuine.

I hesitated. Even though C. C. Wang was Sotheby's consultant, I didn't accept blindly all of his pronouncements. I always consulted with other experts before I decided how to catalogue a painting. In this case, since nobody else I showed it to thought the painting had a chance of being Yuan, let alone by Huang Gongwang, I included it in a minor sale, and labeled it "Style of Huang Gongwang," with an estimate of $3,000–5,000 (fig. 3.18). C. C. ended up buying it for $17,600.

Several months later C. C. excitedly told me that when he was casually flipping through a volume of works collected by the Liaoning Museum, he noticed that there was a colophon to the famous Huaisu calligraphy (fig. 3.19) written by a Yuan dynasty scholar named Zhang Yan, which includes a seal that reads *Zhang Peng Shan zhenshang* 張篷山珍賞 (fig. 3.20). This same seal appears on the Huang Gongwang painting (fig. 3.21).

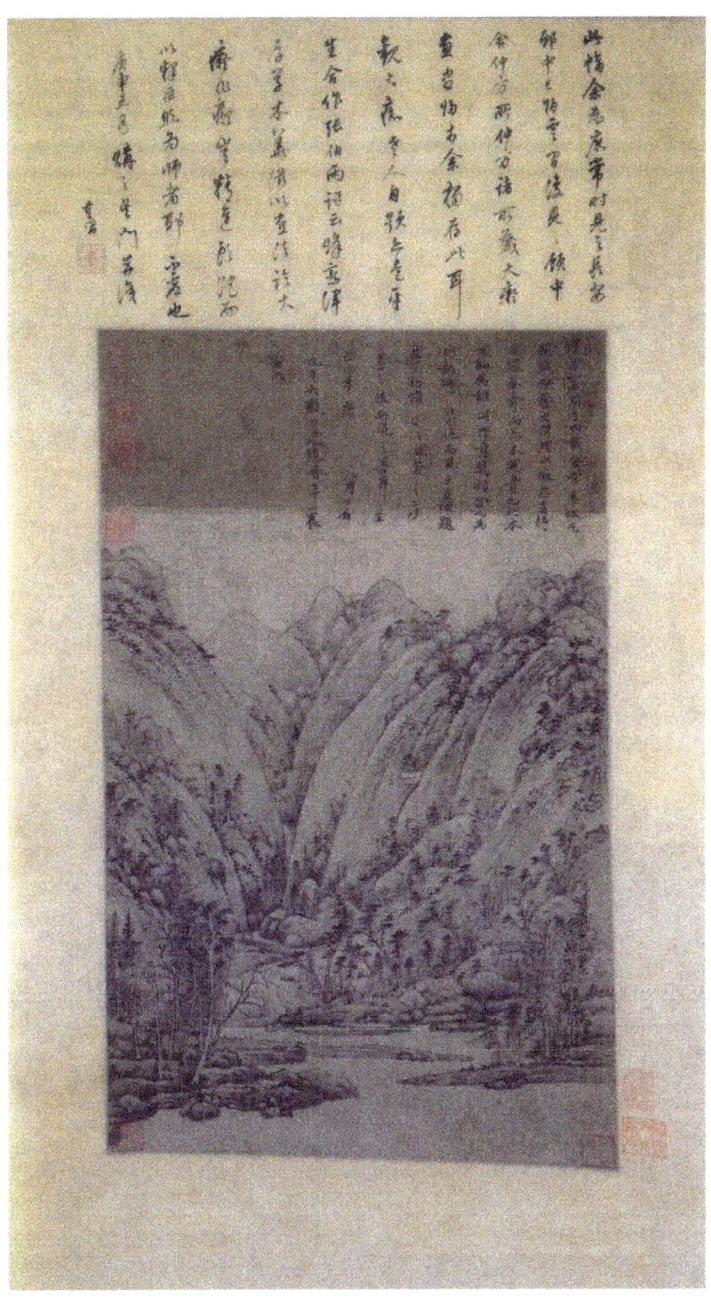

3.17. Huang Gongwang, "Landscape." Photo courtesy of Sotheby's

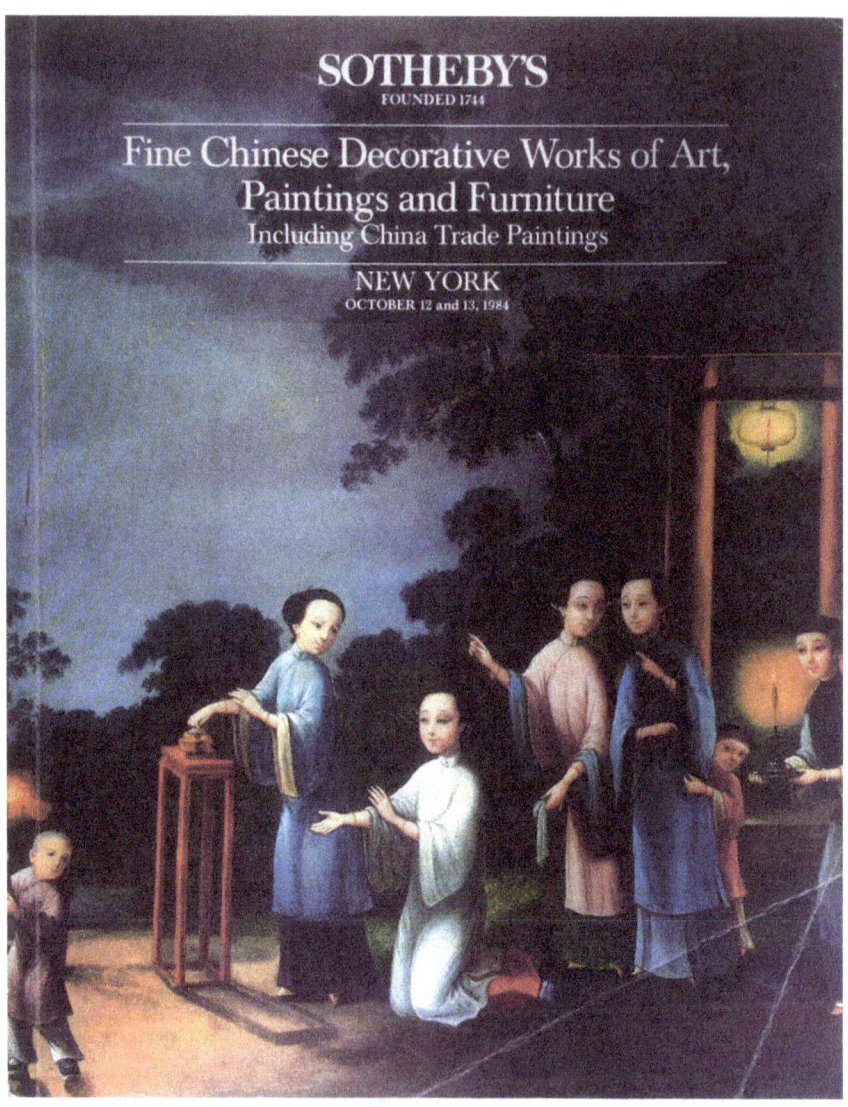

3.18. Cover of sales catalog, Sotheby's, October 12–13, 1984

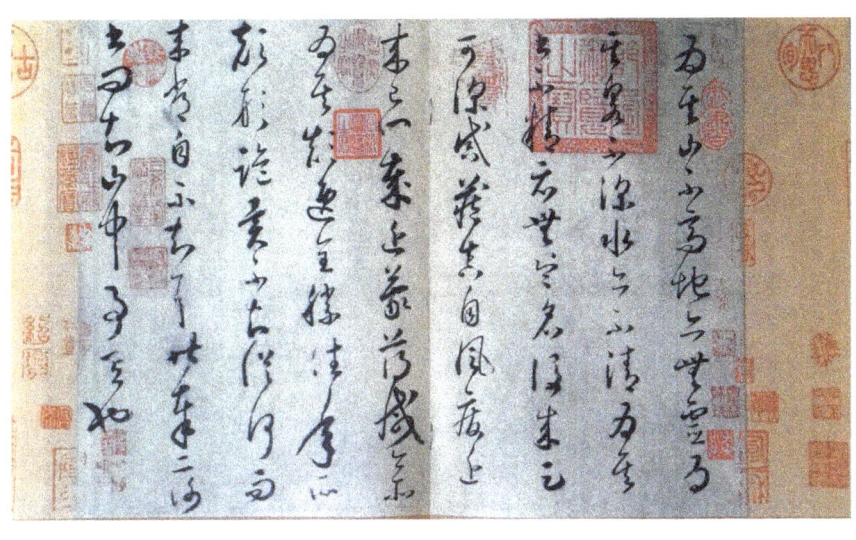
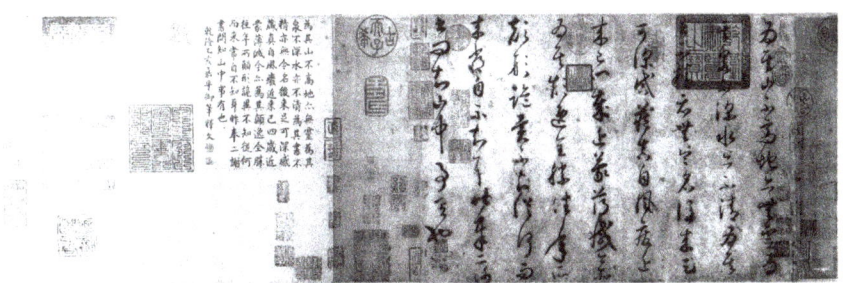
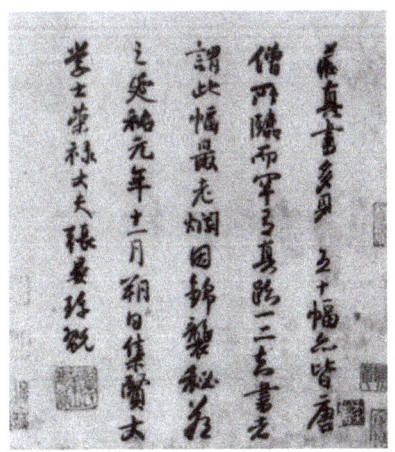

3.19. Huaisu calligraphy, Liaoning Museum, with Zhang Yan colophon dated 1314

80   *Chinese Calligraphy and Painting Studies*

3.20. Seal of Zhang Yan on Huaisu calligraphy, Liaoning Museum, with Zhang Yan colophon dated 1314

3.21. Seal of Zhang Yan on Huang Gongwang painting, detail of fig. 3.19.

This seal does not prove that the painting is by Huang Gongwang but the appearance of a collector's seal by a contemporary of the artist, as well as the colophon by Dong Qichang, certainly makes the work worthy of further study. Nobody else paid any attention to it. C. C. once said to me: "It's bad if you mistake a fake painting for a real one, but calling a genuine painting a fake is a major mistake. Saying something is fake is easy and it makes you sound like you know something, but if the painting is authentic and you declare it a forgery you have misunderstood the artist."

C. C. Wang did not recognize the collector's seal on the Huang Gongwang before he bought the painting; he was relying totally on his understanding of Yuan dynasty *bimo*, brushwork. Unlike Wai-kam Ho or Wang Fangyu, C. C. didn't enjoy doing research for the sake of research. He often began researching a painting only after he had already acquired it, in order to confirm the judgments he had made on the basis of brushwork. I got the sense that he didn't want to waste time researching a piece that he couldn't own when there were so many other things to buy.

So, there you have it. Three experts in Chinese painting, three different approaches, three different personalities. Each of them made important contributions to the field of Chinese art studies and, directly or indirectly, influenced the education of everyone in this room (fig. 3.22).

Wang Fangyu devoted much of his life to the study of Bada Shanren. More than thirty works of Bada's painting and calligraphy were acquired by the Freer Gallery from his estate, through purchase and donation, and we continue to learn from them. Those of us for whom Chinese is not our first language have benefited from Professor Wang's crucial role in developing the methodology and core curriculum for learning the Chinese language in the United States. Wang Fangyu and other dedicated language instructors helped to prepare a whole generation of American scholars to be able to do original research in Chinese.

Wai-kam Ho, working with Sherman Lee at the Cleveland Museum of Art from 1959 through 1983, and Marc Wilson at the Nelson-Atkins Museum from 1984 through 1994, raised the standards of research and scholarship. As Mike Hearn has observed:

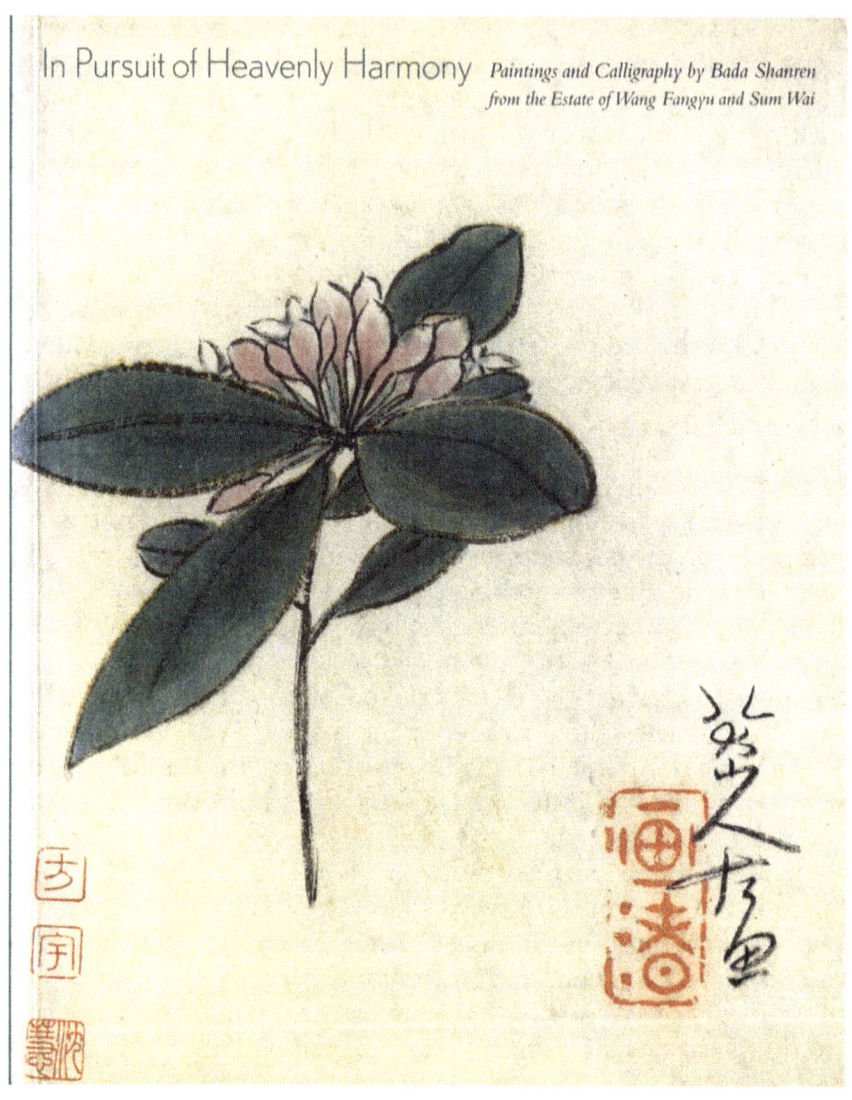

3.22A. Cover of *In Pursuit of Heavenly Harmony: Paintings and Calligraphy by Bada Shanren from the Estate of Wang Fangyu and Sum Wai,* by Stephen Allee and others (Washington, DC: Freer Gallery of Art, 2003)

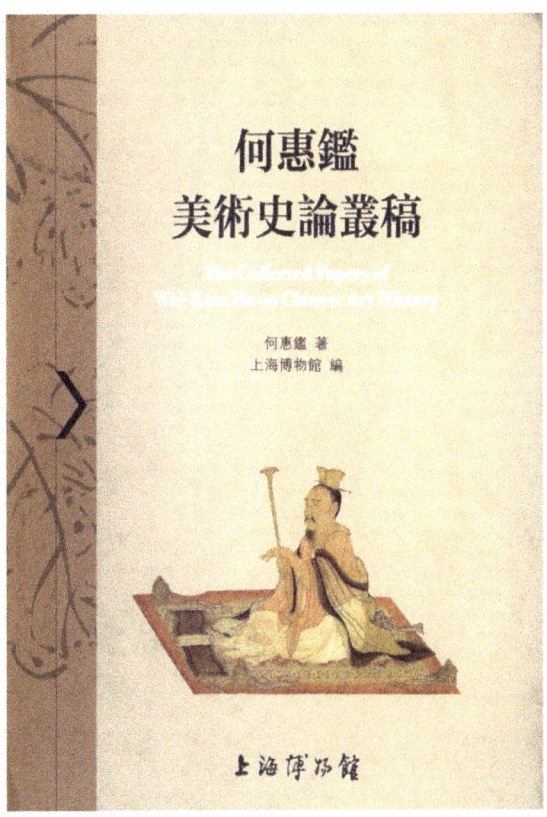

3.22B. Cover of *The Collected Papers of Wai-kam Ho on Chinese Art History* (Shanghai: Shanghai Museum, 2019)

"When Wai-kam came to this country, the survival of actual examples of landscape paintings from the 10th and 11th centuries was widely questioned. Many people thought that everything that had survived were actually later copies that dated from the 15th and 16th centuries. There were all these paintings, but there was no way to prove that they were of an early date, so the whole field was in a terrible morass. It was through the work of scholars such as Ho that these paintings became anchored in time."[4]

C. C. Wang's contribution to the field lives on through the hundreds of paintings that passed through his hands. Kathleen Yang's 2010 book *Through a Chinese Connoisseur's Eye: Private Notes of C. C. Wang* lists 156 works in public American, European, and Australian

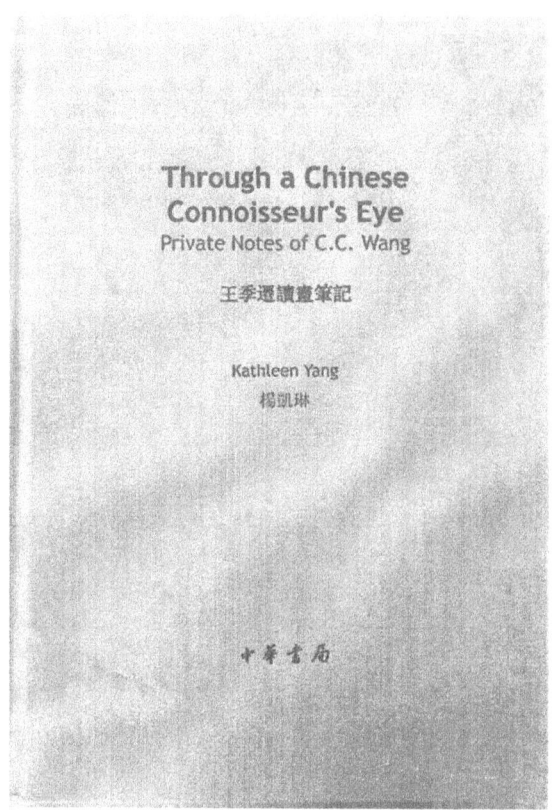

3.22C Cover of *Through a Chinese Connoisseur's Eye: Private Notes of C. C. Wang,* by Kathleen Yang (Beijing: Zhonghua shuju, 2010)

collections that were formerly in the collection of C. C. Wang. In addition, C. C. also worked with art historians and curators, helping them to evaluate and improve their collections. He generously shared his collection with several generations of students who came to visit him in New York.

Notes

1 New Haven: Institute of Far Eastern Languages, 1958.
2 *The Century of Tung Ch'i-ch'ang, 1555–1636*, edited by Wai-kam Ho, with Judith G. Smith, 2 vols. (Kansas City, Mo.: Nelson-Atkins Museum of Art in association with the University of Washington Press, 1992).
3 See in this volume the discussion by Giuffrida on *bimo*.
4 Margalit Fox, "Wai-kam Ho, Authority on Chinese Art, Dies at 80," *New York Times*, national edition, January 1, 2005, C7.

Chapter 4

Collecting and Exhibiting Chinese Paintings in Postwar America: Sherman Lee and the 1954 *Chinese Landscape Painting* Exhibition

Noelle Giuffrida

During the twentieth century, museums in the United States amassed and exhibited distinguished collections of Asian art. Several scholars have examined the history of American collecting during the first three decades of the century. However, comparatively little attention has been paid to the decades following World War II, when the United States blossomed as an international hub for the study and presentation of Chinese art.[1] During the late 1940s and 1950s, political and economic changes affecting the international art market prompted a new wave of collecting and, with it, the production of museum shows and new scholarship in the United States. By reaching a critical mass of individuals, institutions, and paintings, America emerged as a new international center for Chinese painting studies, scholarship, and exhibitions. Publications produced by experts living in the United States and shows at American museums affected the development of the field of Chinese art history. Among the individuals behind these postwar collections and exhibitions, American curator and museum director Sherman E. Lee (1918–2008) stands out as one of the central figures of the era (fig. 4.1).

Through his collecting, exhibitions, and writings, Lee achieved prominence in the field of Asian art history during the second half of the twentieth century. His acquisitions of Asian art for museums in Detroit, Seattle, and Cleveland, as well as his collaboration with John D. Rockefeller III (1906–1978) and Blanchette Rockefeller (1909–1992), whose assemblage formed the basis for the Asia Society

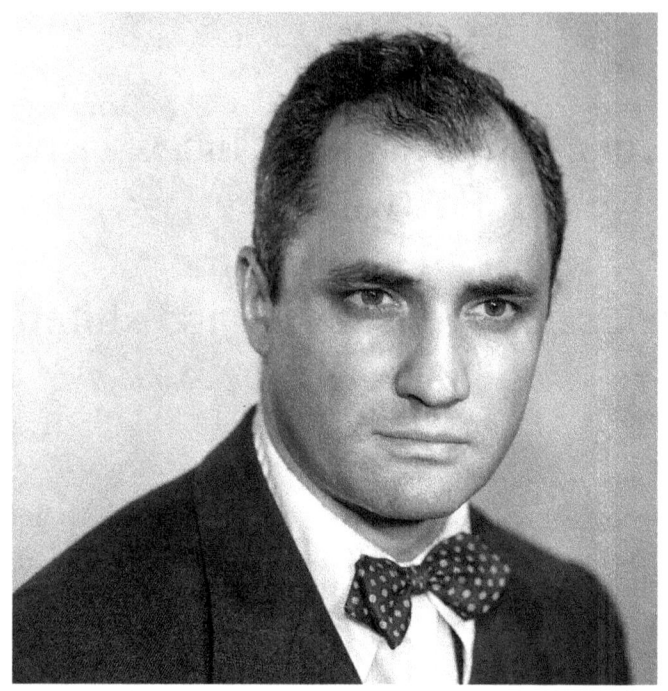

4.1. Sherman E. Lee, 1952. Cleveland Museum of Art Archives

Museum in New York, gave him a leading role in collecting during the post–World War II era. Lee's involvement in major exhibitions and catalogues of Chinese, Japanese, Indian, and Southeast Asian art raised the profile of Asian art and promoted its appreciation by American museum audiences from the 1950s through the 1980s.[2] With his survey *A History of Far Eastern Art*, first published in 1964 and widely adopted up through the 1990s as an introduction for university students and the interested public, Lee helped to shape American and European understandings of Asian art.

In 1954, just two years into his new role as curator of Asian art at the Cleveland Museum of Art, Lee organized *Chinese Landscape Painting*, one of the first major postwar exhibitions of Chinese paintings. While several scholars have highlighted the importance of the *International Exhibition of Chinese Art* at the Royal Academy in London (1935–1936) and the yearlong American tour *Chinese Art Treasures* exhibition from the National Palace Museum in Taiwan

(1961–1962) for the study of Chinese art in Europe and the United States, the significance of exhibitions in the immediate postwar decade remains largely unexplored.[3]

This chapter uses Lee and the *Chinese Landscape Painting* exhibition as a lens through which to explore two questions. What factors affected curators' choices of Chinese paintings to acquire and exhibit during the 1940s and 1950s? And, which strategies did curators and scholars use to present Chinese paintings in exhibitions and publications at the time?

Postwar Exhibitions of Chinese Paintings

Abundant opportunities to obtain pictures, an increase in curatorial and dealer expertise, and the growing interest in China from publics beyond its borders, spurred painting to emerge as a dominant focus for Chinese art exhibitions in the postwar decades. *Chinese Landscape Painting* stands out among the cluster of exhibitions held internationally during the 1940s and 1950s as the largest and most lasting in its effects on American understandings of Chinese painting. For *Chinese Landscape Painting*, Lee secured loans from over thirty-five different museums, private collectors, and dealers, including some from Europe and Japan.[4] By incorporating a large number of paintings from a diversity of lenders, the show achieved more consequence than earlier postwar exhibitions. And Lee's catalogue for the show amplified its significance in the 1950s and subsequent decades.

In the immediate postwar decade, exhibitions featuring Chinese paintings occurred across the United States and in Europe, at different kinds of institutions, all with substantial sway from dealers and collectors. Two exhibitions during the late 1940s that preceded *Chinese Landscape Painting* had a sizeable impact on Lee's ideas about Chinese painting, affecting his choices and interpretation of works in his 1954 exhibition. These shows influenced his views about the historical importance of Ming and Qing pictures. Near the end of 1948, the Nelson-Atkins Museum of Art in Kansas City held an exhibition with twenty-five Chinese paintings, chiefly from its own already impressive collection. The show focused on Ming dynasty works rather than the museum's early paintings from the Northern and Southern Song dynasties.[5] In the small catalogue, Laurence Sickman penned a short essay to introduce basic forms, materials, and methods to an American audience unfamiliar with Chinese painting. In the remainder of the booklet for the show, Sickman and Wang Shixiang 王世襄 (1914–2009), then curator of the department of antiquities at the Palace Museum in Beijing, collaborated on the entries, each of which consisted of a short descriptive text accompanied by a list of inscriptions, colophons, and seals. This exhibition presented a strong contingent of Ming literati paintings, including works by Shen Zhou 沈周 (1427–1509), Wen Zhengming 文徵明 (1470–1559), and Wen Boren 文伯仁 (1502–1575). Lee's visit to this exhibition exposed him to a larger selection of Ming literati pictures than he had seen during his stay in Japan from 1946 to 1948 as a member of the East Asian branch of the Monuments, Fine Arts, and Archives (MFAA) program, the members of which became known as "monuments men."

The following year, French collector-dealer Jean-Pierre Dubosc (1903–1988) organized *Great Chinese Painters of the Ming and Ch'ing Dynasties*, commonly known as the "Wildenstein show" for its venue at one of the premiere galleries in New York (fig. 4.2). Held in March 1949, the exhibition featured seventy-five paintings, most from Dubosc's own collection. Dubosc had lived in Beijing and worked as a diplomat at the French legation during the 1930s and 1940s. He married Janine Loo, daughter of well-known Chinese art dealer C. T. Loo 盧芹齋 (Loo Ching Tsai, 1880–1957) in 1937. During his stay, he earned a reputation as a collector and expert on Chinese art, particularly of Ming and Qing painting, even partnering with his father-in-law as a dealer. Dubosc quickly became the most active, self-appointed campaigner for collecting and appreciating Ming and Qing painting, a reputation he would maintain from the 1930s through the 1950s. During this time, he promoted painting with a series of exhibitions featuring works from his own collection.[6] Dubosc consistently argued against what he saw as Euro-American preferences for Tang, Song, and Yuan paintings and the denigration of later works. In his essay for the Wildenstein show catalogue, Dubosc ranted that "the prejudice persists that the painters of the Ming and Ch'ing dynasties were merely following

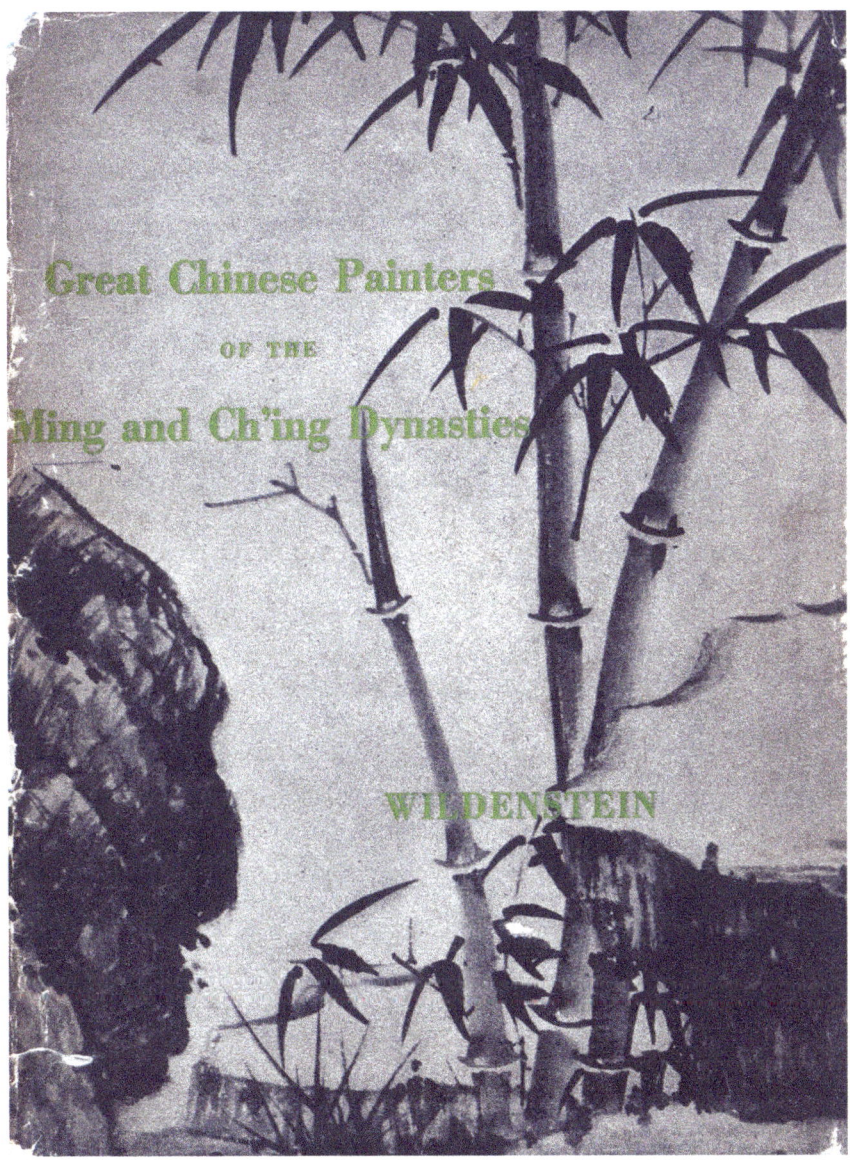

4.2. *Great Painters of the Ming and Ch'ing Dynasties,* by Jean-Pierre Dubosc (New York: Wildenstein, 1949). Photo by author

in the steps of their brilliant Sung and Yüan predecessors and produced nothing but slavish copies entirely lacking in originality."[7]

Lee's most significant exposure to Ming and Qing literati paintings came from his visit to Dubosc's Wildenstein show in 1949. Immediately following the exhibition, Dubosc and Sickman exchanged letters about Lee. Dubosc reported that Lee had attended the show, saying, "He was rather nice about it and seemed inclined to correct his former preconceived ideas about Ming and Qing painting."[8] Sickman responded that he thought Lee had been trained in the "classic precision sort of painting much admired in Japan—the Ma Yuan, Xia Gui gang and their followers in the Zhe School. He is, however, open to convincing and [I] think may swing our way one of these days and say that everything is rubbish save the four Wangs."[9] In fact, in 1951, Lee wrote to Sickman and admitted that his previous judgments of Ming and Qing painting had been "badly in error."[10]

In an earlier article, "The Story of Chinese Painting" (published in 1948), Lee had dismissed the theories and preferences of one of the quintessential Ming literati figures Dong Qichang 董其昌 (1555–1636), who helped to shape practices of Chinese painting and its study in the late Ming dynasty and into the twentieth century.[11] In his article, Lee expressed his visceral reaction to Dong's denigration of Southern Song and early Ming Zhe school paintings that he had learned to valorize during his time studying collections in Japan. Seeking to defend such paintings, Lee declared, "[E]xplicitly or implicitly...the traditional Chinese division of painting into [Dong Qichang's] 'Northern' and 'Southern' schools is a hopeless shambles of prejudiced critical opinion based upon the non-pictorial criteria of calligraphy, morality and social position."[12]

As a youthfully exuberant twenty-nine-year old, Lee's pronouncement, "in later Chinese art we witness the almost total death of a pictorial tradition with the substitution of an amateurism based on literary accomplishment," sounded purposefully provocative.[13] Lee was not alone in declaring Dong's Northern and Southern schools as problematic. For instance, art historian Alexander Soper (1904–1993) recognized that Dong's categories unfairly colored judgments about Chinese painting:

The manipulators of the scheme, themselves "Southerners," used it to separate the masters of the past whom they admired from those whom they disliked…. The division [of Northern and Southern] has approximately as much historic value as would a modern zealot's separation of European political theorists from St. Augustine on, into two camps, labeled "fascist" and "democratic." It has survived to plague accounts of Chinese art even in the advanced twentieth century….[14]

Nevertheless, Lee's earlier hubristically harsh judgment of Ming and Qing literati painting took things too far. His open disparagement of Dong had raised the hackles of Dubosc and Sickman, both of whom had assiduously collected Ming and Qing literati paintings in the 1930s and 1940s. In the catalogue for the Wildenstein show, Dubosc criticized Lee for comments in "The Story of Chinese Painting," taking issue with what Dubosc called Lee's "dislike of so-called 'amateur-aesthetes' of the Ming dynasty, whose integrity he questions and whose importance in the field of Chinese painting he flatly denies."[15]

Before he became curator in Cleveland in 1952, Lee had already begun to recalibrate his ideas about Ming and Qing painting. His early acquisitions of Chinese pictures for Cleveland in the 1950s and his selections for *Chinese Landscape Painting* reflected his new appreciation for Ming and Qing painting gained through his experiences at the Nelson-Atkins and Wildenstein exhibitions just a few years earlier. By 1954, Lee had acquired Wang Hui's 王翬 (1632–1717) *Tall Bamboo and Distant Mountains after Wang Meng* (fig. 4.3) and Wang Yuanqi's 王原祁 (1642–1715) *Landscape in the Color style of Ni Zan* for Cleveland, both of which were featured in *Chinese Landscape Painting*.[16] These two pictures were, in fact, by two of the Four Wangs Sickman had suggested to Dubosc that Lee would eventually embrace. Less than five years after the Wildenstein exhibition, in which Dubosc justifiably criticized Lee for dismissing Dong Qichang specifically, and Ming and Qing painting more generally, Lee had come around to acquiring and praising such pictures.[17] Lee's selection of works for *Chinese Landscape Painting* and his catalogue text evinced shifts in his thinking about Ming and

Qing pictures. Works by literati artists Shen Zhou, Wen Zhengming, and others accounted for over half of the Ming paintings in the show—twenty-three in all. He also incorporated six Qing orthodox pictures by three of the Four Wangs and allocated a fourteen-page section in the catalogue to "Qing Orthodox Painting." Lee even offered contrition for his earlier judgments about Dong Qichang, saying, "There is little doubt that we must speak of later Chinese painting as 'before Tung Ch'i-chang' and 'after Tung Ch'i-chang.' His literary, critical, and calligraphic influence is paramount, and so is his painting, like it or not…. We must not assume, as this writer once did, that the appearance of Tung Ch'i-chang's pictures results from a lack of competence."[18]

Lee dedicated well over half of the show to Ming and Qing works, and among those, more than one third were literati paintings. The higher number and greater attention to later pictures also reflected the availability of loans for *Chinese Landscape Painting*. Works from American collections dominated the show, and even though five Song dynasty paintings from the Nelson-Atkins appeared in the show, the inability—due to lending restrictions in Washington and Boston—to bring in pictures from the Freer Gallery and the Museum of Fine Arts limited the number of Song works to twelve.

Other exhibitions of Chinese paintings occurred during the late 1940s and early 1950s, but they did not have the same initial or lasting impact as *Chinese Landscape Painting*. In 1948, curator Henry Trubner (1920–1999) organized a show of forty-six Chinese paintings drawn from American-based lenders at the Los Angeles County Museum of Art, to which art dealer C. T. Loo contributed the greatest number. The show included some admirable works, but on the whole, Trubner's choices did not amount to a particularly distinguished group of paintings.[19] His acceptance of the attributions of the lenders resulted in numerous entries identified as "Southern Song style," even for paintings obviously from later centuries.[20] The show endeavored mainly to promote cultural understanding about China and to offer an opportunity for southern Californians to see Chinese pictures locally, at a time when museums in the area had yet to build Chinese painting collections.

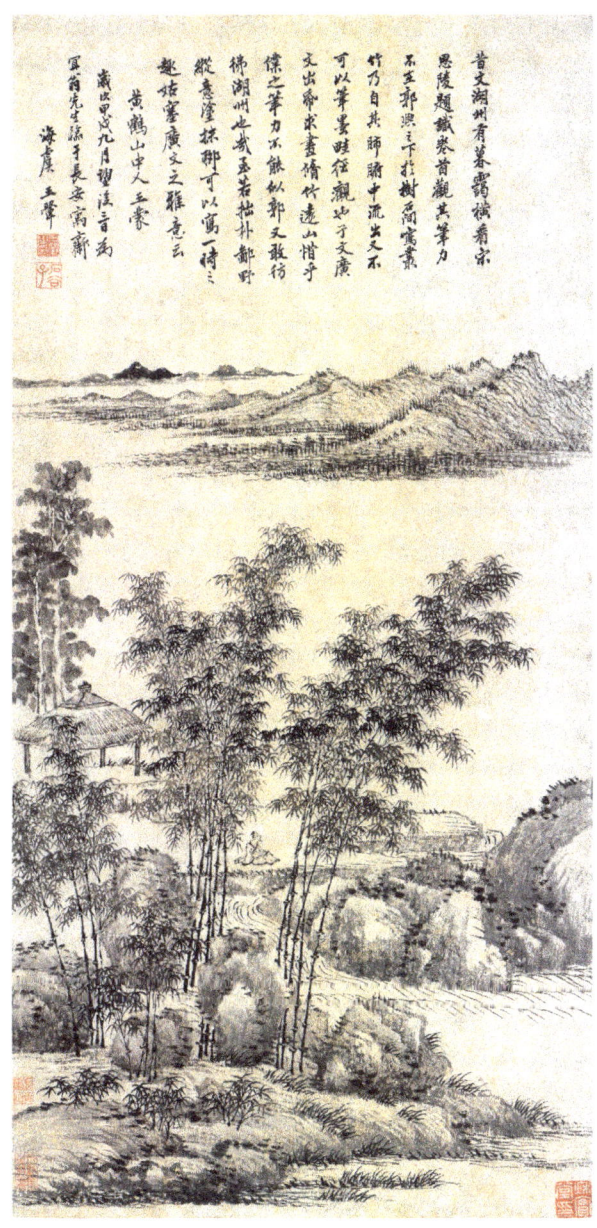

4.3. Wang Hui (1632–1717), *Tall Bamboo and Distant Mountains after Wang Meng*, 1694. Hanging scroll, ink on paper, 79.3 × 39.5 cm, John L. Severance Fund, Cleveland Museum of Art. Photo courtesy Cleveland Museum of Art

More significantly, in August 1954, just months before Lee's *Chinese Landscape Painting* exhibition opened, a massive show of Chinese art commenced in Venice, orchestrated to commemorate the seven hundredth anniversary of the birth of Marco Polo. With over 950 objects in multiple media such as bronze ritual vessels, Buddhist statues, jades, ceramics, textiles, cloisonné, glass, and paintings, *Mostra d'arte cinese* (Exhibition of Chinese Art) drew international attention.[21] It included over one hundred pictures, ninety-four of them from the Ming and Qing dynasties. Eighty were either from the collection of Jean-Pierre Dubsoc or had formerly been part of it.[22] Dubosc, in fact, had organized the painting section, and, unsurprisingly, its content reflected his preference for works by Ming and Qing scholar-amateur painters. The incomplete and uneven character of Dubosc's assemblage, as well as its being submerged within the much larger exhibition, resulted in the Venice show having far less impact on the direction of shifts in the collecting of Chinese painting beyond East Asia than his smaller, more focused Wildenstein show several years earlier.

Few exhibitions of premodern Chinese painting were held in Mainland China during the 1940s and 1950s. In September 1959, however, the Palace Museum in Beijing organized a show of over four hundred paintings called *Tang Song Yuan Ming Qing lidai minghua* 唐宋元明清历代名画 (Famous Paintings from the Successive Dynasties of Tang, Song, Yuan, Ming, and Qing) to celebrate the tenth anniversary of the People's Republic of China.[23] Unfortunately, the show did not have a catalogue and few from outside the country saw it, thus limiting the exhibition's effects beyond the PRC at the time.

With *Chinese Landscape Painting*, Lee assembled a wider range and more consistent caliber of works than previous shows. The exhibition showcased Lee's recent and future acquisitions for Cleveland together with loans from over thirty-five other museums, private collectors, and dealers in the United States, Europe, and Japan. The renowned early twelfth-century handscroll *Streams and Mountains without End* was one of the most significant of Lee's early acquisitions for Cleveland, and *Chinese Landscape Painting* served as its debut showing in the galleries.[24] The painting also served as the focus of an eponymous scholarly book co-written by Lee and then-Princeton graduate student Wen Fong 方聞 (1930–2018) during the summer of 1953 and published shortly following the exhibition.[25] In all, the show also gave Lee the chance to include twelve paintings he had already acquired by the time of the exhibition, such as Bada Shanren's 八大山人 (ca. 1626–1705) *Fish and Rocks* and five more that he would add to Cleveland's collection during the 1950s.

Chinese Landscape Painting offered lenders the opportunity to tout their treasures beyond their own walls, and in very good company. Many of the paintings in the exhibition became part of a newly forming postwar canon of Chinese paintings in the United States.[26] For instance, Wen Zhengming's *Seven Junipers* scroll and Hongren's *The Coming of Autumn* made the trip to the Midwest from Honolulu.[27] The Nelson-Atkins lent several of its best early paintings from the Northern and Southern Song periods—none of which traveled to Venice. Xu Daoning's 許道寧 (ca. 970–1051) magnificent handscroll *Fisherman's Evening Song* and *Solitary Temple amid Clearing Peaks*, attributed to Li Cheng 李成 (919–967), as well as Li Song's 李嵩 (1190–1230) fan-shaped album leaf *Red Cliff* and the renowned handscroll *Twelve Scenes from a Landscape* by Xia Gui all appeared in Cleveland. As one might expect, Lee also brought in some of his favorites from Seattle, including a deftly brushed hanging scroll by Wen Boren and Lan Ying's tour-de-force *River Landscape after Four Masters*. And despite the challenges of securing loans from Japan so soon after the extended American tour of *Japanese Painting and Sculpture* the previous year, Lee tapped his connections for a pair of Wen Boren paintings, classified as Important Cultural Properties, from the Tokyo National Museum, along with additional pictures from the Sumitomo and Abe collections.[28] The Cleveland show incorporated ten works from painter-collector C. C. Wang 王己千 (Wang Jiqian, 1907–2003), including Du Jin's 杜堇 (active ca. 1465–1509) early Ming hanging scroll *Lin Bu Wandering in Moonlight* (fig. 4.4), Lee's first purchase from him, made just in time for the show. Lee also persuaded Wang to lend *Twin Pines, Level Distance* by the Yuan painter Zhao Mengfu 趙孟頫 (1254–1322), which became part of the Metropolitan's collection in 1973 (fig. 4.5). Other significant lenders included New York dealer Frank Caro (1904–1980) and German expatriate dealer-collector

98 Chinese Calligraphy and Painting Studies

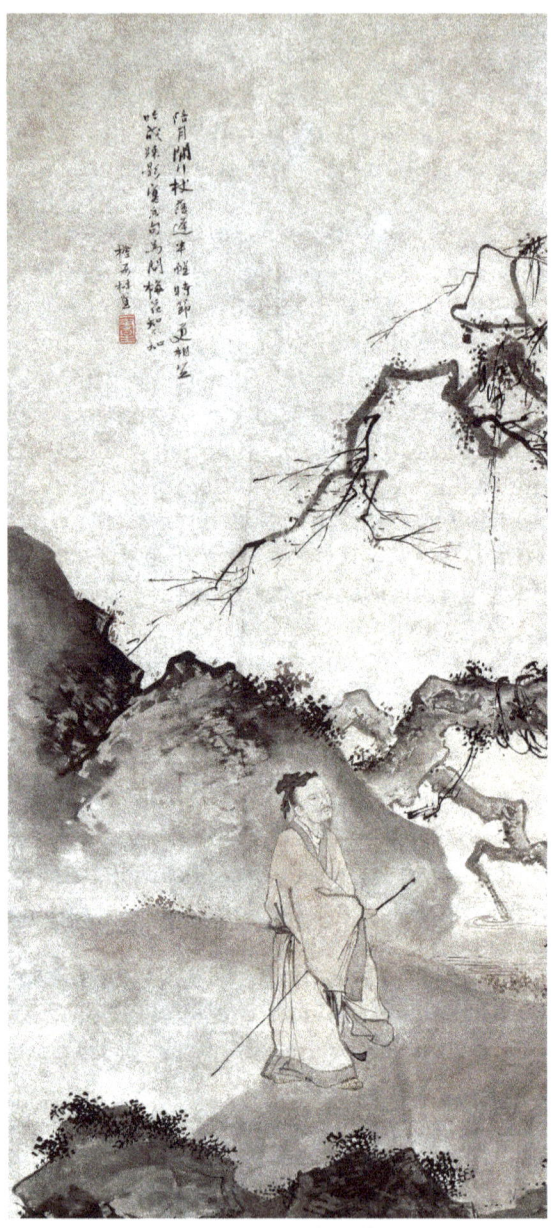

4.4. Du Jin (active ca. 1465–1509), *Lin Bu Wandering in Moonlight*, late fifteenth century, handscroll, ink and colors on silk, 156.4 × 72.4 cm, John L. Severance Fund, Cleveland Museum of Art. Photo courtesy Cleveland Museum of Art

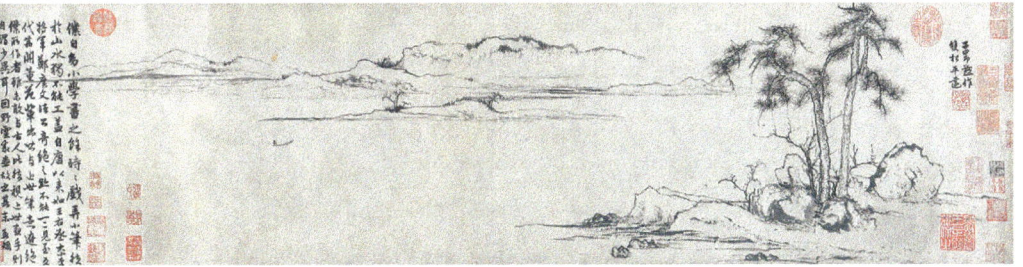

4.5. Zhao Mengfu (1254–1322), *Twin Pines, Level Distance*, ca. 1310, handscroll, ink on paper, 26.8 × 781.5 cm, from the collection of the C. C. Wang Family, Gift of the Dillon Fund, 1973, Metropolitan Museum of Art. Photo courtesy Metropolitan Museum of Art

Walter Hochstadter (1914–2007). Caro supplied nine paintings, five of which Lee eventually purchased for the museum, including Yao Tingmei's 姚廷美 (active mid-fourteenth century) *Leisure Enough to Spare*. *Chinese Landscape Painting* also included Xiao Yuncong's 蕭雲從 (1596–1673) *Pure Tones among Hills and Waters*—one of eight paintings that Lee had already acquired from Hochstadter—along with seven more that would join Cleveland's collection over the next decade.

Presenting Chinese Painting in America

Like many exhibitions and their accompanying catalogues, *Chinese Landscape Painting* aimed to reach Chinese art experts, museum visitors, and interested readers. Its gathering of a large group of pictures guaranteed its appeal for scholars, students, and collectors. And its limited duration prompted many specialists from around the world to travel to Cleveland. Some of Lee's goals for the show centered on fellow experts. For instance, gallery photographs reveal that paintings were displayed fairly close together, mainly on white walls (fig. 4.6). Lee believed that such arrangements would facilitate scholars' ability to compare works attributed to a specific painter, saying, "We cannot ever get enough of the side-by-side comparison of *original* Chinese paintings. Our painful process toward the light in the study of this difficult field owes much to pho-

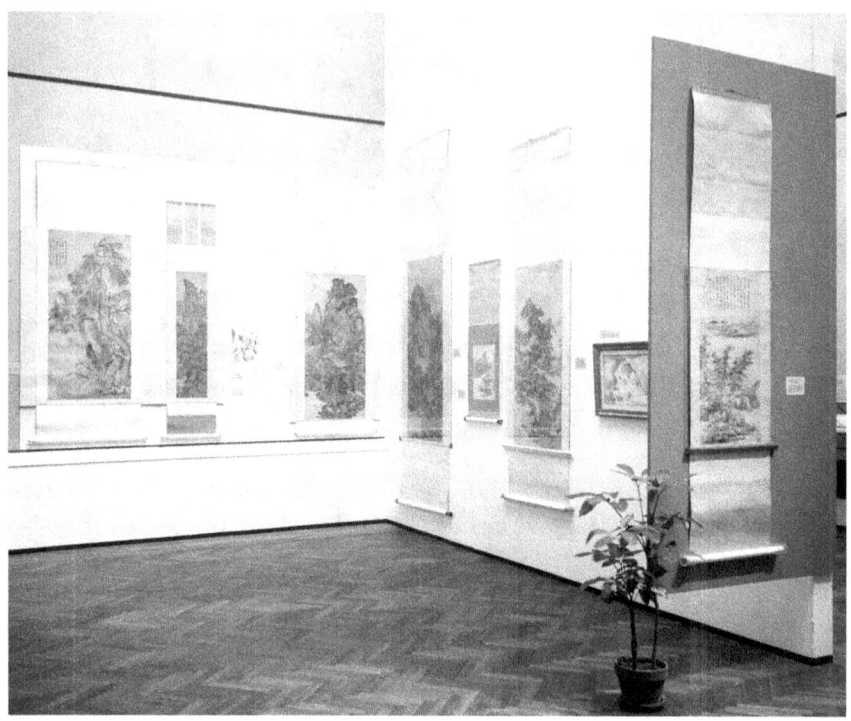

4.6. Gallery view, *Chinese Landscape Painting*, Cleveland Museum of Art, 1954. Cleveland Museum of Art Archives

tographs; but the cliché, as so often, is true: there is no substitute for the original. The close juxtaposition of works attributed to a single master gave much food for thought, even if conclusive decisions were not always reached."[29]

Since museums, private collectors, and dealers in the United States had acquired many of the pictures in the exhibition during the 1930s, 1940s, and early 1950s, few of the works had been publicly displayed beyond their possible inclusion in a rotation at their home institution. *Chinese Landscape Painting*, therefore, offered a momentous opportunity to see 126 paintings—mostly recent acquisitions from an American museum and U.S.-based collectors and dealers—together in one location.

With *Chinese Landscape Painting*, Lee also aimed to raise the profile of Chinese painting and earn it greater acceptance and understanding among American audiences. Rather than incorporating a combination of media from China across millennia, this show signaled that Chinese landscape painting was—in and of itself—an important subject worthy of a dedicated exhibition. At the time, there was still a need to assert that Asian art in general, and Chinese painting in particular, had a history, and that the focus of painting exhibitions should not be confined to the works of European or American artists. Lee's catalogue introduction put readers immediately on notice, saying, "Landscape is the great subject of Chinese painting and Westerners are properly amazed at the very early date of its first full execution."[30]

Along with other curators and scholars of the era, Lee acknowledged the challenges Euro-American audiences would likely face when trying to appreciate Chinese pictures. In 1948, Laurence Sickman warned visitors that their preconceived ideas about the conventions of perspective might make Chinese pictures seem unpleasantly flat.[31] Several years later, in a talk at China Institute in New York, sinologist and collector Victoria Contag (1906–1973) cautioned that a Chinese picture without much color might not match "our concept of painting."[32] Such statements operated under the assumption that many American museumgoers of the time already possessed a basic familiarity with European and American painting, its famous artists, and its pictorial conventions, and accordingly, that viewers felt such affinity with those pictures and identified with them as "their own." Lee echoed those sentiments, while also advocating for different, yet mutually valid, perspectives on Chinese painting:

> We are not Chinese nor ever can be, but we can discipline ourselves to understand something of that country's approach to her own painting. This can be done with integrity only if we, at the same time, maintain our "Westernness," especially in the sense of our objective knowledge of materials and technique and, above all, of style, of forms. Each Chinese painting exists. There it is before us. If to each successive generation of Chinese it was a different painting, how much more so for us. But now it is "our" painting. We can try to see what it was; we see what it is. Both visions are valid and both are taken for granted here.[33]

In pointing out that understandings of Chinese pictures need not be considered static or temporally fixed, he encouraged Americans to embrace Chinese painting. Lee also insisted that one did not need to be Chinese to learn to appreciate these pictures.

At the time, Lee believed that visual engagement with Chinese painting, through its forms, materials, techniques, and styles provided the most expeditious point of entry for Americans uninitiated in the appreciation and understanding of Chinese pictures. Even though Lee's own earlier conversion to Chinese art occurred simultaneously through formal, material, and cultural understandings—particularly in conjunction with Chinese painting, ceramics, and Buddhist art—his perspective as an art historian with basic training as a painter spurred him to guide American viewers in the 1950s to look at Chinese paintings as paintings rather than consider them as something strange and exotic: "This stuff isn't really very different from western art.... I want people to come out here and look at these paintings as paintings. People should remember that the Chinese artists put their pants on one leg at a time just the way western artists do."[34]

Lee's insistence that viewers should try to see Chinese painting as painting can be linked to his exposure to the writings of English art historian and critic Roger Fry (1866–1944), whose promotion of post-Impressionist works by Paul Cezanne (1839–1906) and others advocated the appreciation of painting in terms of its "significant form" as opposed to an exclusive focus on subject matter and meaning.[35] Nevertheless, Lee did not suggest that one should look at Chinese pictures without attempting to understand how one might see painting from a Chinese perspective. For instance, he attempted to explain the concept of *bimo* 筆墨 (lit. brush and ink), commonly rendered as "brushwork" in English, by likening it to the idea of "touch."[36] He claimed that touch differentiated one artist from another, and the artist from the "non-artist."[37]

In the catalogue for *Chinese Landscape Painting*, Lee spoke to readers chiefly in his own native language of visual analysis. Even so, he did not exclude consideration of cultural contexts and textual information. Lee incorporated short sections on Confucianism and Daoism as well as numerous translations of passages from historical Chinese texts on painting, Chinese poetry, and inscriptions on paintings into his discussions.[38] Several curators whose museums loaned pictures to *Chinese Landscape Painting*, including Sickman, Aschwin Lippe (1914–1988), Gustav Ecke (1896–1971), as well as Richard Edwards (1916–2016), each supplied translations of inscriptions and other information on works from their own collections.[39] In addition, Wen Fong contributed translations for some of the colophons on Cleveland's paintings in the show and James Cahill (1926–2014) advised Lee about Yuan painting. Thus, Lee's consultation with other scholars in his work on the exhibition and catalogue was an important step in building key relationships that would benefit his organization of future exhibitions of Chinese art. In the years to come, Lee would continue to collaborate with other sinologically oriented scholars.[40]

Presenting Chinese Paintings

Lee considered the exoticism surrounding perceptions of Asian art among many American museum visitors as a serious impediment to their ability to understand and appreciate it. He also used his dry wit to encourage visitors to come to the museum: "The Western spectator may find the infinite number of mountains and waters rather strange, until he remembers *his* numbers of nudes and apples without end."[41] He challenged audiences to confront their own clichéd ideas about Chinese painting such as the "metaphysical significance of the empty silk" or the "lovely and decorative colors of the later Chinese professional painter-artisan."[42]

In both the catalogue and galleries, Lee employed strategies aimed at de-exoticizing Chinese paintings. By incorporating photographs of real Chinese landscapes, he hoped to dispel the "strangeness" of the paintings, while, at the same time, allowing viewers to access aspects of the visual experience of exploring real Chinese landscapes. Just as painters' journeys into the landscape served as precursors to painting it, readers and viewers exposed to the topography of China might become more attuned to paintings of it. Lee juxtaposed particular paintings and landscape photographs to encourage readers and viewers—in both the catalogue and the gallery installation—to see parallels among them. For instance, a

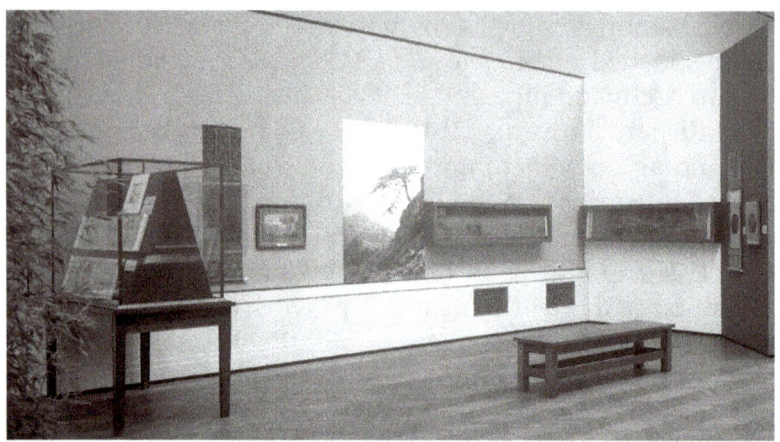

4.7. Gallery view, *Chinese Landscape Painting*, Cleveland Museum of Art, 1954. Cleveland Museum of Art Archives

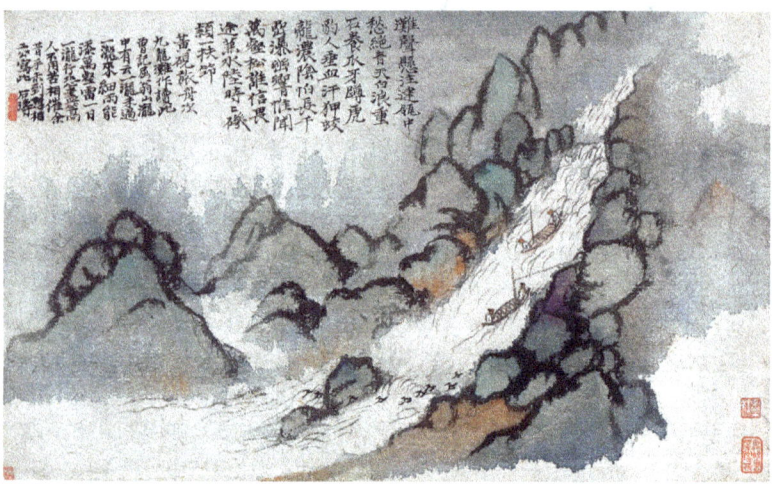

4.8A. Shitao (1642–1707), *Landscapes Depicting Poems of Huang Yanlü*, 1701–2, album leaf, ink and color on paper, 20.32 × 34.29 cm, formerly in the collection of Richard Hobart, Cambridge, MA. Chih Lo Lou Collection, Hong Kong Museum of Art

photograph of a pine growing sideways out of a rock at Mt. Tai (Shandong province) appeared alongside the Nelson-Atkins's Xia Gui handscroll depicting trees growing out of rocks (fig. 4.7). Still, Lee made it clear that even the most naturalistic-looking Chinese painting did not strive for photographic likeness. He cautioned that rather than striving to copy nature, Chinese artists constructed their paintings based upon a complex of brush symbols or "type forms" for nature.

As part of his strategy to both de-exoticize and promote appreciation of Chinese painting, Lee set up striking visual resonances between Chinese pictures and about a dozen European and American drawings and watercolors in the galleries and the catalogue. Lee used these juxtapositions as heuristic tools of engagement. Lee referred to both the landscape photographs and the Euro-American pictures as "secondary aids" to assist in making the scrolls seem "less strange."[43] One of the most compelling visual juxtapositions in the show—that between Shitao's 石濤 (1642–1707) early eighteenth-century album leaf (fig. 4.8A) and a 1914 watercolor by American John Marin (fig. 4.8B)—recreates Lee's own earlier

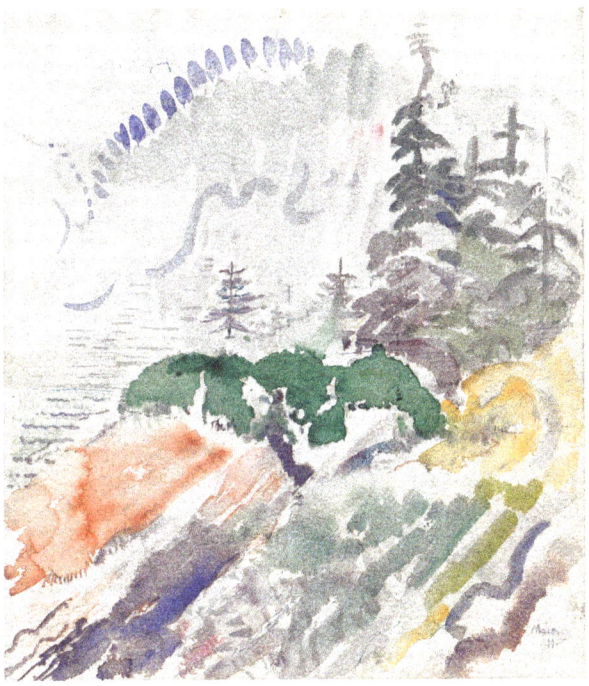

4.8B. John Marin (1872–1953), *Marin Island*, 1914, watercolor, 41.5 × 36.6 cm, Norman O. Stone and Ella A. Stone Memorial Fund, Cleveland Museum of Art. Photo courtesy Cleveland Museum of Art

experiences in interpreting American painting through the lens of East Asian painting.[44]

Throughout his 1941 dissertation, "Critical Survey of American Watercolor Painting," Lee repeatedly answered a question, not posed directly, but undoubtedly on his mind: What is Chinese about American watercolor painting? He frequently referred to East Asian ink painting in his discussions of American watercolors, often holding up Chinese and Japanese techniques, traditions, artists, and individual works as worthy models for American artists to emulate. Lee was the first to connect American watercolorists like Charles Demuth (1883–1935) and John Marin to Chinese and Japanese ink painting. Already advocating for the further study of East Asian painting, Lee asserted that study of Chinese and Japanese paintings and their methods seemed to be "essential" to broaden the effects that American watercolorists could achieve.[45] In his chapter-long treatment of Marin, he described the painter's brushwork as "broad and cursive calligraphy, appropriate to the beach combers in the Maine landscape while also recalling the swirling clouds and water of Chinese dragon scrolls."[46] The aforementioned likely refers to a well-known handscroll in the collection of the Museum of Fine Arts, Boston: *Nine Dragons*, a thirteenth-century Southern Song dynasty work by Chen Rong 陳容, acquired in 1917. While Lee admired the exuberance of Marin's works from the 1910s, he also noted a quality of stillness in those of the 1920s. By invoking the paintings of Southern Song artist Xia Gui 夏珪 (fl. 1195–1224), he complemented such quietude in Marin's *White Mountain Country*.

Another of Lee's uncanny juxtapositions in *Chinese Landscape Painting* paired Zhao Yong's 趙雍 (ca. 1289–ca. 1362) *Fisherman-Hermit in Stream and Mountain* loaned by New York dealer Frank Caro (1904–1980) with Wolf Huber's (ca. 1480–1553) drawing *Rapids of the Danube near Grien* from the National Gallery of Art in Washington, D.C. (fig. 4.9A–B). The compositions resonate strongly: both feature trees emerging from rocks clustered in the foreground, an expanse of water with boaters in the middle ground, and distant hills as a background. Huber's horizontal composition also has some of the same compositional correspondences with Zhao Mengfu's *Twin Pines, Level Distance*, though the positioning of the foreground trees is opposite. Lee's remarkable visual

Noelle Giuffrida 107

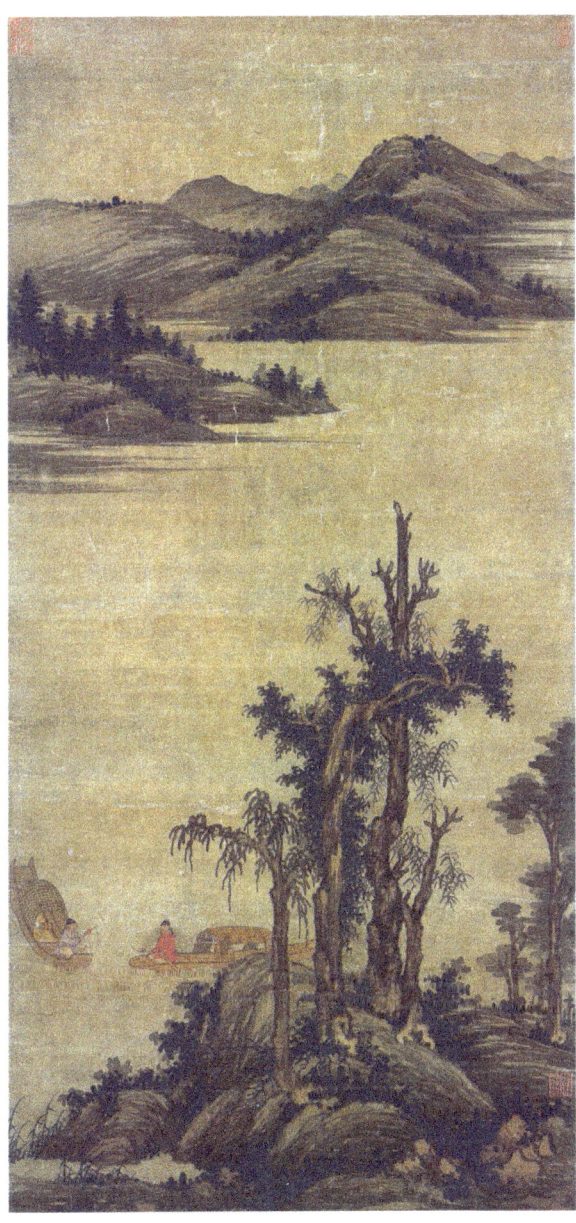

4.9A. Zhao Yong (ca. 1289–1362), *Fisherman-Hermit in Stream and Mountain*, fourteenth century, hanging scroll, ink and color on silk, 86.5 × 42.5 cm, bequest of Mrs. A. Dean Perry, Cleveland Museum of Art. Photo courtesy Cleveland Museum of Art

memory allowed him to compose these convincing juxtapositions, by comparing not merely works in Cleveland's collection but also those loaned from other sources. For individuals today, regardless of nationality or ethnicity, whose path to Chinese painting wound through Chinese art history, literature, history, and religion, rather than through traditional Euro-American art history, Lee's comparisons effectively serve as a bridge to pictures designed for a Western eye. Thus, *Chinese Landscape Painting's* visual resonances work in both directions.

Lee's juxtapositional approach may strike some today as unconventional—even problematic—but it is important to clarify how his pairings differed in intention and message from other "East-West" comparisons during the first half of the twentieth century. His approach was also significant for what it did *not* do when considering Chinese and Euro-American pictures in the same space

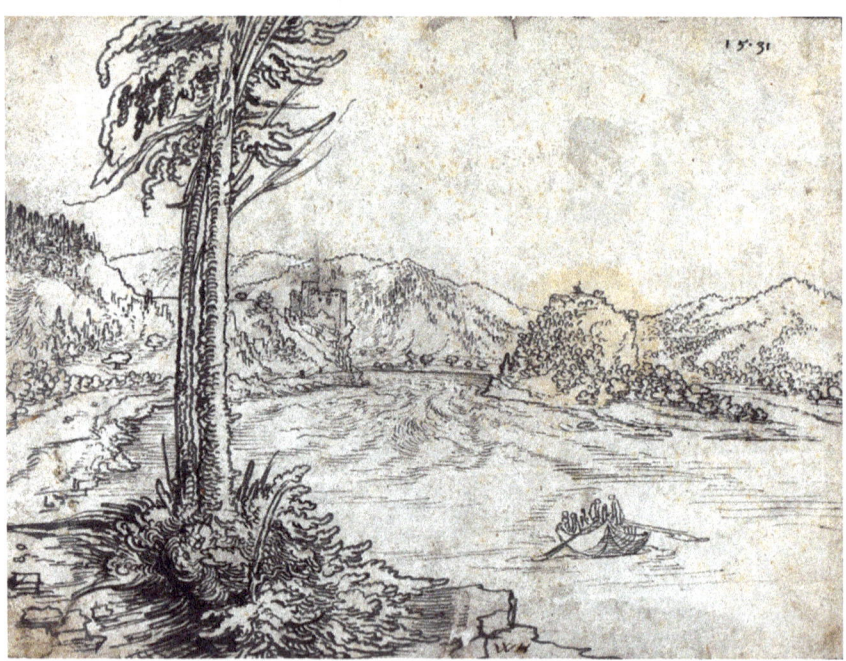

4.9B. Wolf Huber (ca. 1480–1553), *Rapids of the Danube near Grien*, 1531, drawing, pen with black and grey ink, 15.9 × 21 cm, National Gallery of Art, Washington, D.C. Photo courtesy National Gallery of Art, Washington, D.C.

or sentence. Lee rejected the Orientalist notion of Asian art as an "other" that should be defined primarily through its relationship with Euro-American art. And unlike some other exhibitions such as the Royal Ontario Museum's paired shows *East-West* and *West-East* in 1952 and 1953, Lee was not interested in demonstrating "influence" through diffusion or transmission in either direction. By setting up comparisons between Chinese and Euro-American pictures that shared extraordinary visual similarities, Lee offered American audiences a chance to begin to accustom their eyes to Chinese painting. In some ways, Lee probably hoped that the visual resonances that he configured would trigger an initial moment of recognition and lead American viewers to look more closely at the Chinese pictures. After all, once one is able to see similarities in a comparison, one then looks for differences. By drawing attention to basic similarities in form, composition, and brushwork, Lee aimed to cue viewers toward an appreciation of Chinese painting as deserving of the high regard accorded to more familiar European and American painting traditions. While Lee's purely formal and artistic comparisons in *Chinese Landscape Painting* might initially seem superficial, Lee employed them as a kind of icebreaker for his conversation about Chinese painting with American museum audiences and readers of the time. For the most part, in future exhibitions of Asian art, Lee did not use this comparative approach.[47]

Other scholars of Lee's time, such as art historian Benjamin Rowland (1904–1972), also employed cross-cultural comparisons between Asian and Euro-American art in their attempts to introduce Asian art to American novices. In fact, in the same year as *Chinese Landscape Painting*, Rowland published a book designed to accompany one of his undergraduate courses at Harvard: *Art in East and West: An Introduction through Comparisons*. Lee and Rowland's reviews of each other's books appeared back-to-back in a 1955 issue of the *College Art Journal*.[48] Despite a basic similarity in approach, however, Rowland's book was more expansive in scope and types of artworks. Though Rowland's book and Lee's catalogue both used comparisons between Chinese art and European and American art, Rowland's entire volume was dedicated to these comparisons, covering landscape painting as well as figure painting, still life pictures, and sculpture. Rowland chose particular themes and selected artworks to compare not just in terms of composition and style but also in terms of the cultural contexts for each pair of objects. Some of his landscape themes, for instance, included "Romanticism Anticipated in France and China" and "The Totality of Nature in Germany and China." Lee's comparisons, on the other hand, were not the primary *raison d'être* for his exhibition or catalogue, and he used them very sparingly: 126 Chinese paintings compared with eleven European and American pictures. Thus, Lee's juxtapositions served as one of many devices he used to speak to American readers and visitors. In the few pairings he employed, Lee focused on comparing how artists "see in form" and how they choose to render those forms in pictures, rather than trying to compare the artistic intentions of an Asian and European painter as Rowland did.[49] Lee's review complemented Rowland's approach, saying, "Oriental art is admittedly different from the art of our own past, and yet there are grounds for honest probing of likenesses as well as differences."[50] On this fundamental point, Lee and Rowland agreed. After all, one of the basic tools for teaching the history of art has long been the comparison.

With *Chinese Landscape Painting,* Lee employed a blended strategy that de-exoticized Chinese painting for American viewers without essentializing Chinese pictures as a homogenous mass. Lee emphasized Chinese paintings' distinctiveness as Chinese (not European or American) while also highlighting the variety and history of paintings by Chinese artists. Lee's approach resembled—in some ways—that of art historian George Rowley (1893–1962), who had also aimed to present Chinese painting to readers and audiences familiar with aesthetic and visual traditions of Euro-American pictures in his 1947 book *Principles of Chinese Painting.* Rowley used selected contrasts between Chinese and Euro-American ideas about painting, explaining that "comparisons with western attitudes are apt to be more misleading than helpful, and yet the Chinese approaches defy our understanding unless we relate them to western orientations."[51] While Lee's strategy of emphasizing distinctive qualities of Chinese painting parallels some of Rowley's approaches, Lee sought to de-exoticize Chinese pictures, whereas Rowley set up Chinese painting as "other," claiming that the distinctive character of Chinese painting derived from "the importance of the mysterious, the intangible, and the elusively expressive."[52]

Lee's goals regarding American audiences prompted him to assert similarities between Euro-American and Chinese paintings, connecting the concept of form used by French art historian Henri Focillon (1881–1943) in *The Life of Forms in Art* (1957) and Chinese landscape painter Zong Bing's 宗炳 (375–443) *Hua shanshui xu* 畫山水序 (Introduction to Painting Landscapes). In the introduction to his *Chinese Landscape Painting* catalogue, Lee compared Focillon's idea that artists recollect, think, and feel in forms to Zong's commentary that "the lovers of landscapes are led into the Way by a sense of form."[53] Thereby Lee asserted, "Chinese painting then is concerned with forms seen or imagined by the eyes of a Chinese, but still *forms*."[54] In the 1950s, Lee was convinced that "stressing the antipathetic nature of eastern and much western art is not only no help but a substantial distortion."[55] His own ability to operate as an art historical polymath predisposed him to employ visual cross-cultural comparisons as one tool in his efforts to increase American understanding and appreciation of Chinese painting.

Although the reception of historical exhibitions can be difficult to reconstruct, reviews of the *Chinese Landscape Painting* catalogue and show suggest that Lee's approach achieved some success — or at least that one of the aims for the show was adroitly disseminated. Several newspaper reviews specifically commented on the juxtapositions. For instance, one columnist wrote: "He has dug up pictures by Rembrandt, Cezanne, John Marin, and other Western boys to match some of the Chinese brushwork. To an extent he is right. These pictures must be measured by artistic rules. Shed exotic notions and look hard enough and you will notice that some artists solve artistic problems much more successfully than others."[56] Another reviewer noted the "simplification of naturalism [in Shi tao's painting] not too unlike the handling of *Marin Island, Maine*, a sweeping watercolor by John Marin."[57] Fellow Chinese art historian Michael Sullivan (1916–2013) called Lee's comparisons "apt and illuminating."[58] Rowland's praise for the *Chinese Landscape Painting* catalogue confirmed the viability of Lee's approach at the time:

> Except for their descriptive enumeration by Osvald Sirén, later Chinese landscape paintings have never been subjected to analysis based partly on Western stylistic methods,

partly on the Chinese interpretation through brush structure. In this respect the writer's contribution is both original and notable in providing a sound framework of appreciation for this one important category of Chinese painting. This objective analysis is consistently maintained throughout, and there is no attempt to coerce the development of Chinese landscape into a Wöfflinian formula, a didactic approach totally inapplicable to the study of any phase of Oriental art.[59]

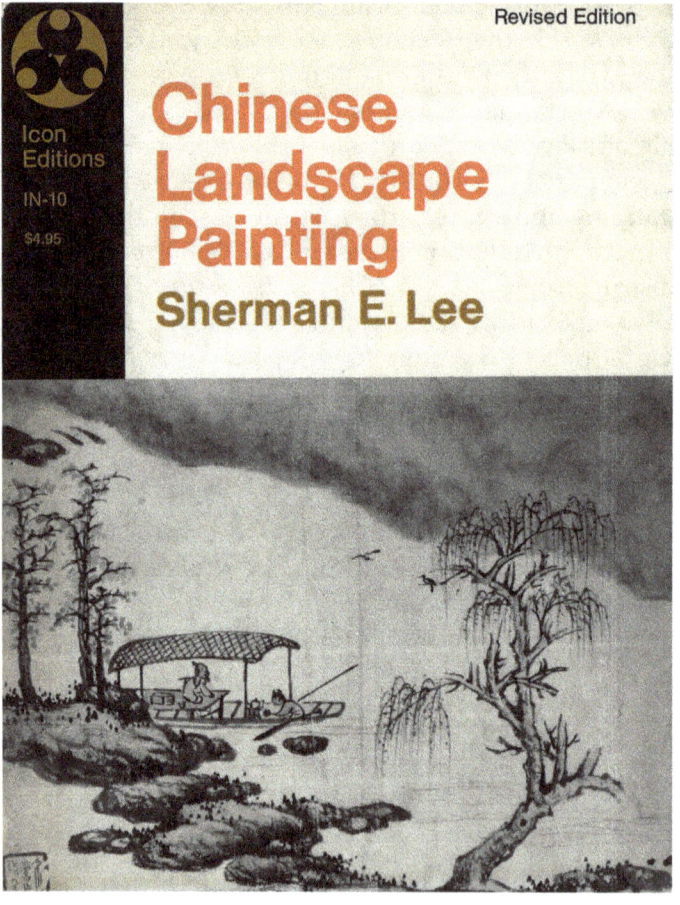

4.10. Paperback edition of *Chinese Landscape Painting*, by Sherman E. Lee (New York: Harper and Row, 1980). Photo by author

When the original catalogue for the show sold out quickly, Lee subsequently revised the book. With some minor changes in the painting selections, it was reissued in a 1962 deluxe edition distributed by Harry Abrams publishing.[60] This edition also sold out, likely on account of the increased interest in Chinese painting triggered by the yearlong American tour of the *Chinese Art Treasures* exhibition in 1961–1962. Following the success of the revised edition, publisher Harper and Row turned the book into a paperback that it reprinted each year from 1977 through 1980 (fig. 4.10). These post-exhibition versions of the catalogue helped to perpetuate the impact of the exhibition on the understanding of Chinese pictures in postwar America.[61] With *Chinese Landscape Painting*, Lee acted not only as curator but also as ambassador for Chinese art, endeavoring to build a bridge for American museumgoers from the shores of Euro-American art to the realms of Chinese painting.

Conclusion

Before and after World War I, Europeans had a leading role in building Chinese art collections at the British Museum, the Museé Guimet, and the Berlin State Museums. And from the late 1920s to the middle 1930s, important exhibitions were held in Berlin and London, positioning Europe as a hub for Chinese art. After World War II, however, dire economic and social conditions in Europe meant that most museums there did not have the financial resources to buy Chinese art. In China, the War to Resist Japan (1937–1945), civil war between the Guomindang and Communists, and the tumultuous early years of the People's Republic of China prompted the sale and export of many artworks to Japan, Hong Kong, and the United States. Economic conditions for museums and collectors in postwar America were more favorable.

The immediate post–World War II decade marked a shift in the balance of power in collections, exhibitions, and scholarship on Chinese art. German émigré art historians such as Ludwig Bachhofer (1894–1976) and Alfred Salmony (1890–1958), who came to America in the 1930s, were joined by members of a new generation with significant sinological skills, including Max Loehr (1903–1988) and Gustav Ecke, who took up academic and museum positions in America after World War II. Sherman Lee, Michael Sullivan (1916–2013), Richard Edwards, and a younger generation of Chinese art historians, including James Cahill, gained experience in Asia in the 1930s and 1940s that they brought with them to museum and academic posts in the United States. Dealers of Chinese art increasingly based themselves in the United States. Because of political and economic circumstances in China during the 1930s and 1940s, dealers and collectors such as Walter Hochstader, Frank Caro, and C. C. Wang built up an ample inventory of paintings that they offered to American museums for acquisition and exhibition.

In the late 1940s, exhibitions organized by Sickman in Kansas City and Jean-Pierre Dubosc in New York drew attention to the importance of Ming and Qing paintings and away from the emphasis on Song pictures that had characterized the attitudes of most Euro-American collectors and curators during the pre–World War II decades of the twentieth century. Curators, collectors, and scholars, including Contag, Dubosc, Sickman, and Lee, recognized the necessity of mediating Chinese paintings for Euro-American audiences. Lee's selections for *Chinese Landscape Painting*—ranging from Song to Qing—evinced the growth in the number and quality of Chinese paintings in American collections. In 1957, in an article that served as a debrief of the exhibition, Lee noted with optimism, "We in the United States cannot complain too much, however. The heartening fact, revealed in part by the exhibition, which was after all limited to landscape subjects, is that American museums have, and are continuing to acquire, a relatively rich variety of Chinese paintings of good quality. These provide us with the aesthetic delight and the historical sources that are the very heart of our study."[62]

Notes

1 Some examples include: *Collecting China: The World, China, and a Short History of Collecting*, ed. Vimalin Rujivacharakul (Newark: University of Delaware Press, 2011); *Collectors, Collections, and Collecting the Arts of China: Histories and Challenges*, ed. Jason Steuber with Guolong Lai (Gainesville: University Press of Florida, 2014), Minna Törmä, *Enchanted by Lohans: Osvald Sirén's Journey into Chinese Art* (Hong Kong: Hong Kong University Press, 2013), and Lara Netting, *A Perpetual Fire: John C. Ferguson and His Quest for Chinese Art and Culture* (Hong Kong: Hong Kong University Press, 2014).

2 "American audiences" is used in this essay to indicate those who visited museums and read exhibition catalogues in the United States as opposed to those who did so in East Asia or Europe.

3 See *Catalogue of the International Exhibition of Chinese Art, 1935–36* (London: Royal Academy of Arts, 1936). On the domestic Chinese versions of this show, see *Canjia lundun zhongguo yishu guoji zhanlanhui chupin tushuo* 参加伦敦中国艺术国际展览会出品图说 [Illustrated Catalogue of Chinese Government Exhibits for the International Exhibition of Chinese Art in London], 4 vols. (Shanghai: The Commercial Press, Ltd., 1935) and Ellen Huang, "There and Back Again: Material Objects at the First International Exhibitions of Chinese Art in Shanghai, London, and Nanjing, 1935–1936," in Rujivacharakul, ed., *Collecting China*, 138–54. On *Chinese Art Treasures*, see Jane Ju, "Chinese Art, the National Palace Museum, and Cold War Politics," in *Partisan Canons*, ed. Anna Brzyski (Durham: Duke University Press, 2007), 115–34, and Noelle Giuffrida, "The Right Stuff: *Chinese Art Treasures'* Landing in Early 1960s America," in *The Reception of Chinese Art across Cultures*, ed. Michelle Y. L. Huang (Newcastle: Cambridge Scholars, 2014), 201–28.

4 In the midst of the Cold War, loans from the People's Republic of China were not possible and the National Palace Museum collection that had been spirited away from the mainland was still crated and stored in caves on Taiwan for its own protection.

5 The show lasted from October 1948 through January 1949. See *Exhibition of Chinese Paintings*, pamphlet, (Kansas City, Mo.: Nelson-Atkins Museum of Art, 1949).

6 See *Exposition de peintures chinoises de la collection J.-P. Dubosc* (Paris: La Bibliothèque, 1937).

7 Jean-Pierre Dubosc, *Great Chinese Painters of the Ming and Qing Dynasties* (New York: Wildenstein, 1949), 10.

8   Dubosc to Sickman, 20 April 1949, Box 1b, Laurence Sickman Papers, 1898–1989, Nelson-Atkins Museum of Art, MS 001. See Sherman Lee, "The Story of Chinese Painting," *The Art Quarterly* 11, no. 1 (1948): 9–31.
9   Sickman to Dubosc, 20 April 1949, Box 1b, Laurence Sickman Papers, 1898–1989, Nelson-Atkins Museum of Art, MS 001. The Four Wangs (Wang Hui, Wang Yuanqi, Wang Jian, and Wang Shimin) are associated with the orthodox school of literati painting in the Qing dynasty.
10 Lee to Sickman, 26 February 26 1951, Box 25, Folder S19, Seattle Art Museum Archives, Special Collections Division, University of Washington Libraries, Seattle, WA (hereafter SAM Archives).
11 For a full discussion of Lee's article and his advocacy of pictorial over textual connoisseurship as well as late 1940s debates about methods for the study of Chinese painting, see Noelle Giuffrida, *Separating Sheep from Goats: Sherman E. Lee's and Collecting Chinese Art in Postwar America* (Berkeley: University of California Press, 2018), 69–75.
12 Lee, "Story of Chinese Painting," 21.
13 Ibid., 28.
14 Alexander Soper, "Eberhard on Chinese Art," *Journal of the American Oriental Society* 71, no. 1 (January–March 1951): 70.
15 Dubosc, *Great Chinese Painters of the Ming and Qing Dynasties*, 11. Dubosc directed his most vehement criticism toward Ludwig Bachhofer's treatment of Ming and Qing literati painting in his 1947 volume *A Short History of Chinese Art*. For more on methodological debates in the late 1940s, see Giuffrida, *Separating Sheep from Goats*, chapter 2.
16 Both pictures hailed from the renowned Shanghai collection of Pang Yuanji 龐元濟 (1864–1949), from which Hochstadter and earlier collectors such as Charles Lang Freer acquired many works. For a study of Pang, see Katharine Burnett, "A Study of the Collection of P'ang Yüan-chi 龐元濟 (1864–1949)" (M.A. thesis, University of Michigan, Ann Arbor, 1989).
17 Certainly, changes in the art market also affected Lee's collecting. Japan's Cultural Property Protection Act of 1950, which Lee and other members of the Arts and Monuments division helped to shape, placed additional restrictions on the export of artworks, and the exchange rate for dollars-to-yen became much less favorable for American buyers. These factors impacted the market for both Japanese and Chinese art.
18 Sherman Lee, *Chinese Landscape Painting* (Cleveland: Cleveland Museum of Art, 1954), 93, 95.
19 Although Trubner received loans from reputable sources like the Nelson-Atkins, the Art Institute of Chicago, Mr. and Mrs. Otto

Burchard, and Tonying and Company, the overall quality of the works he arranged was fairly low. Other lenders included dealers not known for their expertise in Chinese painting such as Dikran Kelekian, Jan Kleijkamp, and C. Edward Wells.

20 Trubner chose to avoid scholarly or connoisseurial examinations of the works in the show. Henry Trubner, *Chinese Paintings Lent by American Museums, Collectors and Dealers* (Los Angeles County Museum of Art, 1948), vii.
21 *Mostra d'arte cinese* [Exhibition of Chinese Art] (Venice: Istituto italiano per il Medio ed Estremo Oriente, 1954).
22 Dubosc sold many of his paintings to the Museé Guimet and Swiss collector Franco Vannotti.
23 *Gugong bowuyuan kan* 故宮博物院院刊, vol. 2 (1960), 193. The National Palace Museum in Taiwan did not hold significant exhibitions on the island until 1966.
24 This painting and many others that Lee purchased in the 1950s and 1960s came from the dealer Walter Hochstadter. For an overview of Hochstadter's life, activities as an art collector and dealer, as well as his key role as a supplier of Chinese paintings for Lee, see Giuffrida, *Separating Sheep from Goats*, chapter 3.
25 Sections in the book are not credited to a specific author, however, consideration of subsequent writings by Lee and Fong suggest that parts I, II, and V reflect mostly Lee's ideas, while parts III and IV can be attributed to Fong. Sherman Lee and Wen Fong, "Streams and Mountains without End: A Northern Sung Handscroll and Its Significance in the History of Early Chinese Painting" *Artibus Asiae, Supplementum* 14 (1955). The publication was revised and republished in 1967.
26 Scholars continue to explore the ideas and processes involved in the construction of artistic canons as well as the fluidity and simultaneous existence of multiple canons. See Gill Perry and Colin Cunningham, eds., *Academies, Museums, and Canons of Art* (New Haven: Yale University Press, 1999); Anna Brzyski, "Introduction: Canons and Art History," in *Partisan Canons*, ed. Anna Brzyski (Durham: Duke University Press, 2007), 1–25; and Hubert Locher, "The Idea of the Canon and Canon Formation in Art History," in *Art History and Visual Studies in Europe: Transnational Discourses and National Frameworks*, ed. Matthew Rampley et al. (Leiden: Brill, 2012), 29–40. For a recent discussion of canons in Asian art, see essays by Frederick Ashker, Vishaka Desai, Jerome Silbergeld, and Nancy Steinhardt in Vishaka Desai, ed., *Asian Art History in the Twenty-First Century* (Williamstown, Mass.: Sterling and Francine Clark Institute, 2007).

27 25 April 1955 invoice, Box 3, Folder 23, Walter Hochstadter Papers, 1876–2002, Leo Baeck Institute, Center for Jewish History, New York, NY.
28 Lee played an important behind-the-scenes role in selecting paintings for this Japanese loan show. See Yoshiaki Shimizu, "Japan in American Museums: But Which Japan?" *The Art Bulletin* 83, no. 1 (March 2001): 123–34.
29 Lee, "Some Problems in Ming and Ch'ing Landscape Painting," 471.
30 Lee, *Chinese Landscape Painting*, 5.
31 *Exhibition of Chinese Paintings*.
32 Victoria Contag, "The Unique Characteristics of Chinese Landscape Pictures" *Archives of Chinese Art Society* 6 (1952): 47.
33 Lee, *Chinese Landscape Painting*, 7.
34 "China Show a Museum Triumph" by Jim Frankel, *Cleveland News*, Nov. 6, 1954. Lee Family Papers.
35 These ideas are expressed in many of Fry's writings, including *Vision and Design* (London: Chatto and Windus, 1920). Fry and art historian Clive Bell (1881–1964) overlapped in their views on significant form; see https://dictionaryofarthistorians.org/fryr.htm. For an examination of some of Fry and Bell's ideas about Chinese art, see Lin Hsiu-ling 林秀玲, "Reconciling Bloomsbury's Aesthetics of Formalism with the Politics of Anti-Imperialism: Roger Fry's and Clive Bell's Interpretations of Chinese Art" *Concentric: Studies in English Literature and Linguistics* 27, no. 1 (2001): 149–90.
36 For further explorations of how *bimo* has been explained and discussed by Chinese and American experts, see Arnold Chang, both in this volume and in "Returning to Brushwork: A Personal Exploration" *Kaikodo Journal* 7 (1998): 17–26 and Joan Stanley-Baker 徐小虎, *Huayu lu: Wang jiqian jiao ni kan dong Zhongguo shu hua* 畫語錄: 听王季迁谈中国书画的笔墨 [C.C. Wang Reflects on Painting] (Taipei: Diancang yishu jiating gufen youxian gongsi, 2013).
37 Lee, *Chinese Landscape Painting*, 7.
38 Passages from the writings of painters included Xie He, Zong Bing, Guo Xi, Jing Hao, Shitao, and Kuncan. Like many Euro-American and Chinese scholars of the time, Lee referred to Confucianism and Daoism as philosophies, rather than as religious traditions.
39 Each individual was specifically recognized for their contributions in the preface and acknowledgments of the catalogue.
40 For instance, in 1959, Lee hired Wai-kam Ho 何惠鑑 (1924–2004) to join him as assistant curator of Chinese art in Cleveland. Lee and Ho would collaborate on several major exhibitions through the early 1980s.

41 "China Show a Museum Triumph."
42 Lee, *Chinese Landscape Painting*, 7.
43 Ibid., 8–9.
44 Ibid., 120.
45 Sherman Lee, "A Critical Survey of American Watercolor Painting" (Ph.D. diss., Western Reserve University, 1941), 18.
46 Ibid., 260–61.
47 One notable exception was a special exhibition in Cleveland in 1983, *Visions of Landscape: East and West*, in which Lee and several curators from the Asian, European, and American departments collaborated to create a fully comparative show using paintings from the museum's collection. See William S. Talbot, "Visions of Landscape: East and West," *Bulletin of the Cleveland Museum of Art* 70, no. 3 (1983): 112–35.
48 Sherman E. Lee, "*Art in East and West: An Introduction through Comparisons* by Benjamin Rowland," *College Art Journal* 15, no. 1 (Autumn, 1955): 68–69 and Benjamin Rowland, "*Chinese Landscape Painting* by Sherman E. Lee," *College Art Journal* 15, no. 1 (Autumn, 1955): 69–70.
49 Lee derived this idea of seeing in forms from French art historian Henri Focillon (1881–1943); see *Vie des Formes* [The Life of Forms] (Paris: Presses Université de France, 1934). Focillon's book was translated into English by C. B. Hogan and George Kubler and first published in 1957.
50 Lee, "*Art in East and West*," 68.
51 Rowley, *Principles of Chinese Painting*, preface.
52 Ibid., 30–32, 51, 77.
53 Lee, *Chinese Landscape Painting*, 7.
54 The passage that Lee uses from Zong Bing's text is part of Zong's response to a passage from the Confucian *Lunyu* (Analects): the wise man finds pleasure in water; the virtuous find pleasure in mountains.
55 Lee to Plumer, 7 Feb 1952, SAM Archives, Box 25
56 "China Show a Museum Triumph."
57 "Art Today," column by Paul B. Metzler, *Cleveland Plain Dealer*, 7 November 1954.
58 Michael Sullivan, "Chinese Landscape Painting by Sherman E. Lee," *Bulletin of the School of Oriental and African Studies* 26, no. 2 (1963): 459.
59 Rowland, "*Chinese Landscape Painting* by Sherman E. Lee," 70.
60 Like many curators and collectors, Lee made his share of misjudgments about paintings. In the 1962 edition, he retracted and replaced several pictures that he had admitted into the original show, such as a "Dong Qichang" from the collection of anthropologist Brenda Zara Seligman (1882–1965). Milton Fox (1904–1971) served as editor for Harry Abrams at the time and his friendship with Lee, whom he

got to know at the Cleveland Museum of Art when he was working in the education department and Lee was working on his doctorate and with Howard Hollis, likely facilitated the publication of the catalogue's revised edition. Lee worked with Fox again on several books, including his seminal survey volume *A History of Far Eastern Art*.

61 For the remainder of the 1950s, Dubosc and Frank Caro continued to stage exhibitions of their works. In 1956, Caro organized a show of sixty paintings at the Royal Ontario Museum, chiefly from his own stock. Two years later, Caro also presented a one-month exhibition of a wide range of Chinese art, including some paintings, at the Wadsworth Atheneum in Hartford, Connecticut: "4,000 Years of Chinese Art," October–November 1958.

62 Lee, "Some Problems in Ming and Ch'ing Landscape Painting," 471–72.

Chapter 5

Patrimony and Posterity: The "Confucian" Legacy of James F. Cahill (1926–2014)

Xiaoqing Zhu

Professor James Cahill, on numerous occasions, made special reference to one of his earliest essays, "Confucian Elements in the Theory of Painting" (1960).[1] He considered this essay his "first attempt at formulating a coherent theory of literati painting" and acknowledged his early devotion to this genre, for which, in his words, "I was sometimes accused, not undeservedly, of setting myself up as a spokesman…a true believer."[2] In one of his unpublished lectures, Cahill defines Confucianism and explains the "doctrine or ideology of *ru*儒 or *junzi*君子." "Junzi" refers to "a group of educated and learned men, [a] scholarly class who were obligated by this ideology to try, at least, to put their learning to the benefit of society…to perfect and preserve [a] kind of stable, stratified society that Confucius envisioned as ideal."[3] Over his six decades as a scholar, collector, and great teacher, he did just that, and "put [his] learning to the benefit of society."

It is difficult to fully acknowledge Cahill's voluminous contributions to the field of Chinese art and to the public knowledge of Chinese painting. In sheer quantity alone, Cahill's contribution finds hardly any match. He authored more than ten books and a dozen or so exhibition catalogues, some in collaboration with his students and other scholars. Most of his books were translated into Chinese, Japanese, and other languages. He penned hundreds of essays and articles, including many unpublished papers now available on Cahill's website. Also available to the public on his website are his nearly thirty hours of video lectures organized between two titles: "A Pure and Remote View: Visualizing Early Chinese Landscape Painting" and "Gazing into the Past—Scenes from Later Chinese & Japanese Painting." All completed after his retirement, these lectures were made with the aid of new technology and can be streamed on YouTube. Cahill also left an extensive body of his letters, notes, and other papers in the care of the archives of the National Museum of Asian Art, Washington D.C., a resource that greatly benefited the research behind this paper. He donated his personal library to the China Art Academy (Hangzhou), including his collection of 13,000 slides, to be digitized and to be made available to Chinese students.[4] In addition, the finest of his collection of Chinese paintings has formed the core collection of Chinese art at the Berkeley Art Museum and Pacific Film Archive. Cahill was also instrumental in building the Chinese art collection for the Allen Art Museum of Oberlin College, Ohio, and the Willard G. Clark Center for the Study of Japanese Art, in Hanford, California.[5]

To this enumeration of his achievements should be added the controversies he engendered (particularly the famous ones pertaining to *The Compelling Image* and *Riverbank*) and his correspondence, which bridged nationalities and disciplines. And the record must recognize the impact of his students and the young scholars he helped.[6] Many of them are now teaching Chinese art in leading universities, or directing Asian art museums across the country and beyond.

Throughout his life, Cahill remained steadfast in what he saw as his "fundamentally Confucian" philosophy of teaching, "a belief that knowledge and wisdom transmitted from generation to generation is the basis for human society and culture; that minds can be improved, mostly through self-cultivation but also with some help from outside."[7] The abundant gift, or patrimony, that Cahill has left will indeed reverberate for generations to come. As one who has benefited intellectually from Cahill's volumes of writing and often taken enormous pleasure in reading them, I harbor no doubt that Professor Cahill exemplified a model member of the Confucian *junzi*: benevolent, humanistic, and unflinchingly dedicated to his public responsibility as a scholar and a teacher (fig. 5.1). A true *junzi*, according to Confucius, is someone who strives to, "when looking, see clearly; when listening, hear distinctly; in his expression, be

Xiaoqing Zhu 123

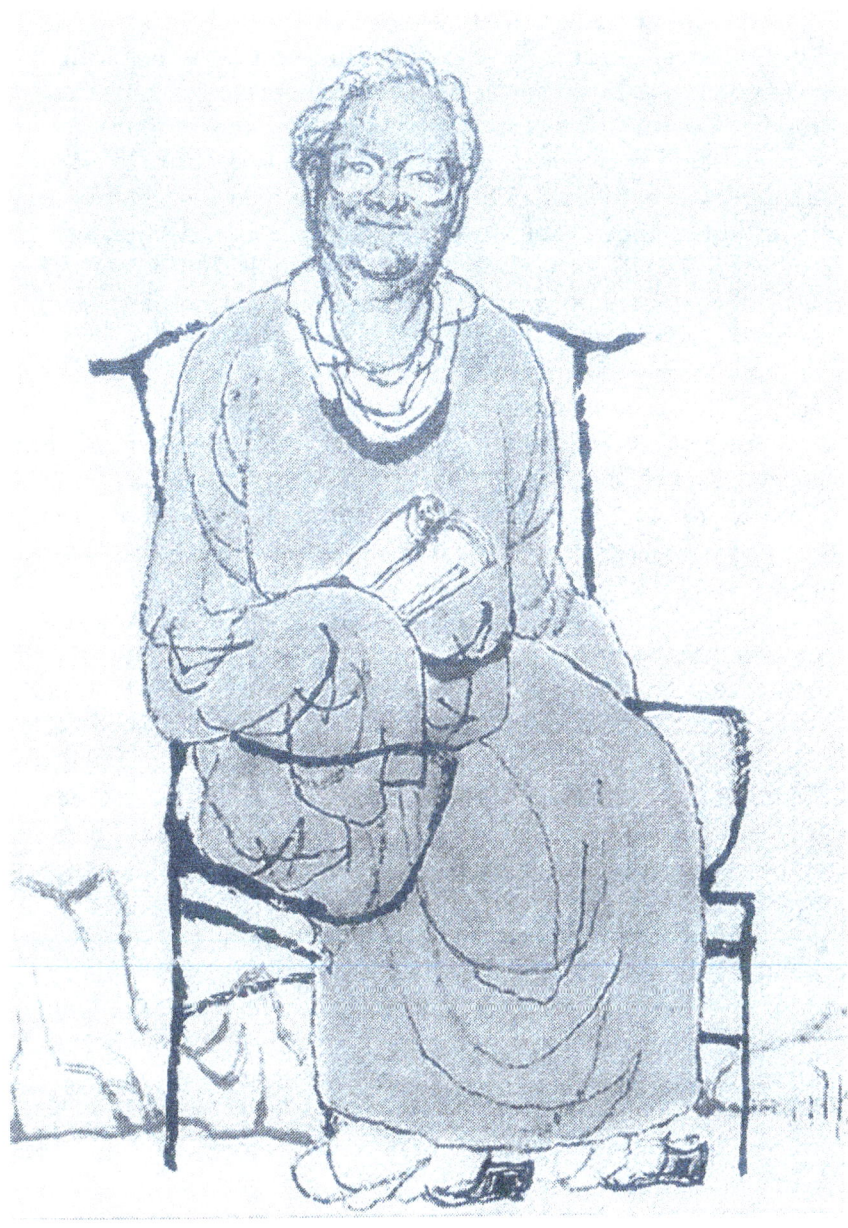

5.1. Wan Qingli, *Portrait of Cahill as a Chinese Scholar*, in James Cahill, "In Defense of the Visual: Reflections on an Illustrious Career," *Ars Orientalis* 41 (2011): 22

amiable; in his attitude, be deferential; in his speech, be loyal; when on duty, be respectful; when in doubt, question...."[8] One particular precept of a true Confucian scholar—one that is often subverted by orthodox Confucianism in favor of virtues of loyalty and filial piety, unity and harmony—is the intellectual's moral duty to criticize the ruler (even at the risk of their lives) when the ruler becomes corrupt and unyielding.[9] The eleventh-century poet and statesman Su Dongpo (1036–1101), for example, whom Cahill admired and referenced in his many books, and later questioned concerning his doctrine of literati painting, was such an intellectual who was demoted and forced into exile after criticizing the emperor. The Confucian legacy is thus complicated, and sometimes contradictory. While observing loyalty and filial piety, and emphasizing harmony and cohesion, ideal Confucian scholars should also follow the precepts of "social justice," "political dissent," and an intellectual's moral duty to question and criticize the ruling establishment of which they have, over time, often become a part.

In "Max Loehr at Seventy," a tribute given at Loehr's retirement from Harvard University, Cahill remarked: "we must begin to stop regarding him as a fixed institution, and take some time to consider this extraordinary man and his effect on Chinese art studies."[10] Thirty years later, in November 2005, invited to a University of Maryland graduate symposium titled "The Making of a Postwar American Historian of Chinese Painting: A Critical and Historiographical Study of James Cahill," Cahill mused, "now I feel like an institution."[11] Instead of regarding Cahill as "a fixed institution," or the "Cahill School" as it is commonly known in the field of Chinese art history, perhaps it serves us well if we can celebrate his enormous repertoire of publications, which reveal both his "filial piety" to his teacher's scholarship and what he claimed to be his "radical departure" from Loehr's focus on "leading masters."

To understand the complexity of Cahill's "Confucian" legacy, I first trace in this paper the lineage of his former teacher Max Loehr (1903–1988) and focus on how this relationship of patrimony was passed to posterity, from Loehr to Cahill. Drawing parallels between Cahill's late-life Haley Lecture (1999) and his teacher's periodization paper, "Phase and Content in Chinese Painting" (1970), I examine how Cahill carried forward Loehr's commitment to a "style history." At the same time, I consider how Cahill, with his independent and critical spirit, or his "Berkeley style," as his longtime student Howard Roger put it, broke from this patrimony to produce alternative histories of Chinese painting that have benefited future scholars of Chinese art such as myself. The paper will highlight his lifelong commitment to "the defense of the visual" with a focus on his award-winning book *The Compelling Image* and the cross-cultural controversies it created. Finally, it is especially pertinent to this author to celebrate Cahill as a great teacher by following his advice and testimony on how to be a good teacher, which is also part of his enduring legacy. The paper will conclude by turning to Cahill's final book, *Pictures for Use and Pleasure: Vernacular Painting in High Qing China*, and reflect on his legendary patrimony, which both allures future scholars and allows academic expansion, but may also deter and delay a serious critical evaluation of his legacy. In the spirit of a true Confucian scholar, such as Cahill, both respectful and independent of our forebears, we might ask what alternative art histories we can add to this rich legacy of Chinese painting studies that Cahill has left us.

Lineage and Style History

Cahill belonged to that deservedly revered "great generation of men" whose World War II and postwar experience definitively shaped their career and their character. For Cahill, that was the discovery of Chinese and Japanese painting. When he was stationed in postwar Japan, and later Korea, he began collecting Chinese paintings, which initiated his lifelong devotion to their study. After completing his undergraduate degree in Oriental Languages at the University of California, Berkley and working one year at the Freer Gallery of Asian Art as a fellow, he went on to become Max Loehr's disciple at the University of Michigan.[12] Loehr's academic lineage traced back directly to Heinrich Wölfflin, whose canonic status in the discipline of Western art history needs no elaboration here; his *Principles of Art History* is usually the first book assigned in a graduate methods seminar. Heinrich Wölfflin's student Ludwig Bachhofer was Max Loehr's teacher in Chinese art studies at the University of Munich between 1931 and 1936.[13] This genealogy would place Cahill in the fourth generation of the Wölfflinians, and the first generation in the United States.

Throughout Cahill's long and illustrious career, he frequently referred to Loehr as an important influence and memorialized his mentor in many of his writings. He fondly recalled the "elegant gatherings" at Ann Arbor, where people were enchanted by Loehr's trim European manner or, in Cahill's own words, the "old world polish."[14] He admired Loehr's deep erudition in Chinese classics and proficiency in Chinese language while often lamenting his own inadequacy in Chinese.[15] He remembered Loehr's precision and, in Cahill's words, "lapidary quality" in his lecture and writing, and recounted the time when he was seeking his mentor's advice on his own "verbose and facile" style of writing for his dissertation.[16] What resonates the most in Cahill's publications is Loehr's "grand design," which Cahill purposefully set himself to fulfill and carry forward.[17] Cahill wrote in 2005, "Like Loehr and others, I still like to treat works of art sometimes *in series*."[18]

In his 1975 tribute to Loehr, Cahill summarized his teacher's contribution to Chinese art studies, chiefly in two areas. Cahill wrote, "On the one hand, he has greatly increased our knowledge of the *historical processes*...and our understanding of the objects that are its substance. On the other, he dealt more systematically and effectively than has anyone else with the theoretical and methodological problems that must, implicit or stated, underlie any responsible study."[19] For Loehr's foremost contribution, Cahill cited his "brilliant tracing of the stylistic development of the bronze styles of the *Anyang* period through a series of clearly defined stages, a study based on stylistic analysis and still largely hypothetical when it was written, but later to be borne out by the excavation of earlier sites than were then known."[20]

Cahill acknowledged, "as to formal and stylistic analysis, I learned from Loehr, I do it more as he did it than anybody else did it."[21] Cahill's preference to "put things in their place" and his commitment to formal and stylistic analysis led him to write his eloquent 1960s *Chinese Painting* and three surveys on Chinese painting from Yuan to Ming, all poetically titled: *Hills beyond a River: Chinese Painting of the Yuan Dynasty, 1279–1368* (1976), *Parting at the Shore:*

Chinese Painting of the Early and Middle Ming Dynasty, 1368–1580 (1978), and *The Distant Mountains: Chinese Painting of the Late Ming Dynasty, 1570–1644* (1982). Lamenting, at various occasions, on the lack of interest on style history among the younger generations of scholars, he warned, "it is as though we had abandoned the practice of architecture before we had built our city." To this failure, he sighed, "our generation, then, can be charged with having collectively failed to build on the achievements of the pioneers sufficiently to construct a history as solid and detailed as had been done (over a much longer period, to be sure) for European painting." That sentiment was expressed at the age of seventy-three, in 1999, at his Haley Lecture at Princeton, titled "Some Thoughts on the History and Post-History of Chinese Painting."[22] By Cahill's own account, this late-life lecture echoed Loehr's late-life periodization paper "Phase and Content in Chinese Painting," delivered for the first international symposium on Chinese painting in 1970, when Loehr was sixty-seven.[23]

In his periodization paper, Loehr argued that, looking at pictorial art alone, we should notice "a fairly clear division" in its history. This "clear division" within Chinese pictorial art, for Loehr, spanned into two cycles. The first was "concerned with representation of nature, lasted till the end of Sung; the second, concerned with images of a supra-representational order, began in Yuan period."[24] The consequence of this Yuan achievement, in Loehr's view, was "the existence of four or five unique and dissimilar styles created by the leading masters."[25] Loehr then asked thoughtfully, "whether it is at all possible to dismiss the 'chronological history' without sacrificing the idea of a history altogether," for which he proposed a "cycle theory" for Chinese painting.[26]

Cahill, in his 1999 Haley lecture, added a firmer note to Loehr's notion that the Chinese pictorial tradition moved from representation to a "supra-representational order" at the Song and Yuan juncture. Cahill wrote, "the dynastic change from Song to Yuan in the late thirteenth century, however, is more than a wrenching historical disjuncture brought about by the Mongol conquest of China: it marks, for Chinese painting, *the end of its history*."[27] Cahill further expounded, "[T]he achievements of the later [post-Yuan] Chinese artists can often be described in terms of reconciling seemingly *in-*

compatible choices, and more specifically, as following up some stylistic direction into the range of *extremism* without sacrificing the power of the picture as an image."[28]

Cahill's "incompatible choices" paralleled what Loehr considered to be two irreconcilable traditions, Song and Yuan, which post-Yuan painters had to choose from or reconcile. The following is what Loehr wrote in 1970:

> The post-Yuan painters, therefore, especially, those of early Ming, look back upon two traditions which in principle are *irreconcilable*.... What happened now, in early Ming? *No new style* was likely to appear that was not linked to either of the two traditions [Sung and Yuan]. A choice was unavoidable...Accordingly, *eclecticism* becomes a matter of course.... Painting became a strongly intellectual pursuit: a learned discourse with the past, more naïve here, more critical there. Individuality was expressed in the personal statement on ancient styles. To some extent, the painter becomes a historian.[29]

Cahill called the post-Yuan "a *post-historical* period," which, he believed, adjusting Loehr's view, continued to flourish on "a high innovative level."[30] Both Loehr and Cahill considered that this epiphany of innovation arrived with the genius of Dong Qichang (1555–1636), a late Ming bureaucrat, art critic, painter, calligrapher, and connoisseur, whose historical significance has been widely celebrated in the field of Chinese art history.[31] Loehr, in his 1970 paper, considered Dong to be the "only great genius...within the world of learned painting in the Ming period." He claimed, "Out of well-worn technical means derived from the past he forged a new imagery of landscape, whose character and strength lies in its very *abstractness*...[after him] there was no such thing as a *development* in Ming painting."[32]

Cahill arrived at a similar accolade for Dong's place in Chinese art history in his much more decorative verbiage: "[T]he next truly radical move within this series [after Yuan] is made by Dong Qichang in the early 17th century, the late Ming.... [T]hroughout the later phases of this series, it is as if the system of forms is being progressively stripped of its softening and naturalizing overlays of looser brushwork to reveal the stark underlying structure. And this process obviously implies an ever-increasing tolerance, or even preference, for unnaturalistic, all-but-*abstract*-form."[33]

In his *The Compelling Image*, Cahill attributed, with detailed formal analysis, Dong's "radical move" to this "all-but-abstract-form," to his historically conscious "imitation" (*fang*) and "transformation" (*bian*). Again in Cahill's eloquence, "the highly schematic character of a debased imitation of antique style is transmuted into a purposeful and aesthetically effective formalization," on the one hand, and "[Dong's] engagement with the past to be a true dialogue," combined with "a deep sense of his place in history," on the other, resulted in his paintings' "historical validity" and turned his "borrowed forms" [from the past or elsewhere] to "new uses in a fundamentally new structure."[34] This new structure is what Loehr called "abstractness," and in Cahill's words, "all-but-*abstract*-form."

The Compelling Image, a focused study on the seventeenth-century Ming painters, was written for the prestigious Charles Eliot Norton Lectures delivered at Harvard, 1978/79, around the time Loehr was completing his last book, *The Great Painters of China* (1980). Loehr's book focused mostly on pre-Ming artists, with the last fifth of the book on the Ming and Qing painters. Loehr, in his preface, remarked: "the author, who with Konrad Fiedler believes that art exists not to express its time but to give content to its time, attempts here to present the story of Chinese painting in *a meaningful sequence*: phases of unified content or intrinsic meaning, *independent of extraneous, non-artistic factors*."[35] Cahill, in his Norton lectures, began to question "the meanings attached to style" and "the association of style with status." Observing that styles in the late Ming were manipulated by the cultural elites, such as Dong Qichang, to "evoke associations in the minds of one's cultural peers," Cahill considered that "style choices" were not always innocent and were often relational. He argued, "Styles are created or adopted from the past for reasons of critical taste and doctrine as well as personal preference, and not for their effectiveness in producing better images or better paintings by traditional standards. Stylistic choices made in the freer context did, indeed, reveal more about the artists who made them."[36]

Starting in the late 1970s, Cahill began to diverge from "the grand design" laid out by Loehr. Nonetheless, in his loyalty to his teacher, and in principle, Cahill held on to the belief that Loehr's "grand design," whether consciously used or not, "will continue to underlie studies of the subject for generations to come."[37]

In his late-life Haley lecture, Cahill pronounced the responsibility to build a style history for Chinese art a collective failure, and in numerous later occasions, Cahill repeated the importance of doing style history, pleading that "someone should continue doing it." He explained, "I hold myself as responsible as others for this situation, having made the move from heavily stylistic studies following Max Loehr into later writings that take a more contextual approach, for which the principal model was Michael Baxandall's variety of social art history and his inferential criticism...."[38]

A "Berkeley Style" and Departure from Style History

Cahill's decision to decline the offer of the Harvard University Professorship in Chinese art, which was left vacant by Loehr, perhaps best manifested his independent character, or his "Berkeley style."[39] At Berkeley, Cahill found himself in a collaborative academic atmosphere of a public university and in the company of innovative art historians such as Svetlana Alpers, Michael Baxandall, and T. J. Clark, who have all blazed the trail in contextualizing art history and writing social art history.[40]

Cahill's major turn to a contextual approach to Chinese painting studies would have distressed his teacher, given Loehr's firm conviction in the Kantian "pure aesthetic" formulation. In Loehr's own pronouncement:

> "[W]orks of art, as mysteriously individual entities, do not possess, according to Konrad Fiedler, any intrinsic historical significance.... [T]o view [art works] primarily as historical monuments, in their historical context, is to do them an injustice.[41]
>
> ....

[P]ainting, like music or calligraphy, is a more or less closed system; much of those background matters remain extraneous and are unsuited to explain creative events.[42]

This conviction reveals Loehr's unwavering commitment to the German heritage of formalism and perhaps also the limitation of his time. Cautioning that one should avoid getting "stuck in any single way of doing art history," Cahill made his early effort to expand beyond style history in a 1976 symposium paper on Wen Cheng-ming. He discovered "there was a very clear correlation between the life patterns or the patterns of the career of an artist and the kinds of paintings the artist did."[43] He considered this case study a key methodological turning point in his career. His contextualization of Wen's works generated controversies and challenged the convention of formalism that still reigned in the field of Chinese painting history.

His participation in the 1980s workshop on patronage organized by Chu-tsing Li (1920–2014) at the Nelson-Atkins Museum of Art, Kansas City, marked his further step onto this path toward social art history. His essay, "Types of Artist-Patron Transactions in Chinese Painting," laid out various types of artist and patron relationship before delving into further investigation into how these relations affected artistic production.[44] His further investigation into the socioeconomic context of artistic production led to another eloquent book, *Three Alternative Histories of Chinese Painting*, published in 1988, the year Max Loehr passed away. Reflecting on his "radical departure" from the singular "style-history" to "social art history," Cahill attributed his development to the liberal environment at Berkeley, starting when his students in the late 1960s and early 1970s began asking about Chinese political propaganda pictures and subsequently inspired their teacher to look into this genre more closely. At the time, student-led rebellions made U.C. Berkeley one of the nation's most active centers of the anti-war, anti-establishment movement.[45]

In his *Three Alternative Histories of Chinese Painting*, Cahill wrote, "art history can validly be written in a diversity of ways or modes… without admonishing the importance of other modes of writing art history, such as the more conventional style-history mode and the biographic-and-documentary mode.... [W]e ought to give at least 'equal time' to other alternatives."[46] His commitment to alternative art historical approaches achieved another volume, *The Painter's Practice: How Artists Lived and Worked in Traditional China* (1994). In light of the seminal writing by his Berkeley colleague Svetlana Alpers on Rembrandt and the socioeconomic conditions of seventeenth-century Netherlands, Cahill played an instrumental role in dispelling the myth around the Chinese literati artists.[47] Using newly recovered personal diaries, letters, local records, and other unofficial and little-tapped materials collected and translated in collaboration with his students,[48] Cahill raised questions on this myth, perpetuated from the eleventh century onward, that Chinese literati artists refused to work for money, to preserve their artistic and moral integrity. With his usual literary agility, Cahill told stories in *The Painter's Practice* of Chinese painters who worked in different circumstances as artists-in-residence, ghost-painters, or freelancers for commissions and gifts of all sorts, from monetary payment to doses of elixir pills, from silk scrolls to aged liquor, from rice to the service of an attractive courtesan; the list goes on.[49] Cahill called for more realistic and penetrable readings and interpretations of Chinese paintings in their socioeconomic and political contexts. His determination to shed light on the "truth" behind the writings of Chinese educated elites represented by Dong Qichang and the like is reflected in the following passage: "I have all along been trying, in various ways, to expand our purview beyond the boundaries of what the Chinese literati critics allow as respectable painting but in recent years, I've pursued this project with greater intensity and tried to make stronger arguments."[50]

Cahill, in a letter to Loehr dated December 28, 1977, when he was preparing *The Great Painters of China*, commented with care on his teacher's preference for "the oeuvre of the individual master what I and some others would incline to spread out over several centuries and see as representing stages in the development of a school or tradition rather than a single artist."[51] Moving away from the "individual master" and "style history," the two approaches linked to his teacher, Cahill not only restored lesser-known artists such as Zhang Hong and Wu Bin to the landscape of Chinese painting history, while collecting their works, but also applied more intense scrutiny on Chinese literati writing on painting and their "text-reading" offspring.

"In Defense of the Visual" and The Compelling Image

In his speech titled "In Defense of the Visual," given at the Freer on the occasion of accepting the prestigious Charles Lang Freer Medal for his lifetime achievement in Asian art, Cahill, at the advanced age of eighty-four, urged his younger colleagues to pay more attention when looking at art: "And if there is anything I would impress with the utmost urgency upon young specialists in Chinese art, it is that no approach that does not involve prolonged and analytical looking at the work of art, and attention to its visual properties, can produce an adequate account of it."[52]

This "prolonged and analytical looking" along with Cahill's verbal eloquence best characterizes *The Compelling Image,* which he would describe as "my best book" in an autograph to one of his Chinese colleagues in 2011.[53] Admitting in an earlier interview that he was "fond of controversies," Cahill singled out his Harvard Norton lectures, an occasion where he indulged in his guilty pleasure of causing controversies by introducing the notion of plausible Western influence on seventeenth-century artists.[54] He argued that their exposure to Western topographical and pictorial images served as an impetus behind the late Ming revival of the Northern Song representational and naturalistic style. Juxtaposing paintings by Suzhou professional artist Zhang Hong and the late Ming court painter Wu Bin to European topographical engravings, most likely available in Nanjing and Beijing after 1608 via Jesuit missionaries, Cahill demonstrated striking visual similarities in their compositions, for example, the pictorial plane's diagonal recession into the distance and shading techniques used to depict volume of rocks and folds of clothing. Cahill argued that these visual correspondences, possibly coincidental, revealed at least "a mysterious convergence of separate artistic traditions,"[55] the outcome of which is "the most striking and art-historically momentous case in seventeenth-century painting of a convergence of old Chinese practice and response to foreign stimuli."[56]

His inference, based on keen formal comparisons, of "Western influence" as stimuli to late Ming "revival of Northern Song landscape style," exposed him to much criticism from Chinese art historians. His usual contender, Professor Wen Fong (1930–2018) of Princeton, charged Cahill with "cultural relativism" and "seeing the non-Western world as part of the expanding Western world."[57] Wen Fong wrote in his review of Cahill's book:

> Since this [the concern with the "representation of the physical world" in late Ming] introduces a complexity not dealt with *by Loehr's neat scheme*, Cahill decides that "the impetus of this new direction of descriptive naturalism was…contact with European pictures.
>
> ....
>
> Skeptics, of course, will remain unconvinced, precisely because the late-Ming panoramic views cited by Cahill derive structurally from 12th- or 13th-century Sung "flat-distance" compositions, many of which show exactly the same kind of diagonal pattern of recession as seen in the late 16th-century Northern European picture-maps.[58]

Anticipating criticism from Chinese art historians, Cahill warned in *The Compelling Image*, "[keep] always in mind the penchant of the Chinese for giving priority to their own tradition."[59] When arguing that Dong Qichang's picture "depends on sources" other than Huang Kung-wang's, "possibly Western," Cahill postulated that "[Dong] would have been less willing to acknowledge" such sources. "[I]f charged with using elements of Western style in his paintings, [Dong] would doubtless have found Chinese precedents for them, however specious. Some of his spiritual heirs among contemporary Chinese scholars are still committed to the same stratagem."[60] Professor Wen Fong was likely in Cahill's mind when he wrote those lines. Despite a myriad of criticism from various Chinese art historians, Professor Fan Jingzhong of the China Art Academy (Hangzhou) applauded *The Compelling Image*, "the most extraordinary book of the 20th century on Chinese painting history and a landmark in the transformation of research approaches in the discipline."⁶¹

Disheartened by younger scholars' preoccupation with theories at the expense of "looking at the pictures," or "close readings and analyses of the works of art themselves," Cahill kept his "detached view of theories."⁶² Unlike his teacher Max Loehr, who cited at ease theories of Immanuel Kant (1724–1804), Konrad Fiedler (1841–1895), Max Dvořak (1874–1921), Erwin Panofsky (1892–1968), and Susanne Langer (1895–1985), Cahill, on various occasions, admitted being not a "theory man" or "widely read in theories."⁶³ He once noted that his entry to Chinese art theory was initiated by Loehr, who persuaded him to "not only translate Chinese art theoretical texts, understand them and be critical of them even."⁶⁴ Undertaking this critical bend to demystify Chinese art theories that were constructed by the Chinese literati elite, Cahill consequently formulated his own theory. His proposition of European influence as an impetus behind the revival of the northern Song "representational style" in the late Ming was substantiated by his theory on "artistic imitation," corresponding to Baxandall's writing on artistic influences.⁶⁵ Cahill wrote:

> The likelihood of conscious imitation is small; a better supposition is that the idea of constructing a landscape picture on this new model was implanted in the Chinese artist's mind by a viewing of the European print, or of others like it. Such a process is unconscious and irreversible; even if the artist tries consciously not to be influenced, he cannot, once he has seen a picture, return to the state of not having seen it. Once absorbed into his visual memory, the new image or structure can be called up at will or can appear unwilled.⁶⁶

His persuasive postulation on "artistic imitation," lucidly stated, rings largely true when seen against the preponderance of supporting visual evidence he discovered in his compelling images. His refusal to "write anything that is beyond what [I] really, fully understand," precisely gives his writing and even his formulation of "a theory" a discernable clarity.⁶⁷

When Cahill wrote, on the occasion of honoring his teacher, that "Loehr has formulated and stated large truths about Chinese art… truths that others had been too near-sighted or too timid to discern, but which, once stated, seem almost to have been always with us," he might have just spoken of himself precipitously.[68]

In Praise of the Verbal and a Great Teacher

In 1985, Cahill received the Distinguished Teaching Award at the University of California, Berkeley. In his acceptance speech, he reflected on his strengths as a teacher: "My strengths are probably in having a real liking and respect for students, letting them realize that we are involved in a collective enterprise, trying to learn about and understand Asian art, and that although I'm farther along in that enterprise, we are on the same track."[69]

Cahill was widely known in the field for referring to and praising his own students' works and publicly crediting their achievement in conferences, lectures, and in his own books, albeit sometimes in the footnotes. For the 1971 exhibition catalog *Restless Landscape: Chinese Painting of the Late Ming Period*, Cahill included entries written by his seminar students, providing his students the opportunity to see their works in print.[70]

In one of his 1972 letters to Loehr, on the occasion of recommending his student Richard Vinograd's master thesis for publication, Cahill wrote:

> I read [Vinograd's thesis] with the same kind of warm feeling, *in recognizing formulations and perceptions based on my own*, that you must feel when I or another of your students develop ideas of yours in new and interesting ways. Really, I am sending this with the kind of feeling that Wang Shih-min would have had if he had been able to introduce Wang Hui to Tung Ch'i-ch'ang, as he wished he had been able to do.
>
> ………….

> Frankly, I find some of his writing *positively dazzling*. I mean both his precise use of language (a phrase like "desiccating refinement," for Ch'ien Hsuan is the kind of thing that makes one smile with pleasure as he reads) and the clarity of structure.[71]

Cahill's writing and his verbal capacity to convey the visual is legendary. It is only natural that he would highly appreciate the verbal aptitude of his students. He believed that what essentially an art historian does is "to sensitize people to certain qualities of a work of art, once pointed out, others can see."[72] He often used Baxandall's "man in the bus phenomenon" to exemplify the function of a teacher in art history; "for he/she is the one who points out what everyone else can see but fails to discern…. While standing before a painting, any good art historian, knows that ideally we are doing much more: we are *conveying a reading of the painting*, perhaps some kind of analysis of it, that opens new areas of perception in the viewer-listener's mind."[73]

"Teaching and writing," Cahill reflected at the 2005 University of Maryland symposium, "the two practices have scarcely been separate in my work." Some of his major writings were completed when he was lecturing: the aforementioned *The Compelling Image* written for the Norton Lectures at the Harvard, 1978/79; *Three Alternative Histories of Chinese Painting* for the Franklin D. Murphy Lectures at University of Kansas, 1988; *The Lyric Journey: Poetic Painting in China and Japan* for the Reischauer Lectures at Harvard, 1993; and his final book, *Pictures for Use and Pleasure,* followed after his 1994 Getty Lectures titled *The Flower and the Mirror: Representations of Women in Late Chinese Painting*. "History being written in the class room" was his students' comment on Cahill's lectures.[74] In Cahill's own words of testimony:

> A good teacher, who has arrived at a clear and convincing set of formulations of all these and conveys them effectively to her or his students, can take the students a long way in this process. The student does not, of course, accept the teacher's account as the final word, as I did not accept Loehr's; but he or she has a model and a tentative structure

to accept, modify, or reject—any of these being better than beginning "cold".... What matters is that the students will have a visual grounding into which they can fit their experiences with paintings, and which they can in turn adapt and use if they themselves become teachers.[75]

No fitting words, except the famous Chinese phrase *tao li man tian xia* 桃李滿天下—[teacher's] "peaches" and "plums" fill abundantly what is under the heaven—can better honor and celebrate this great teacher.[76] It is widely known that many of Cahill's students have become distinguished scholars, teachers, and museum curators. The aforementioned Richard Vinograd, one of Cahill's principal students, went on to teach Chinese art history, first at Columbia University, later at Stanford University, leading the discipline since 1989. One must note that many of Cahill's female students have become leading scholars in the field; some have significantly expanded the field, such as the Distinguished University Professor Julia Andrews (The Ohio State University), who opened up the studies of Chinese art beyond the Qing to the Republican (1911–1949) and PRC (1949–) periods. Patricia Berger, professor emeritus, a Buddhist art specialist, became Cahill's successor at U.C. Berkeley. Senior curator of Asian Art Julia White, at the Berkeley Art Museum/Pacific Film Archive, collaborated with her teacher in many projects, the last one being the exhibition *Beauty Revealed: Images of Women in Qing Dynasty Chinese Painting* (2013).[77] Professor Anne Burkus-Chasson (University of Illinois at Urbana-Champaign), an Ailsa Mellon Bruce Senior Fellow (2017–2018) at the Center for Advanced Study in the Visual Arts, National Gallery of Art, Washington, D.C., is an accomplished leading expert on the late-Ming artist Chen Hongshou (1599–1652). Many of Cahill's students went on to work in prestigious auction houses and museums of Asian art.

Cahill's "requisites of good teaching" sound alarmingly simple upon first reading, but they are as valuable as difficult to fulfill. Cahill wrote, "simply being there: spending enough time with students; being around when they want to talk with you...always read the papers myself...."[78] "The true successful art historian," Cahill pronounced, is "the one whose lectures and writings are exciting to listeners and readers, the one who gets letters saying 'you have changed my life'."[79] Cahill's larger-than-life presence in the field of Chinese art history has changed and will change many lives. Any art historian who has arrived at the field of Chinese painting studies, whether we believe ourselves to be the formalists, the contextualists, or the deconstructists, the amateur or the professional, the insider or the outsider, or the somewhere in-between-it-all, will find something meaningful from Cahill's writing: to learn and to unlearn, to buttress and to unsettle, to supplicate and to problematize.... Without Cahill's and Loehr's generations of art historians laying the ground for the field, where do we stand?

Patrimony and Posterity

With the recent passing of luminary and founding figures in Chinese art history—Michael Sullivan (1916–2013), James Cahill (1926–2014), Chu-tsing Li (1920–2014), Richard Edwards (1916–2016), and Wen Fong (1930–2018)—on an "etiological impulse," one could almost say that the discipline of Chinese art history has felt rather "fatherless."[80]

Posterity in the field of Chinese painting studies was always in Cahill's mind. In his final book, *Pictures for Use and Pleasure*, Cahill made it all too clear that it was written for the future generations of art historians. Cahill wrote:

> For the benefit of future researchers who may want to follow up on particular subjects and types discussed here, I have provided many references in notes to paintings of the same kinds as those reproduced.... Since the book is intended to chart initially an expansive subject area—long essays or even books could be devoted to topics and issues I touch on only lightly—I hope it will inspire a great many writings, from term papers to advanced scholarly disquisitions, and want to provide whatever assistance I can to those who undertake them.[81]

In his acknowledgement, he began by thanking prominent specialists in Chinese women's studies, from whom he called on for help and advice. At the onset of the first chapter, Cahill recounted his early devotion to the theory of literati painting which promoted literati doctrines that favor the scholar-official amateur artists over the technically trained professional painters. In his later career, he came to two realizations. The first was that "the great corpus of Chinese painting theory and criticism…*is heavily biased in favor of the literati artists* and their works—understandably so, since the authors of it were virtually all members of the literati class themselves, and so strongly inclined to favor the kinds of painting practiced and promoted by their fellows." His second realization was that the Chinese painting that has survived has been "severely censored by this same elite, *the Chinese male educated class*, who have exercised control over its transmission, deciding which paintings should be preserved." He continued, "[a] good part of my later career has been devoted to attempts to recover and reconstitute, insofar as possible, 'lost' areas of Chinese painting by identifying and bringing together pieces that have somehow survived, against the odds. A closely related interest in recent years, and another that has led me away from orthodox Chinese attitudes about painting, has been *the pursuit and study of pictures of women*." He claimed, "no one had written seriously about them."[82] In words of urgency, Cahill continued:

> At this time *innovative studies by social historians* and others of women's changing role in Chinese society, especially in the Ming-Qing period, were adding rich revelations that were revising our old stereotypes of the *stable Confucian society* and *its pattern of male dominance. Scholars engaged in women's studies* of this kind were making heavy use of Chinese vernacular and popular literature, a field that had also opened up remarkably in recent decades. But *no one* was looking seriously at the paintings, or taking account of what they could reveal about these new concerns.[83]

Carefully reading these paragraphs, one cannot help but be moved by an elder and magnanimous scholar/teacher who was earnestly worried about the posterity of the field. In the last years of his life, looking back on his own academic career, Cahill was still ceaselessly trying to build resources for the future scholars, and he genuinely cared about and respected contributions made by female scholars or by female subjects. Here comes to mind the famous painting by Chen Hongshou, "Scholar Teaching Girl Students" (fig. 5.2),[84] one of the first paintings to enter the collection of the U.C. Berkeley Art Museum, an acquisition for which Cahill was instrumental. Who is to say Professor Cahill is far from the scholar depicted in this beloved painting of his? "Respectfulness, magnanimity, truthfulness, acuity, and generosity," the five virtues which Confucius supposedly enumerated for a *junzi* scholar-gentleman are perhaps suited to sum Cahill's character as a teacher. One should also add: his modesty and humility to learn from his younger colleagues and scholars of other fields, his openness to change his own course of scholarly undertaking, his intellectual curiosity, and his sheer joy and pleasure in looking at and describing beautiful paintings, whether they are of lofty landscapes or of beautiful women.[85]

Conclusion

Professor Cahill's texts and irreplaceable words have guided the undertaking of this paper. With his keenness for the visual, he would be the first to point out that this is an art history paper that has only two pictures. When we examine art historical writing and its impact on the formation of a discipline, one is reminded of art historian Elizabeth Mansfield's caution in her introduction to *Art History and Its Institutions: Foundations of a Discipline*, historiography "must decipher, analyze, and interpret rather than *mythologize* a disciplinary culture. This involves examining the culture from within as well as without. *Ideally*, the historiographer maintains a *critical* position at once inside and outside a discipline. But this diffuse self-positioning cannot take place independently of institutional critique."[86]

Cahill would be the one to warn us about mythologizing him or treating him as a "fixed" institution. He would, as he did

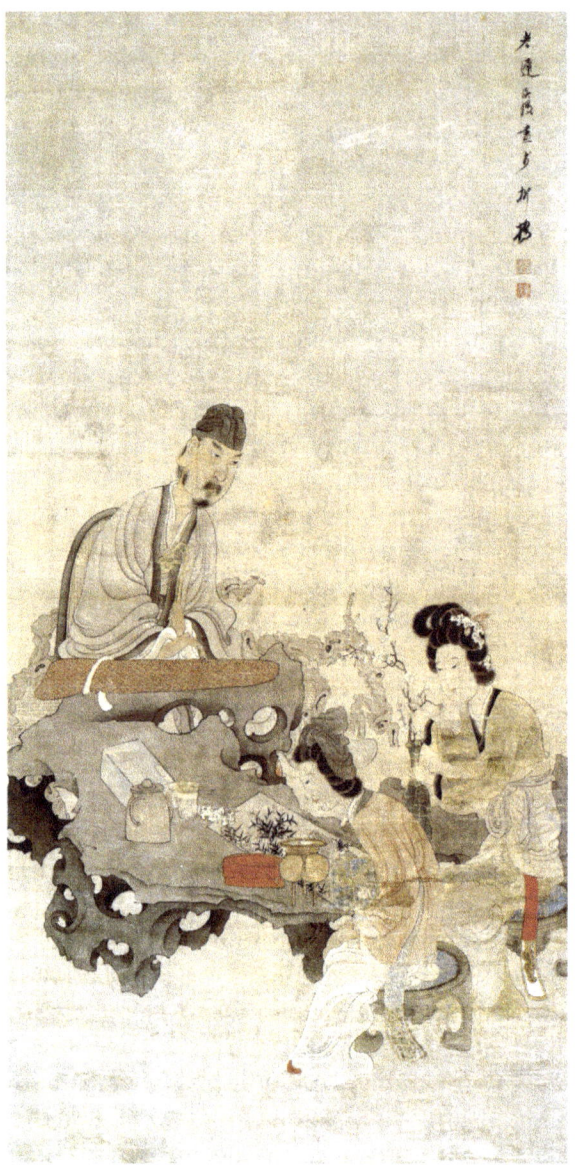

5.2. Chen Hongshou, *Scholar Teaching Girl Students*, first half of 17th century, hanging scroll, ink and colors on silk, 35 ¾ × 18 in., University of California, Berkeley Art Museum and Pacific Film Archive, Gift of Elizabeth Hay Bechtel, Class of 1925. Photo courtesy University of California, Berkeley, Art Museum.

throughout his career, urge us to move the discipline forward by questioning and examining the conventions set by our predecessors, no matter how illustrious. With that in mind, I want to imagine what Cahill would envision for the discipline to expand and evolve continuously and considerably.

At the end of his paper "Visual and Verbal Approaches in Chinese Painting Studies" given at the 2005 Maryland symposium, Cahill stated three things he would like to see happen before too long. The first is the removal of the visual and the verbal "divorcement... from the arena of the controversy over foreign versus indigenous traditions." The second is that his Chinese colleagues would recognize that the Chinese painting studies conducted in the United States are not simply "western" but draw insights from many traditions, Chinese, Japanese, and Western. The third is that the availability of digital imagery and other new technologies would "encourage Chinese scholars to move toward a better balance of visual and verbal in their work and their teaching, they will develop distinctively Chinese ways of looking...."[87]

Cahill defended the importance of "object-looking" throughout his career. One would think he would not object to us raising questions on the subjects and objects in the act of looking. Who is looking and who is being looked at when we study Chinese painting? We might consider the cultural power of the observer and the lack thereof of the observed; the interrelationship between visuality and our cultural positioning and identity. Or whether there are "distinctively Chinese ways of looking" or "Western ways of looking," especially as we enter the age of globally polarized, technologically enhanced visuality.[88]

Cahill's generation, with its access to the visual limited by historical and political conditions throughout most of the twentieth century, built the discipline largely on viewing personal collections. Such an approach to teaching and scholarship relied heavily on painting and connoisseurship. The availability of digital imagery, as Cahill anticipated and took advantage of, has already expanded subject areas that now engage the current generation of scholars. Perhaps our "looking" will be less colored by our visual preferences, or by our socioeconomic and cultural status, and our objective independence would, hopefully, be less compromised when we write about the art we do not collect or have the possibility to collect.[89]

Throughout his academic career, Cahill drew inspiration from social art historians, such as T. J. Clark and Michael Baxandall, and scholars of women's studies, and noted their many innovative studies. He would have wanted to see this interdisciplinary trend among Chinese art historians continue, to have the dialogues spread to other disciplines. As we celebrate Cahill's superb eloquence in writing Chinese painting history, let us imagine how he would also likely encourage art historians of all nationalities (as he helped many) to avoid perpetuating the primacy of the descriptive (however dazzling) and documentary modes of doing Chinese art history, and urge scholars to write innovative and critical alternatives, as he did.

Some of the contentious connoisseurship debates in the postwar history of Chinese painting studies, between the seemingly irreconcilable "object-looking" or "text-reading" traditions has exposed us to an institutional culture that has so far centered around strong personalities, a patrimony that simultaneously benefits and burdens us. We need to remember Cahill's example, and draw insights from scholars in other disciplines, in women's studies for example, and from his collaboration with his many distinguished female students and fellow art historians. Cahill would be happy to see that the large majority of presenters and attendees at the 2018 University of Maryland symposium, where he was celebrated and repeatedly referred to, were female art historians and students of Chinese art history, and many of them came from the People's Republic of China and other sinophone locales. Such a sight would have happily anticipated for him a more congenial and compatible marriage between the visual and the verbal traditions.

When we inherit and honor the great patrimony passed on from Cahill and others, it is equally important, in order to expand and advance the field, to recognize their limitations, reflective of their time and our common humanity. Perhaps it is also imperative to engage in a reflexive art history—one that is aware of our collective internalized Confucian values, our respect for our ancestry or our "etiological impulse," and our loyalty to our teachers and our forbears—that will free us to be more innovative and critical. Perhaps in the next symposium on Chinese Calligraphy and Painting Studies in Postwar America, we can begin to celebrate the many female art historians of Chinese art and their quiet and steady dedication to the field.

Notes

I want to thank my fellow art historian and friend Marie Leduc for helping me refine the title and make my ideas more coherent through her reading and over our conversations. And a note of thanks must go to Professor Jason Kuo, whose graduate seminar in 2005 initiated the early stage of this essay and who gave me the opportunity to present some of my ideas at the 2018 symposium "Chinese Calligraphy and Painting in Postwar America," at the University of Maryland. I am grateful to his unfailing patience with me, which has made this rewriting and completion possible.

1 "Confucian Elements in the Theory of Painting" was included in Arthur F. Wright, ed., *The Confucian Persuasion* (Stanford: Stanford University Press, 1960), 115–40. It was largely derived from Cahill's dissertation, completed in 1958. To cite but his two latest mentions of this essay: "In Defense of the Visual: Reflections on an Illustrious Career," *Orientalis* 41 (2011): 6–25, at 10 and *Pictures for Use and Pleasure: Vernacular Painting in High Qing China* (Berkeley: University of California Press, 2010), 2. References also surfaced at the 2005 graduate symposium at the University of Maryland and in "James Cahill [in Conversation with Kuo]" (1998), included in Jason Kuo, ed., *Discovering Chinese Painting: Dialogues with American Art Historians* (Dubuque, Iowa: Kendall/Hung Publishing Co., 2000), 31–37.
2 Cahill, *Pictures for Use and Pleasure*, 2.
3 CLP (Cahill Lectures and Papers) 69: 1983 "Confucian Aspects of Edo Art." Lecture, LACMA, January 15, 1984: http://jamescahill.info/the-writings-of-james-cahill/cahill-lectures-and-papers/241-clp–69–1984 (accessed March 2, 2019).
4 Zaixing Hong, "James Cahill and the Study of Chinese Painting," *Journal of Art Historiography* 10 (2014): 8–9.
5 Howard Rogers, "Jim Cahill at Eighty," *Orientations* 37, no. 1 (2006): 52–53.
6 Archival research reveals that Cahill wrote many reference letters for students who were not his own. Also see Cahill's students' tributes for his eightieth birthday, in *Orientations* 37, no. 1 (2006): 42–57.

7   Cahill, "What Good Teachers Say about Teaching," University of California, Berkeley, 1985.
8   Simon Leys, trans. *The Analects of Confucius* (New York: W.W. Norton & Company), 83 (16.10). Chinese original: 君子有九思：视思明，听思聪，色思温，貌思恭，言思忠，事思敬，疑思问，忿思难，见得思义,《論語》"季氏第16."
9   Ibid., xvi.
10 Cahill, "Max Loehr at Seventy," *Ars Orientalis* 10 (1975): 1.
11 Jason Kuo, ARTH 778, Seminar in Chinese Art: "Discourse, Power, Art Historical Knowledge, and the Making of a Postwar American Historian of Chinese Painting: A Critical and Historiographical Study of James Cahill," University of Maryland, fall 2005. In connection with the seminar, a symposium was organized by Professor Kuo on November 13–14, 2005. Professor Cahill delivered two lectures and held discussions with graduate students. His lectures can be found at http://jamescahill.info/the-writings-of-james-cahill/cahill-lectures-and-papers/106-clp176–2005 and are also included in Jason C. Kuo, ed., *Stones from Other Mountains: Chinese Painting Studies in Postwar America* (Washington, D.C.: New Academia Publishing, 2009), as James Cahill, "Visual, Verbal, and Global (?): Some Observations on Chinese Painting Studies," 29–66 and, James Elkins and James Cahill, "The Cahill-Elkins Exchange," 119–66.
12 "James Cahill in [Conversation with Kuo]," in Kuo, *Discovering Chinese Painting*, 31–37.
13 Ibid., 31–32.
14 Cahill remarked on Loehr's "old world polish" humorously: "Ann Arbor professors' wives have never forgiven the person who traitorously informed him that kissing hands on meeting was not expected in American society." "Max Loehr at Seventy," 3. Regarding the reference to "elegant gatherings," see J. P. Park with James Cahill, "Max Loehr, James Cahill and the Flying Dragon: A Moment in Chinese Art History," *Orientations* 42, no. 6 (2011): 99–104.
15 "James Cahill [in Conversation with Kuo]," in Kuo, *Discovering Chinese Painting*, 74. Cahill expressed his regret at not learning conversational Chinese.
16 Cahill, "Max Loehr at Seventy," 4.
17 Cahill, "Some Thoughts on the History and Post-History of Chinese Painting," *Archives of Asian Art* 55 (2005): 17. Cahill referred to Loehr's late-life periodization paper "Phases and Content in Chinese Painting" (presented at the International Symposium on Chinese Painting, held at the National Palace Museum, Taipei [June 18–24, 1970]) and remarked "it is time to attempt another one." "Grand design" was also used in Cahill's "Max Loehr at Seventy," 5.

18 "James Cahill [in Conversation with Kuo]," in Kuo, *Discovering Chinese Painting*, 67; emphasis added.
19 Cahill, "Max Loehr at Seventy," 4.
20 Ibid.
21 "James Cahill [in Conversation with Kuo]," in Kuo, *Discovering Chinese Painting*, 53–54.
22 Cahill's Haley lecture was subsequently published as "Some Thoughts on the History and Post-History of Chinese Painting," *Archives of Asian Art* 55 (2005): 20. In both his response to "Elkins's Proposals for 'Globalizing' Chinese Painting Studies," given at the graduate symposium at the University of Maryland, on November 14, 2005 (published in Kuo, *Stones from Other Mountains*, 45–65), and his symposium response paper for the section "Art-Historical Methodology" at the Conference on the History of Painting in East Asia at the National Taiwan University, Taipei, 2002 (published in *The History of Painting in East Asia: Essays on Scholarly Method* [Taipei: Rock Publishing International, 2008], 499–96), he called for continuation of style history.
23 Cahill, "Some Thoughts," 17.
24 Max Loehr, "Phase and Content in Chinese Painting," in *Proceedings of the International Symposium on Chinese Painting* (Taipei: National Palace Museum, 1972), 286–88.
25 Ibid., 290.
26 Ibid., 293.
27 Cahill, "Some Thoughts," 20; emphasis added. This acclamation recalls Hans Belting's *The End of the History of Art* (Chicago: University of Chicago, 1987).
28 Ibid., 27; emphasis added.
29 Max Loehr, "Phase and Content in Chinese Painting," 291; emphasis added.
30 Cahill, "Some Thoughts," 18.
31 Wai-kam Ho, ed., *The Century of Tung Ch'i-ch'ang 1555–1636* (Kansas City, Mo.: Nelson-Atkins Museum of Art in association with the University of Washington Press, 1992), a two-volume catalogue for an exhibition organized by the Nelson-Atkins Museum of Art are dedicated to Dong's works. The catalogue includes scholarly essays and Dong's writing on art, translated into English.
32 Loehr, "Phase and Content in Chinese Painting," 291; emphasis added.
33 Cahill, "Some Thoughts," 22; emphasis added.
34 James Cahill, *The Compelling Image: Nature and Style in Seventeenth-Century Chinese Painting* (Harvard University Press, 1982), 44–63. The book received the Charles Rufus Morey Prize awarded by the College of Art Association of America for the best art history book of 1984.

35 Loehr, *The Great Painters of China* (New York: Harper & Row, Publishers, 1980), preface; emphasis added.
36 Cahill, *Compelling Image*, 62. All the phrases in quotations are cited from the same page.
37 Cahill, "Max Loehr at Seventy," 6.
38 Cahill, "Art Historical Methodology," 3.
39 Rogers, "Jim Cahill at Eighty," *Orientations* 37, no. 1 (2006): 51.
40 Cahill made numerous references in his writing and conversations to these three art historians and their influence on him, especially that of Michael Baxandall and Svetlana Alpers. Svetlana Alpers's *The Art of Describing: Dutch Art in the Seventeenth Century* (Chicago: University of Chicago Press, 1983), Michael Baxandall's *Painting and Experience in Fifteenth Century Italy: A Primer in the Social History of Pictorial Style* (Oxford: Oxford University Press, 1972), and T. J. Clark's *Image of the People: Gustave Courbet and the 1848 Revolution* (New York: New York Graphic Society, 1973), have all been included in the collection *The Books that Shaped Art History: From Gombrich and Greenberg to Alpers and Krauss*, edited by Richard Shone and John-Paul Stonard (London and New York: Thames & Hudson, 2013).
41 Loehr, "Some Fundamental Issues in the History of Chinese Painting," *Journal of Asian Studies* 23 (1963–64): 185.
42 Loehr, *Great Painters of China*, preface.
43 "James Cahill [in Conversation with Kuo]," in Kuo, *Discovering Chinese Painting*, 81 and 42.
44 Chu-tsing Li, ed., *Artists and Patrons, Some Social and Economic Aspects of Chinese Painting* (Seattle: University of Washington Press, 1989), 7–20.
45 Professor Cahill's lunch conversation with graduate seminar students on Nov.13, 2005 at the University of Maryland.
46 Cahill, *Three Alternative Histories of Chinese Painting* (Lawrence, KS: Spencer Museum of Art, University of Kansas, 1988), 9.
47 Svetlana Alpers, *Rembrandt's Enterprise: The Studio and the Market* (Chicago: University of Chicago Press, 1988). Cahill also remarked on the influence of Alpers's essay "Is Art History?" *Daedalus* (summer 1977): 1–13 in his "In Defense of the Visual," 19, as well as on the influence of Baxandall and T. J. Clark.
48 Here I want to thank Professor Anne Burkus-Chasson, who graciously shared some of her insights on May 30, 2018, at the National Gallery of Art's Terrace Café.
49 Cahill, *Painter's Practice: How Artists Lived and Worked in Traditional China* (Columbia University Press, 1994), 35–45.
50 "James Cahill [in Conversation with Kuo]," in Kuo, *Discovering Chinese Painting*, 82.

51 Cahill's letter to Loehr, December 28, 1977 [Archival Material: "Loehr (1973 on)." Correspondence. 1974–1982 in Cahill's Papers at the Freer Gallery Archive, Smithsonian Institute, Washington, D.C. (Box #6, Folder 15)].
52 Cahill, "In Defense of the Visual," 15.
53 Hong, "James Cahill and the Study of Chinese Painting," 10.
54 "James Cahill [in Conversation with Kuo]," in Kuo, *Discovering Chinese Painting*, 83.
55 Cahill, *Compelling Image*, 75.
56 Ibid., 91.
57 Wen Fong, "Review of James Cahill's *The Compelling Image: Nature and Style in Seventeenth-Century Chinese Painting*" *The Art Bulletin* 68, no. 3 (September, 1986): 507.
58 Ibid., 504–5. To support his points, Fong used *A Bridge over a Stream among Steep Mountains*, an early 13th-century fan painting from Liaoning Provincial Museum, artist unidentified. The image of the painting can be found in Wen Fong, ed., *Images of the Mind: Selections from the Edward L. Elliott Family and John B. Elliott Collections of Chinese Calligraphy and Painting at the Art Museum, Princeton University* (Princeton: Princeton University Press, 1984), figure 63.
59 Cahill, *Compelling Image*, 92.
60 Ibid., 83.
61 Hong in his essay notes Fan's comment, "James Cahill and the Study of Chinese Painting," 10, footnote 27.
62 For his impatience with theorists, see his response to "Elkins's Proposals for 'Globalizing' Chinese Painting Studies," given at the graduate symposium at the University of Maryland on November 14, 2005 (published in Kuo, *Stones from Other Mountains*, 45–65), and his symposium response paper for the section "Art-Historical Methodology" at the Conference on the History of Painting in East Asia at the National Taiwan University, Taipei, 2002 (published in *The History of Painting in East Asia: Essays on Scholarly Method* [Taipei: Rock Publishing International, 2008], 499–96). His "detached view of theories" came from Loehr in his letter to Cahill dated April 4, 1967 (archival material: "Max Loehr," Correspondence, 1957–1979 in Cahill's papers at the Freer Gallery Archive, Smithsonian Institution, Washington, D.C. Box #6, Folder 14). In his letter, Loehr praises Cahill's exhibition catalogue *Fantastics and Eccentrics in Chinese Painting*, and Loehr, after joyfully applauding Cahill's book, remarks, "I was glad to see that you take a detached view of theories that would explain as a 'response to the shock of the Manchu conquest.'"

63 "James Cahill [in Conversation with Kuo]," in Kuo, *Discovering Chinese Painting*, 56–57; see also his "Response to Elkins's Proposals," in Kuo, *Stones from Other Mountains*, 45–46.
64 "Cahill in Conversation with Kuo," 59.
65 Michael Baxandall, *Patterns of Intention on the Historical Explanation of Picture* (New Haven: Yale University Press, 1985), 58–59.
66 Cahill, *Compelling Image*, 83.
67 "James Cahill [in Conversation with Kuo]," in Kuo, *Discovering Chinese Painting*, 56.
68 Cahill, "Max Loehr at Seventy," 4
69 Cahill, "What Good Teachers Say about Teaching," lecture delivered at the University of California, Berkeley, 1985.
70 His edited exhibition catalogue *Shadows of Mt. Huang: Chinese Painting and Printing of the Anhui School* is another example of his collaboration with his students, who wrote principal essays.
71 Cahill's letter to Loehr on July 5, 1972. Cahill's Papers at the Freer Gallery Archive, Smithsonian Institution, Washington, D.C. Box #6, Folder 15. Emphasis added.
72 "James Cahill [in Conversation with Kuo]," in Kuo, *Discovering Chinese Painting*, 54.
73 "Response to Elkins's Proposals," 55, emphasis added.
74 Cahill, "What Good Teachers Say."
75 Cahill, "Response to Elkins's Proposals," 59.
76 A famous Chinese phrase in praising teachers, originated in the Tang dynasty (7th–9th century). Peaches and plums are metaphors for students, teachers are often compared to tree and flower planters.
77 Berkeley: University of California Press.
78 Cahill, "What Good Teachers Say."
79 Cahill, "Elkins's Proposals," in Kuo, *Stones from Other Mountains*, 60.
80 Here I am rephrasing what art historian Elizabeth Mansfield remarked on the "etiological impulse" in Western art hagiography. Elizabeth Mansfield, ed., *Art History and Its Institutions: Foundations of a Discipline*: "We have an abundance of fathers. ... An orphan discipline, apparently, art history goes motherless." (New York: Routledge 2002), 1.
81 Cahill, *Pictures for Use and Pleasure*, vii.
82 Since Cahill's pronouncement, more works have been accomplished in the area of women's space in Chinese art. See Kristina Kleutghen, *Imperial Illusions: Crossing Pictorial Boundaries in the Qing Palaces* (University of Washington Press, 2015) and Wu Hung's recent book, 中國繪畫中的 "女性空間" *Feminine Space: An Untold Story of Chinese Pictorial Art* (Beijing: Sanlianshudian, 2019).

83 Cahill, *Pictures for Use and Pleasure*, 2. Emphases added.
84 The image is scanned from the exhibition catalogue *Beauty Revealed: Images of Women in Qing Dynasty Chinese Painting* (Berkeley: University of California Press, 2013).
85 Thomas Cleary, trans. *The Essential Confucius* (San Francisco: Harper Collins, 1992), 4.
86 Mansfield, ed., *Art History*, 1, emphasis added.
87 Cahill, "Visual, Verbal, and Global (?)," in Kuo ed. *Stones from Other Mountains*, 63–64.
88 Works on alternative visuality: Shu-mei Shih, *Visuality and Identity: Sinophone Articulations across the Pacific* (Berkeley: University of California Press, 2007); W. J. T. Mitchell, *Seeing through Race* (Cambridge, Mass.: Harvard University Press, 2012); Craig Clunas, *Chinese Painting and Its Audiences* (Princeton: Princeton University Press, 2017).
89 For example, the lost and "destroyed" Chinese art during the first six decades of the twentieth century.

Chapter 6

Fault Lines: Notes toward a Memoir

Anne Burkus-Chasson

> Yes, with all its greens and blues, its lines running up and across, its attempt at something. It would be hung in the attic, she thought; it would be destroyed. But what did that matter? She asked herself, taking up her brush again. She looked at the steps; they were empty; she looked at her canvas; it was blurred. With a sudden intensity, as if she saw it clear for a second, she drew a line there, in the centre. It was done; it was finished. Yes, she thought, laying down her brush in extreme fatigue, I have had my vision.
> —Virginia Woolf, *To the Lighthouse*

This essay began with an invitation to a conference. The charge: to reflect on my experience learning seventeenth-century Chinese painting in the United States. As I drafted the talk, I did not fully accept the subjective nature of this charge. Nonetheless, to preface my remarks, I inserted a brief reminiscence about the years I spent in Berkeley, where, as a graduate student, I was introduced to vast Chinese literary and visual cultures. The memories of my teachers were intended primarily to demonstrate the institutional power they possessed to shape my knowledge of China. Was this not the point of the conference, which memorialized the men who had dominated the disciplinary field of Chinese painting for decades, fashioning its practice for generations?

So it was that I could not disregard a friend's response to what I had presented at the conference: "Yours was the most academic of all the papers given today." I was astonished. The analytical mode had apparently trumped the autobiographical. Or was the brevity of my reminiscence of classroom experiences more telling than either my friend or I understood? What was it that I was avoiding?

Without a doubt, academic institutions had shaped my experience learning Chinese painting as much as the politics of cold-war America had supported it. But, upon reflection, I came to regret that I had not spoken about the frictions between what I was taught and what I wanted to know and why I wanted to know it. For what I knew was mediated through a diversity of words and pictorial images, not all of which emanated from academic institutions. My image of China began to take shape with the translations of Ezra Pound, which I read in my mid-teens on the recommendation of a friend. In my imagination, it was sustained by a longing to summon the cacophony of the incomprehensible sounds of European languages that I had heard my grandparents speak. But, ultimately, my study of Chinese was an escape—a reckless escape from what I feared would be a tedious and dull art-historical education in formalism. I wanted to gather metaphors—these very words, the salvage of a lost friendship. Surely, the Chinese language would offer me that much. The paintings came much later. But even the landscapes of Dong Qichang (1555–1636), which have never failed to bewitch, appeared to me all the more abstract and contrived as I saw them in relation to the geometric structures of Agnes Martin and Anne Truitt. The latter two were my models in the sculpture studio I occupied in college. Nonetheless, I wanted to become "Chinese," even as I began to comprehend the regretful position of being other, inevitably, to the China I imagined. Haun Saussy has put it this way: "We are always in the midst of mediation, that mediation is our authenticity."[1]

Thus, I decided to rewrite the text of my conference talk as an intimate history. The autobiographical and affective narratives that have reappeared on academic bookshelves lent support to my endeavor. I am deeply inspired by the women who have dared to write them.[2] Still, I feel compelled to provide an excuse, or rather a justification, for what I am about to do. It comes down to my perception of myself as an outlier.[3] In art history departments, I am segregated as "non-Western," estranged from, and irrelevant to, the grand narratives of Euro-American art history. I have never been long supported by elite academic institutions that house extensive curricular programs in East Asian art history. I work at a university whose art museum has relegated its Asian collection to storage, whose curator of Chinese and Japanese art is a "generalist" trained in Dutch seventeenth-century prints. And yet, among sinologists, I am also an outlier because I specialize in using visual evidence rather than verbal evidence. Nonetheless, in their isolation, outliers are relatively free to cross boundaries and to violate disciplinary expectations. In many ways, this has suited me well. Gathering the strands of my history, I am never far removed from Virginia Woolf's fictive creation of Lily Briscoe, the painter with "little Chinese eyes," who dared, in the end, to articulate her vision, even if her canvas were to be hidden somewhere in an attic or otherwise destroyed.[4]

It should be clear by now that this essay cannot be construed as a survey of the literature on seventeenth-century Chinese painting that has been produced during the past forty-odd years. Nor can it be construed as a thoroughly documented presentation of the "state-of-the-field." My own intellectual pleasures and pursuits have shaped the views expressed in this essay; I am drawn to some things and blind to others. I cannot dismiss how I was educated in the practice of art history. But, rather than genealogies, what interests me now are fault lines, especially those that crisscross my own history.

The Seminar

The night had already worn. The seminar stalled. I still see their faces, the eyes darting in fear. The projector droned, its heat scarcely dissipated. Specks of dust drifted through the cone of unbearable bright light that broke onto the screen.

"So. What do you intend to do?"

The eyes turned to the screen, to the image of a male figure, there, ridiculously enlarged. How much more outlandish appeared its nose and large almond-shaped eyes, how much more strident its coloring, how much more sensational its costume of undulate folds and fluttering sashes. How inadequate the words that played on my lips!

But the other face was defiant. Too many things had changed. Was art history, after all, or was it something else?

"I will let you know when I have figured that out."

In the mid–1970s and through the early 1980s, I studied Chinese painting with the late James Cahill at the University of California, Berkeley. Which is to say that I received a thorough training in close looking.

A number of art historians have recently exhorted us to look closely. The "passionate visualist" Barbara Stafford, for example, has advocated "good looking" as a means to bring new relevance to image study in the face of a widespread view that cognition is primarily linguistic. Art historians who adopt the (by now trite) metaphor of "reading" visual images demonstrate this logocentric bias. Writing in 1996, Stafford further observed, "The passionate visualist, roaming the labyrinth of the postdisciplinary age, is haunted by the paradoxical ubiquity and degradation of images: everywhere transmitted, universally viewed, but as a category generally despised. Spectatorship itself has become synonymous with empty gaping, not thought-provoking attention."[5] The challenge, then, is to recover the intelligence of seeing and making.

But not all visualists are equal. Nor do they practice good looking for the same reasons. Consider, by contrast, Jennifer L. Roberts. As a teacher, Roberts promotes "a deliberate deceleration of the learning experience."[6] For one assignment, she requires that students look at a painting of their choice for three hours before they begin to write about it. To assess the effectiveness of this experiment in slow looking, Roberts herself devoted three hours to looking at John Singleton Copley's *A Boy with a Flying Squirrel* (Henry Pelham), an oil painting Copley (1738–1815) completed in 1765 (fig. 6.1). She thus concluded:

> Just a few examples from the first hour of my own experiment: It took me nine minutes to notice that the shape of the

boy's ear precisely echoes that of the ruff along the squirrel's belly—and that Copley was making some kind of connection between the animal and the human body and the sensory capacities of each. It was 21 minutes before I registered

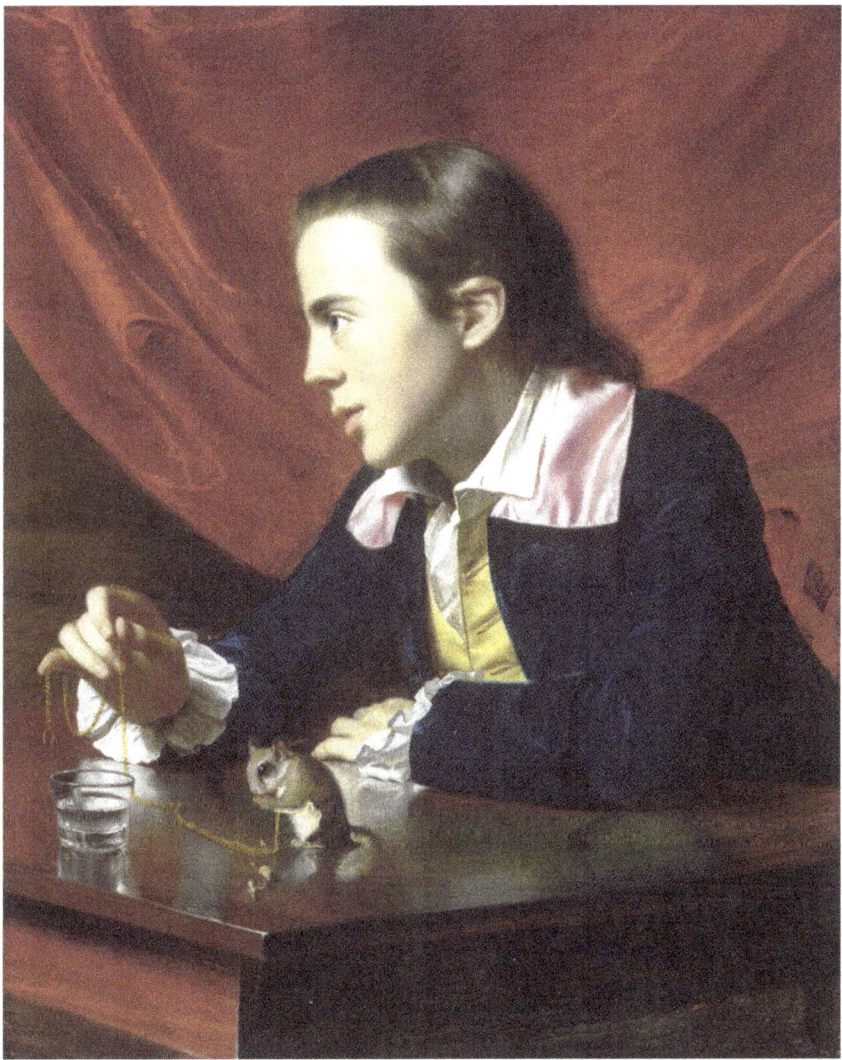

6.1 John Singleton Copley, *A Boy with a Flying Squirrel* (Henry Pelham, 1765), Museum of Fine Arts, Boston. Jennifer L. Roberts, *Transporting Visions: The Movement of Images in Early America*, fig. 1, p. 14.

the fact that the fingers holding the chain exactly span the diameter of the water glass beneath them. It took a good 45 minutes before I realized that the seemingly random folds and wrinkles in the background curtain are actually perfect copies of the shapes of the boy's ear and eye, as if Copley had imagined those sensory organs distributing or imprinting themselves on the surface behind him. And so on.[7]

Unlike Stafford, Roberts is not engaged in a polemical debate about the importance of image study. She questions neither the value of her minute and careful observations nor their power to bring out the significance of Copley's work. The quasi-scientific approach she takes toward visual observation is further developed in the chapter devoted to Copley's painting that appears in her justly celebrated book about the transportation of paintings and prints in British America and the United States in the late eighteenth and early nineteenth centuries.[8] Arguing that the movement of a thing is manifest in the thing itself, Roberts offers the evidence of what she has observed to prove her point. But is the eye a reliable witness?

It is well known that Copley, after having completed his portrait of Henry Pelham, shipped the painting to London. Roberts identifies the potential mobility of Copley's portrait with several of its peculiar compositional attributes. She emphasizes, for example, the "numismatic profile" of the boy. Indeed, the boy was shown with his head turned against the picture plane. However, at the same time, Copley tilted the boy's head toward his shoulder and lifted his jaw, thus leaving his neck in shadow. The boy is distracted; he turns away from the squirrel to peer outside the pictorial field. His state of distraction is only enforced in contrast with the intense concentration of the squirrel that is hunched over its food, its gliding membrane collapsed. Unlike the strict profiles found on medallions and coins, Copley's rendition of Henry Pelham is animated and slightly askew. Nonetheless, Roberts argues that Copley adopted the "numismatic profile" not only to suggest the painting's "portability" but also to permit it "to enter an abstract space of transmission and exchange."[9] Clearly, much weighs on the perception of a strict profile. I do not know what Roberts would make of my observation of Henry Pelham's portrait. I bring it forward simply to suggest that even the closest looking may be biased or blinded in one way or another.[10]

I dwell on these visual practices because the close looking that I was taught to do had a very different goal. The objective was to learn how to isolate certain characteristics of any given painting—primarily, brushwork and compositional structure—to enable a proper dating and authentication of the work. James Cahill took delight in "rocking the boat," as he once put it to me. His attributions were often controversial.[11] However, even without the excitement of rousing controversy, I confess that the dry and analytical exercise of authentication never failed to capture my attention. For Cahill knew how to bring out the sensuality of these paintings. He acknowledged his commitment to the work of Susanne K. Langer (1895–1985), who considered that artful designs or aesthetic symbols gave the viewer insight into a human feeling.[12] A work of art does not assert anything that can be gauged from outside its form.

> *The buzzer sounded. Startled hands stopped writing; books closed. He stood at the lectern to the side of a projected image of Guo Xi's* Early Spring. *I was prepared to hear him continue with words such as these, recorded elsewhere, or, at least, something like them: "The earth forms, swollen to an exaggerated rotundity, fuse and interpenetrate like parts of a vast organism. The strong sense of unrest that activates the picture is intensified by the use of a nervous, wavering line, constantly fluctuating in breadth, and the suggestion of an unnatural illumination, by which rocks can be lit from below, and shadows flicker mysteriously over a surface. Most unsettling of all is the regularity with which ponderous masses are deeply undercut, as if by aeons of erosion."[13] For some time, I had typed my scrawling notes immediately after his lectures; I was familiar with their lyricism. For now, the spell was broken. Shrugging his shoulders, he ended the lecture instead with these words: "What can I say?"*

Nonverbal intuition was sufficient to knowing the feeling represented in a picture. And good looking ensured that a viewer be not fooled by an inferior product.

Many years later, I found a different reason for close looking, one that especially appealed to me. In her introduction to *Reading Rembrandt: Beyond the Word-Image Opposition*, Mieke Bal dwells at length on an obscure detail in Vermeer's *Woman with a Balance* (1662–64): she noticed that a nail and a hole pierce the white wall that backs the figural scene (fig. 6.2).[14] Rendered visible in the light that falls onto the wall through an opened window, the nail and the hole appear adjacent to an image of *Last Judgment*. Bal argues that Vermeer thereby represented the traces of an effort to locate a proper place from which to display the sacred image. Someone experimented at least three times with hammer and nail before an appropriate spot from which to hang the picture was found. Thus, the nail and the hole mirror the mortal and divine acts of weighing and judgment that Vermeer delineated in this painting. For her part, Bal inserts a story into a painting in which nothing seems to have happened. Close looking enables Bal to construct her narrative. Or, as she puts it, "The work no longer stands alone; now the viewer must acknowledge that he or she makes it work, and that the surface is no longer still but tells the story of its making."[15] Thereupon ensues another point, one that is equally intriguing. The nail hole is the sort of detail that enables a viewer to construct an alternative interpretation of a visual image. The detail that does not fit the conventional understanding of a picture shatters the assumption that a picture's significance is fixed and determinate. After all, we generally expect a picture to be coherent; we reject contrary pictorial elements that cannot be conveniently explained.

Bal's interpretation of close looking, together with her extensive writings on narratology, prompted me to reconsider my approach to Chen Hongshou (1598–1652), the difficulty of whose paintings has long been acknowledged. During his lifetime, Chen's work was described not only as striking and unusual but also as freakish and preposterous. But what was it—precisely—that elicited such a response from viewers in the seventeenth century? Was it simply his proclivity to distort form? Or was it the unexpected appearance of a misshapen face in a genre of painting that ordinarily did not accommodate distortion? After all, misshapen faces were familiar in some genres of Buddhist figural painting, but they were ordinarily not described as preposterous. I have thus come to think that the difficulty of Chen's imagery lies in his proclivity to juxtapose incongruous genres and styles of representation in his paintings. Only after I had accepted the degree to which his compositions resisted my attempts to fold them into coherent interpretative schemes could I comprehend what I now see as the source of his ingenuity.

In one of his late works entitled *Yaji* [Elegant Gathering], which Chen composed some time between late 1646 and early 1647 for

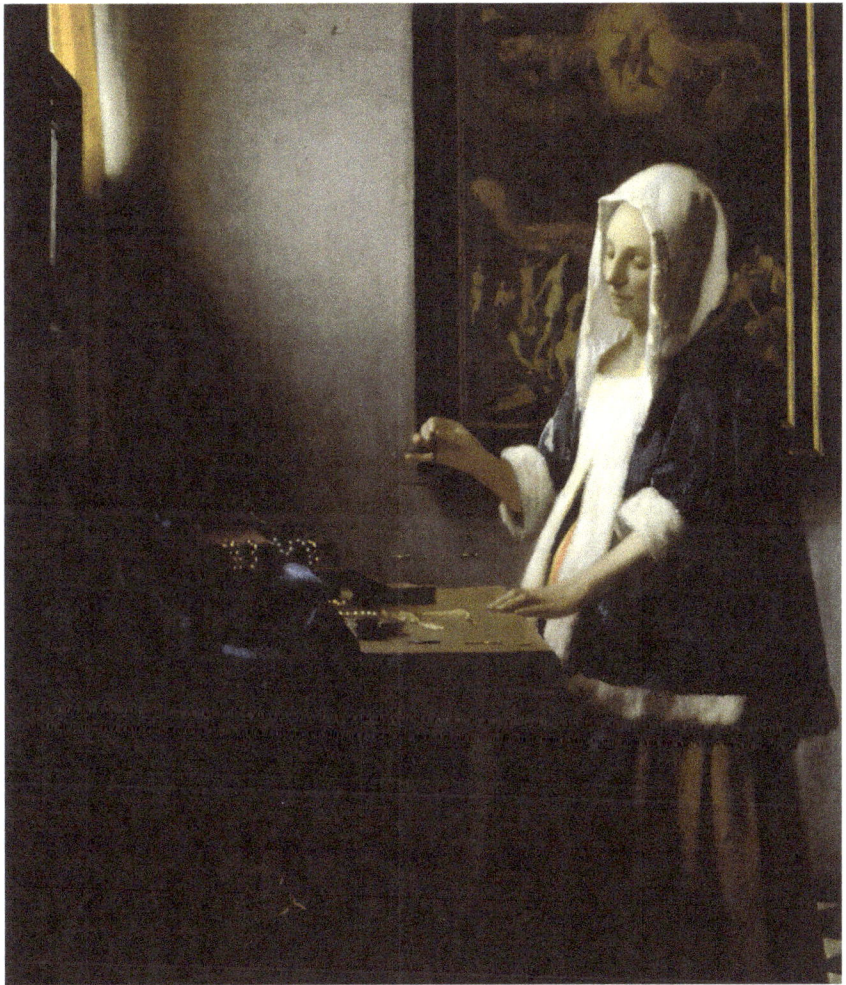

6.2 Johannes Vermeer, *Woman with a Balance*, ca. 1664, National Gallery of Art, Washington, D.C. Photo courtesy National Gallery of Art, Washington, D.C.

an acquaintance named Tao Qubing ("Ridding Sickness" Tao, formally known as Tao Xing [act. mid–17th century]), I noticed that the bodhisattva in the picture occupies an uncertain and ill-defined space (fig. 6.3).[16] Again and again, I looked at the rendering of the divine being, which presides over a gathering of nine men in a thickly wooded close. Why had a draughtsman as skilled as Chen not positioned the bodhisattva's imposing figure either on or behind the stone table, where implements for worship lay scattered? If the bodhisattva was not a sculpted icon designed to fit a clearly marked and measureable space, then what was it?

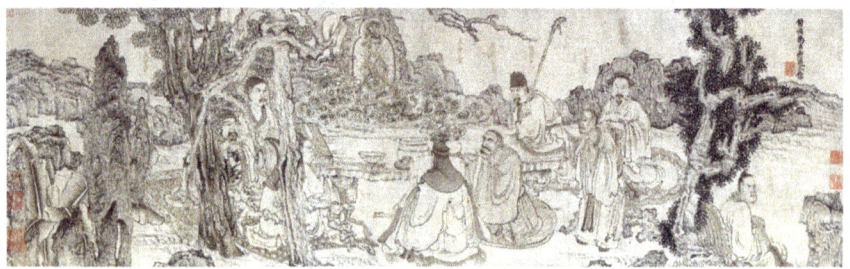

6.3 Chen Hongshou, *Elegant Gathering*, ca. 1646–47, Shanghai Museum, published in *Repentant Monk: Illusion and Disillusion in the Art of Chen Hongshou*, ed. Julia M. White, pp. 122–25.

Chen introduced endless potentialities for misapprehension in *Elegant Gathering*. Ambiguity unsettles the painting in a variety of ways. For example, the nine men he depicted are each identified, their names inscribed in the interstices of the composition with gold paint. Scrutiny of historical documents evidences a complex web of associations among the nine men, but none verifies their ever having convened as a group. In all likelihood, Chen's portrayal of their meeting is an artful fiction.[17] The figure of the bodhisattva that is at once insubstantial and substantial, realistic and artificial, partakes in the same economy of contradiction.

Thus, I concluded that the bodhisattva's appearance among the men who had gathered together to worship was unexpected. It is a visionary event in a story whose plot turns on the perception of the divine being. True, Chen did not utilize the pictorial conventions that ordinarily marked a visionary event: no swirling cloud delivers

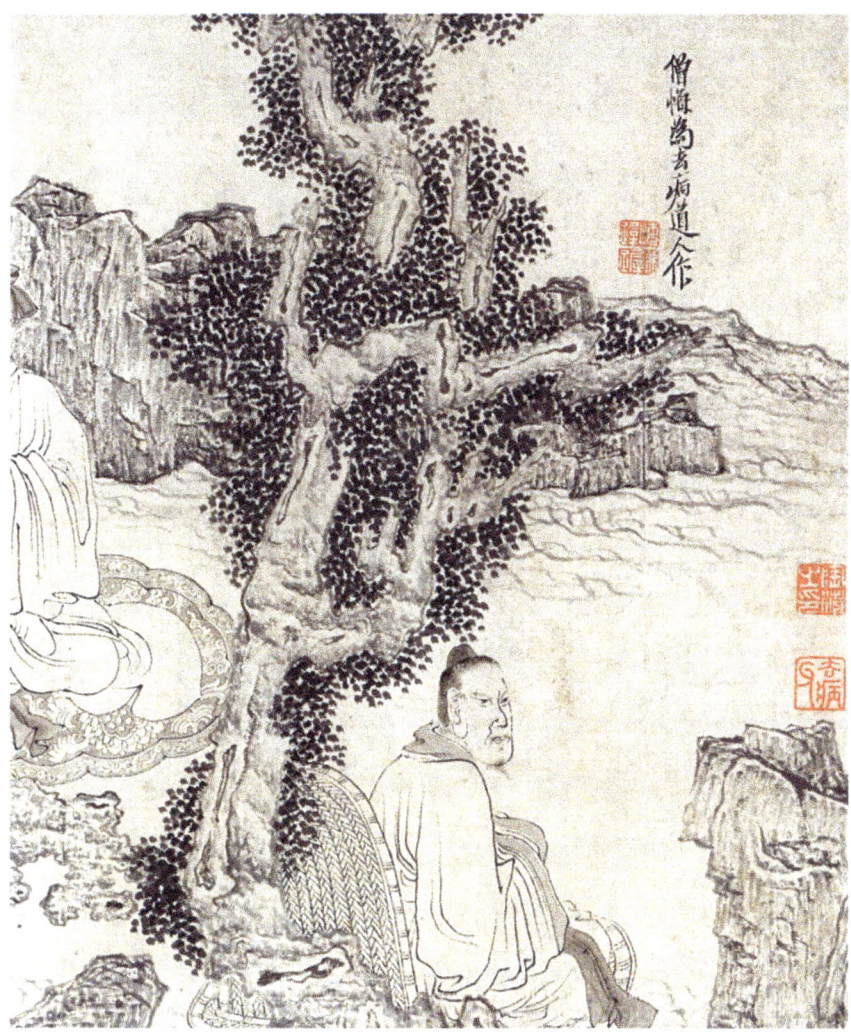

Detail of fig. 6.3

the bodhisattva to this garden scene. Instead, Chen chose to render the bodhisattva's feline vehicle cloudlike. The creature, delineated with dry ink that crumbles on the paper, acquires a ghostly ephemerality. The shape of the feline is indeterminate; it dissolves into a series of linear patterns. The mane and tail are portrayed as tightly wound spirals. These spirals, which cascade onto the

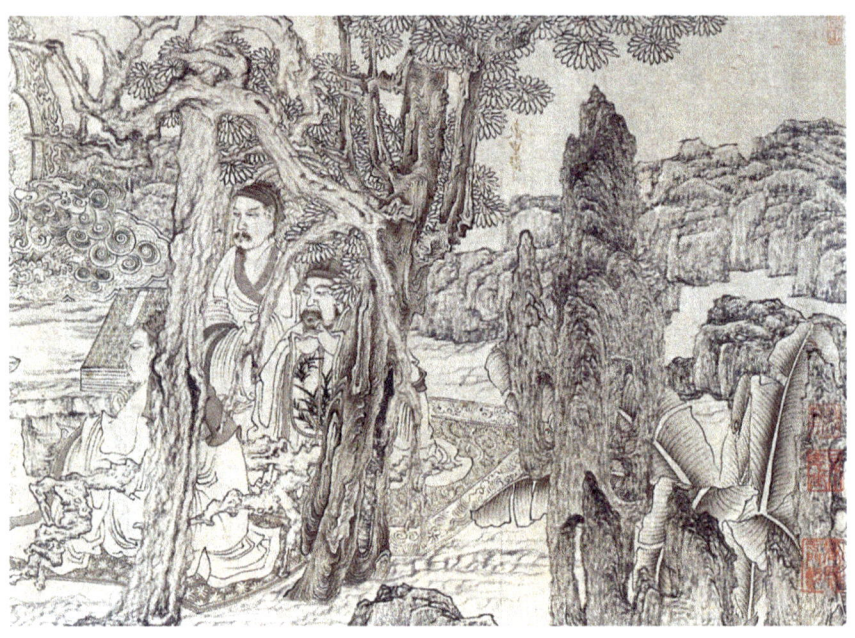

Detail of fig. 6.3 (here and following pages)

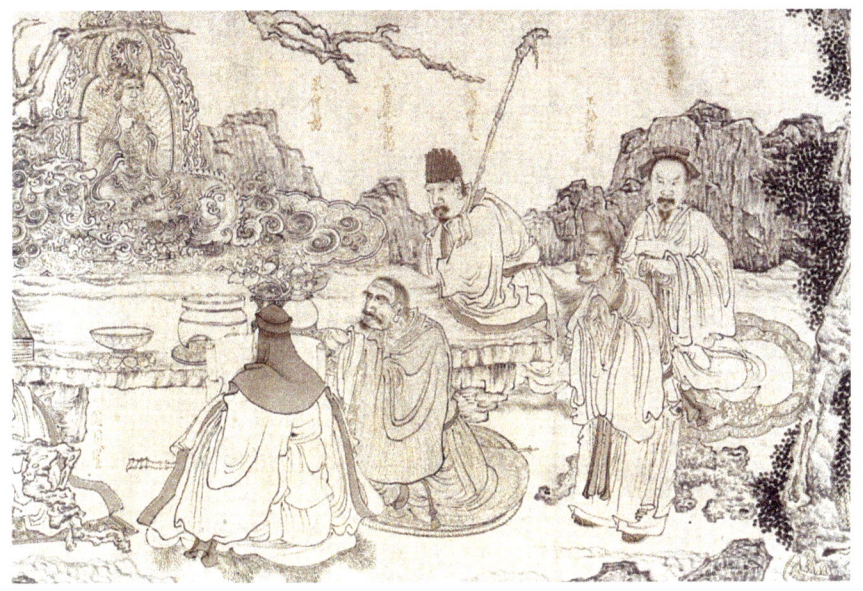

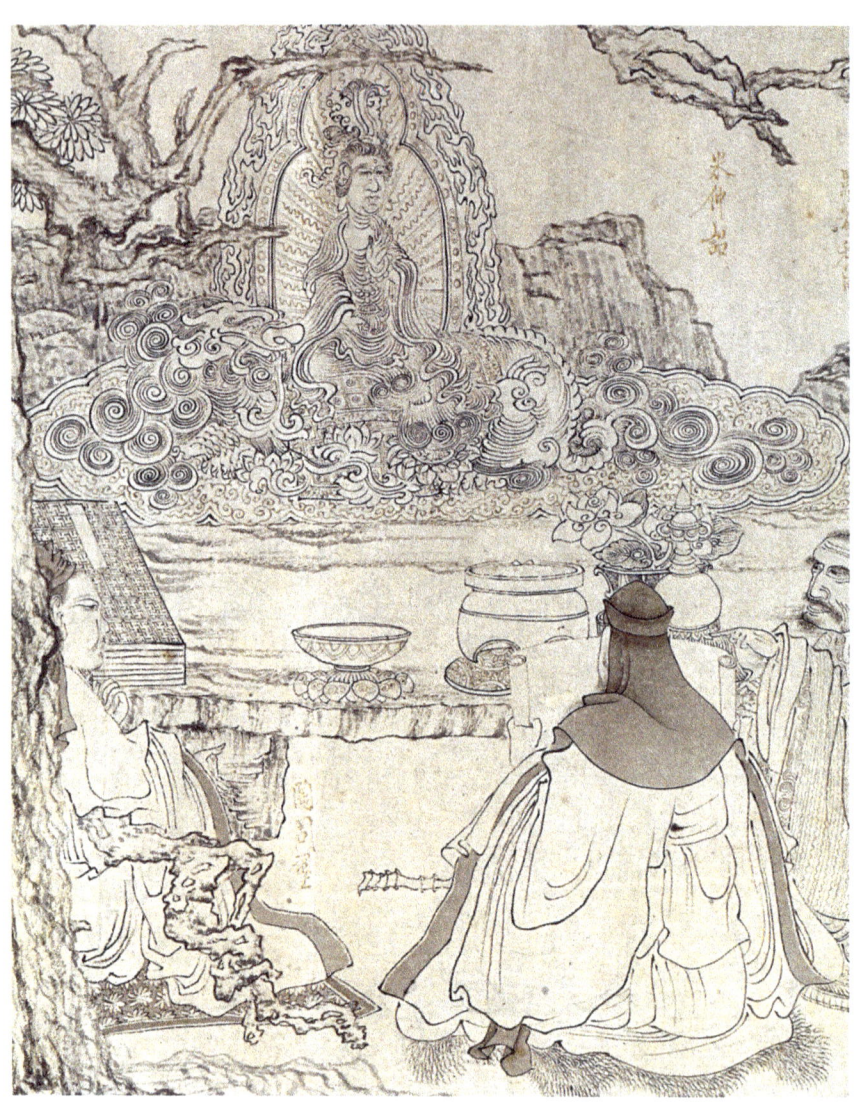

decorated platform that bears the feline, seem capable of endless proliferation. The animal's teeth and forked tongue conjoin and transform into undulating lotus stems. What is this beast? Every time I looked, I noticed another detail that confused the distinction I may have wanted to draw between the body of the fanged animal and the decorated platform on which it appears.

Moreover, despite the bodhisattva's imposing presence, none of the men who had gathered to worship and listen to the recitation of a sacred text show any sign of having noticed her. But even this detail was unsurprising, for not every figure named in this painting was a devout Buddhist. Therefore, I argued that Chen cast doubt on the efficacy of Buddhist practice to bring about salvation, especially in a time of war and devastation. The potential invisibility of the savior in Chen's painting led me to examine notions about seeing and sight that circulated in the first half of the seventeenth century and in particular those that pertained to religious practices.[18] I argued that Chen deliberately positioned a historical painter, "Mi Wanzhong," facing the apparition in *Elegant Gathering*. Seeing the invisible would have confirmed the efficacy of prayer and recitation. And for Chen the only chance of perceiving the visionary bodhisattva lay in a painter's peculiar interest in making things tangible, in rendering things visible.

Not everyone has agreed with my interpretation of Chen's *Elegant Gathering*. Early on, I was challenged to identify whether the Buddhist icon was fashioned with clay or carved from stone. Others, disinclined to engage in dialogue or even reasoned refutation, simply ignore my writing.[19] A far more fruitful debate has arisen from weighing the relative importance of scriptural text and pictorial image in the interpretation of *Elegant Gathering*. In a recently published article, Patricia Berger derives her argument from Buddhist textual sources, which largely displace the work of close looking.[20] Berger, who devoted much of her career to the study of eighteenth-century Chinese Buddhist court art, endeavors to impose an overarching theme onto Chen's *Elegant Gathering*. In short, she argues that the painting is a tribute to late Ming practices of Pure Land Buddhism.[21]

Although Berger concurs with my conclusion that Chen presented the bodhisattva as an apparition, she suggests that the men who had gathered around the stone table have lowered their eyes to concentrate on a mental image of the divine being. What Chen pictured, therefore, was what they had conjured in their minds. This is a fascinating proposal, but Berger does not specify which figure was delineated with its eyelids lowered. As I look at this painting, I see the glances of most of the men openly directed at one other. Their glances knit them together as a group, even though one figure looks outside the picture, while another hooded figure has turned its back to the viewer. Indeed, the glance of an eye was a pictorial device commonly used to define the relations among the actors in pictorial narratives.

Berger's assumption that Pure Land Buddhism imbues Chen's fictive gathering leads her to vacillate with regard to the identity of the bodhisattva. She first identifies her as "Lion's Roar Guanyin," a manifestation of the bodhisattva that she claims was popular in the mid-seventeenth century.[22] She uses this epithet to explain the presence of the feline mount. But the animal is more accurately identified as a fantastic *hou*-beast rather than as a lion; in Ming times, it often accompanied Guanyin.[23] Subsequently, Berger argues that Chen conflated a manifestation of Guanyin with that of a separate bodhisattva, Mañjuśrī, who also bore the epithet "Lion's Roar" and who does ride a lion. Why did Berger discount the spouted ewer that the bodhisattva holds in one hand and the simple robe that she wears pulled over her shoulders, both signs of a manifestation of Guanyin? But the conflation of the two bodhisattvas leads her to propose that Chen alluded to historical reenactments of the *Vimalakīrti-nirdeśa Sutra* promoted by a sixth-century Pure Land Buddhist master. Thus, in *Elegant Gathering*, the painter "Mi Wanzhong," who is shown reading a scroll before the apparition, represents the devout layman Vimalakīrti; in this context, the bodhisattva must, therefore, be Mañjuśrī. If so, then why did Chen not portray the two in dialogue with another? And, if this scene represents a sacred encounter, why are the implements of worship not properly displayed on the stone table? I should like to suggest that Berger's attempt to establish above all an association between *Elegant Gathering* and Pure Land Buddhism obscures the discordant elements in Chen's painting and reduces it to an illustration of the Buddhist texts she cites. Pictorial artifacts do not provide the evidence to support her overarching theme.

In the end, I did figure out what I wanted to do with Chinese paintings. An accidental encounter with a book about Rembrandt gave me a reason to look closely, and I stepped away from the formalism that had governed much of my art-historical education.

Long after I left Berkeley, I am told, James Cahill no longer taught techniques of connoisseurship. In one of his last print publications, devoted to a rare archaeological find from the fifteenth century, he, too, began searching for types or schema (his preferred word) in "reading" Chinese paintings.[24] Considering the paintings discovered in the tomb of Wang Zhen (1424–1496), located in Huai'an in northern Jiangsu Province, he emphasizes the political significance of the paintings that was conveyed through diverse visual signs. Turning to their stylistic features, he stresses that both artisans and members of the educated elite produced loosely sketched paintings on special occasions such as the departure of a friend. And this demonstrable fact, he asserts, should result in a reevaluation of our views of the diverse painters represented in the Huai'an tomb. Yet, on the other hand, Cahill concludes that the tomb paintings prove that the "correlations between the social and economic status of the artist and the subjects and styles of the paintings he makes are real and definable."[25] Moreover, he asserts that the most valuable lesson to be garnered from the Huai'an tomb paintings is that they "might inspire us to attempt some archaeology of our own, identifying and reattributing neglected and misunderstood works in museum basements, auction catalogues, and old publications, and thus reconstructing some of the nearly lost regions of Chinese painting."[26]

The connoisseur, exhorting us to look widely and deeply, did not entirely disappear. Recently, I came across Cahill's curatorial notes from the 1950s, which are kept in filing cabinets that occupy one side of the storage rooms in the Freer Gallery of Art. The content of these records was as familiar to me as the hand that had roughly transcribed Chinese characters in distinct, blocky shapes.

> *He wanted to show me photographs: "She is pensive. You can see that." Later, he took me to dinner. Was it a Vietnamese place? I can still feel the cool air, the nearness of the sea. I wanted to visit the Rose Garden before I left. For years, I had watched from its height clouds of fog move with an uncanny deliberation across the bay, enveloping the hills, enveloping me.*

"You probably thought we were going to talk about your work." Oh. I said nothing, for I had not given it a thought. I had come only for a signature.

These days, I think about Helen Oyeyemi's Mary Foxe, who dared to ask why is it that the women are always killed at the end of the story: "We dream, it is good that we are dreaming. It would hurt us, were we awake. But since it is playing, kill us. And—we are playing—shriek..."

The Archive

It was some time before I got there. The house was nestled in the hills that surround the city, far from where I lived. He had managed to obtain a bicycle for me: a black vehicle with slender wheels that belonged to the son of a local dealer. I stopped and started on the city's narrow streets, desperate to avoid careening cabs. I arrived, the cold having settled deep into my hands. Upstairs, opened books were strewn everywhere. He rose from his chair, again and again, to search for yet another book. Hours passed.
《出てこない》。

During the years I spent in Japan, I dedicated myself to archival research, following the example of the teachers I met there. Everywhere, people opened their libraries to me and responded to my nervous questions. This was not how I was taught to practice art history in the United States. But I was seeking something for my dissertation that required extensive reading in late Ming documents: a cultural history that engaged the rhetoric of self-presentation in the mid-seventeenth century. I was immersed in languages that demanded close attention. The stack of notecards on which I translated and annotated each of Chen Hongshou's poems and essays grew.

Nonetheless, it is also true that the Berkeley I knew in the late 1970s well prepared me for this move. It was an exciting place to be for anyone interested in an interdisciplinary study of the late Ming period. At the time, Cyril Birch was translating *Mudan ting* [The Peony Pavilion]; the late Frederic Wakeman was writing his two-volume study of the Ming-Qing transition; Tu Wei-ming taught seminars on Wang Yangming. When I came across the work of Stephen Greenblatt, I felt as though I had found the key to that for which I had been searching.[27]

Without a doubt, my practice of cultural history resembled nothing more than the choreography of players: I positioned the historical actors I had encountered in books on a stage set of my own intricate, immutable design.[28] I hardly imagined how difficult it would be to retrieve a past so unfamiliar and so little known: the endless hours spent leafing through old books for something yet unknown, the endless hours spent searching through the corners of dictionaries for appropriate words, the endless hours spent sculpting sentences to articulate the delicate balance I had weighed between historical artifact and my imagination.

Disciplinary Structures: An Even Exchange?

The differences among the disciplines that accommodate Chinese painting and their separate shifting positions can be baffling. To straddle them is daunting. Although I consider that the questions posed both by sinologists and by art historians are crucial to my study of Chinese painting, I am keenly aware that my work fits neither disciplinary group. Nonetheless, it is also clear to me that many factors, such as trending studies in material culture and environmental criticism, have in general eroded the disciplinary structures that once guided and restricted work in the humanities. Still, I maintain that pictures are not words. They require a pictorial intelligence. But, to my mind, without sinological research to expand and enrich the work of close looking, a historical explanation of a picture cannot be articulated. Nonetheless, it remains to ask how to conduct sinological research while using analytical tools developed to study Euro-American visual images. Are sinology and art history compatible? Where do Chinese painting studies belong in the curricular structures of a university? My questions are not freshly posed. For decades, scholars have pondered this conundrum.[29]

Jennifer Purtle suggests that there is an "even exchange" between art history and sinology in the writings of Craig Clunas.[30]

Throughout his prolific and influential career, Clunas has attended to artistic objects primarily in terms of the social relations that they exhibit. A painting evidences a debt repaid or a gift bestowed. Clunas rarely, if ever, describes an object. Lavish reproductions embellish his books, a sign of the reciprocal relationship into which he has entered with university presses that expect his books to sell. But the illustrations do not provide the substance for his arguments about artistic exchange. As for the "even exchange" that Purtle understands to occur in Clunas's work, I wonder whether it occurs between art history and sinology or rather between sinology and anthropology.

The following excerpt from Clunas's book on the celebrated painter and calligrapher Wen Zhengming (1470–1559) demonstrates the lengths to which he is willing to go to avoid interacting with a material object, in this case a painting. He argues that Wen's quotation of the old masters partakes in an economy that is analogous to the protocols of the gift-giving society in which Wen lived and worked. Clunas thus observes,

> But we may wonder if even so they take their place in a regime of reciprocity through the exchange that exists, not simply between the painter and the recipient of the picture, but between the painter and Li Cheng, or Zhao Mengfu, or Mi Fu, or any one of the painters of the past who is the object of Wen's reinscription. They are providing something for him, and he is providing something for them, in the form of "transmissions" (*chuan*) or "imitation" (*fang*). This does not make them equals but, as we have seen throughout, reciprocity almost always implies hierarchy, and recompense is always at least rhetorically "not sufficient."[31]

This passage prompts many questions. I shall limit myself to two. First, Clunas borrows the concept of "reinscription" from an article that traces how the military official Guan Yu (160–219) was transformed into a god, after having faithfully served a hapless descendant of the Han house.[32] Does the transformation of a historical painter's work through the hand of a later painter evidence social and religious change such as that comprehended through Guan

Yu's eventual transformation? As for the "exchange" that Clunas posits to have occurred between Wen and earlier landscapists such as Wang Meng (1308–1385), did it comprise primarily layers of verbal inscription? Second, was power exerted only from "above," from the canonical painter, or was the living painter powerless in deciding which old master to emulate? Through the act of transmitting a canonical painting, is recompense from the dead ever conceivable? Or am I missing something?

I have read and re-read these sentences without fully comprehending their import. However, I recollect the words that Dong Qichang once inscribed on a scroll: "Huang Zijiu's [Huang Gongwang (1269–1354)] *Rivers and Mountains on a Clear Autumn Day* resembles this. I do regret that the ancient master does not see me."[33] Although Dong imagines that his rendition of a landscape would have caught the attention of Huang, a painter whose work Dong often quoted, it is unlikely that Huang could have perceived Dong's picture to be the representation of an earthly landscape, much less one that resembled anything that he himself had ever painted. Did Dong consider that he was therefore beneath Huang? Was their painterly relationship hierarchical, as Clunas insists? Or could it be that the exchange between the dead and the living changed over time between the sixteenth and seventeenth centuries?

I do not know what Clunas would make of my questions. His arguments tend to be idiosyncratic or teasingly obscure. Indeed, he once turned a phrase from the writer Gertrude Stein to conclude a chapter on mechanical reproduction (by which he alluded, of course, to Walter Benjamin).[34] That he is not interested in securing a tie between art history and sinology through his history of Wen's "elegant debts" is clear enough in his indifference to visual evidence. After all, Clunas has stated, "But, recently too, pictures have seemed too important to leave to art historians."[35] What does he mean by this? Martha Kingsbury and Debra Pincus may provide insight into Clunas's singular statement. Writing in 1993 in their program statement for the annual meeting of the College Art Association, they suggested that art history is inherently unstable: "Art history continuously redefines itself in relation to other academic fields. But are there factors integral to art history that either subvert or aggrandize the impacts of various disciplines?"[36]

Is the porousness of art history evidence of a true interdisciplinarity? Or do visual images, entangled among the many threads of a society, invite a diversity of interpretation and method that is unique? Has Clunas simply taken advantage of this attribute of a discipline from which he claims to distance himself?

Nonetheless, James Elkins, an ardent admirer of Clunas's work, casts doubt on the wisdom of discounting the visual qualities of a painting.[37] Perhaps more important in furthering our discussion is the context in which Elkins praises Clunas's "revisionist" work on Wen Zhengming. Unlike Clunas, who avoids the issue, Elkins is skeptical that an "even exchange" between art history and sinology is even possible: "Chinese landscape painting presents itself to us as Western art history, even though we know full well that it is not, and that tension animates and generates art historical meaning. To ignore the uncanny resemblance, or to put it in footnotes, is to avoid the full game of art history."[38] Which is to say that an encounter with Chinese landscape painting engenders questions about how we write the history of art. Elkins delineates six hypotheses throughout the course of his book, the last one of which states that European assumptions about art permeate art history.[39] To write art history, while putting aside these assumptions, is to write a history that cannot be recognized as art history. Has any one of us succeeded in writing a history about Chinese painting that is not art history?

The eminent historian of the early Qing, Dorothy Ko, strikes a different kind of balance between sinology and art history in her research on inkstones that were produced and collected in the mid-seventeenth and eighteenth centuries.[40] In particular, Ko emphasizes the value placed on the skill required to carve an inkstone in the early Qing, arguing that for the early Manchu rulers of China "the power of technology—mastery over material processes, product design and making, as well as their attendant knowledge cultures—was coextensive with political power."[41] Consequently, she sees the eighteenth century as an episteme that she terms the "craft of *wen*." Exemplary of this shift is a group of inkstone collectors who not only wrote learned encomia for their stones but also learned how to carve them.[42] Through their practice, which brought together disparate forms of knowledge and making, from epigraphy and calligraphy, to seal carving and inkstone carving, the boundaries that once divided artisan from scholar were no longer meaningful. This leads Ko to coin the terms "artisan-scholar" and "scholar-artisan."[43] The fame of an artisan-scholar lay in his skill as a craftsman, whereas the fame of a scholar-artisan lay in his classical learning. Nonetheless, Ko emphasizes that the distinction between the two was manifest primarily through the *"social and cultural postures"* each assumed. This is fascinating. Indeed, her articulation of this issue only gains in subtlety and nuance in contrast with the drama of difference between so-called professional and amateur painters delineated in art-historical writings.[44]

Ko finds an affinity with the writings of Craig Clunas and the anthropologist Jacob Eyfert, among others. Nonetheless, throughout her book, she uses the tools and language of art history, even as she adopts the perspective of material culture studies to define her subject. For example, she composes meticulous, exuberant descriptions of the stone carvings. About an inkstone from 1679 named *Luminous Dragons* (fig. 6.4), she writes, "A dragon and the swirling clouds it sets into motion occupy the upper half of the front. Its head, dominated by a muscular anthropomorphic face with a strong square jaw, turns toward the right in three-quarters profile. In the opposite direction, the dragon's soft-edged horns arc backward as they hover over its flying mane, chiseled strand by strand as if combed by iron-wire."[45] She later continues,

> As my mind's eye traced the direction of the swirling clouds and my fingers followed the channels on the stone's surface, it dawned on me that the inkstone is a simple hydraulic device: the water pool is the entire crevice underneath the dragon's head and body; upon grinding, the ink is directed into the pool by ways of sluices and channels, one example of which is the channel that bisects the tip of the dragon's tail; the three holes connected by narrow bridges at the upper left corner of the ink pool are the main conduits through which ink sips into the crevice.[46]

Ko's connoisseurship of the inkstones produced by the mysterious carver named Gu Erniang (d. mid- to late 1720s?), a woman who worked in Suzhou, is exhaustive and, as is customary, based on comparison.[47] With the assurance gained through years of observation and practice, she tells how ink-slabs are carved and where the stones were once quarried. At the same time, Ko demonstrates her knowledge of objects that range across diverse media, a necessity given her claim that "intermediality" was a mode of knowledge production that was specific to the early Qing. Why Ko does not fully explain the artistic and social objectives of intermediality is unclear, for a consistent explanation would have been the most satisfying outcome of her descriptive and analytical powers.[48]

Nonetheless, I was struck when I stumbled on the word *disegno* in Ko's chapter on the inkstones produced by the noted court artist Liu Yuan (ca. 1641–after 1691).[49] *Disegno*, from the Italian for "drawing" or "design," is a term that was used in early modern Italy to denote the ability to make a drawing and the intellectual capacity to invent a design.[50] Drawing was a key activity by which Italian artists planned or conceptualized the composition of a painting or a sculpture. Drawing was a form of visual thinking; it put the artist on a footing with God, the ultimate creator, and elevated the status of painting from a craft to a liberal art. Was Liu Yuan's role in the design of an inkstone similarly improvisatory or experimental? Did he not sketch with brush and ink a fixed design to be copied by a stone carver? This was how he had worked with block carvers to produce the leaves in a printed book. Was Liu Yuan's sketch, which embodied a specific outcome, analogous to the drawing of a Leonardo, who as a draughtsman might play with variations on the bend of an arm or consider how water might swirl around an obstruction? I think not. The few sketchbooks that have survived from the seventeenth century indicate that they were conceived as partial records of paintings seen, which may or may not have been later incorporated into another painting.

Despite her sensitivity to the nuance of a word and its translation, which Ko exhibits throughout her discussion of inkstones, her writing confirms James Elkins's hypothesis that our art writing is permeated with assumptions about artistic objects that derive from art history. Rather than *disegno*, might not the word *yang* (model or design), which appears in early eighteenth-century texts and which

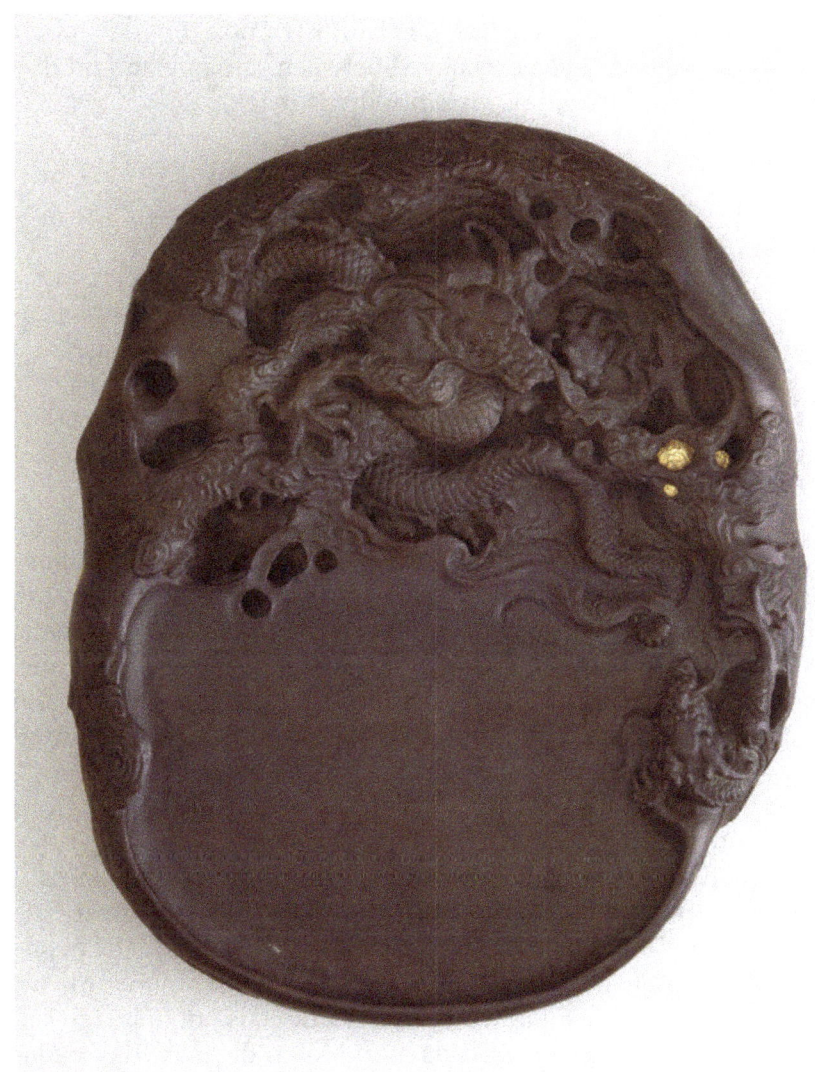

6.4. Liu Yuan, *Luminous Dragons* inkstone, 1679, Palace Museum, Beijing. Dorothy Ko, *The Social Life of Inkstones: Artisans and Scholars in Early Qing China*, fig. 1.6, p. 26.

she cites elsewhere in her book, have better suited her purpose?⁵¹ Although she acknowledges her adherence to sinological methods of textual analysis, as well as her theoretical bias toward material culture, Ko appears to be reluctant to acknowledge her use of the language of art history, whether it is fruitful or not.

It seems that an "even exchange" between sinology and art history still remains beyond our reach. Why is that?

A Global Art History?

> The room darkened. Bright images flashed across the curved screen. I spoke my opening words. Already the sunglasses were pressed against her face. I still see the large purple frames, the dark circles that could not see to see. I am reminded of something that someone said to me the other day: "There is a spirit in Chinese painting." I wondered at the time whether she meant jingshen, but I dared not ask. May I see it, too?

For some time, I have been struck by the philosophical and abstract ways in which students educated in art departments in the People's Republic of China approach objects. Apparently, aesthetic concepts are at the center of education in the arts. In my classrooms, I confess I do not know how to respond to the assertions made about an essential spirit that resides in a Chinese painting. Nothing in my experience better exemplifies the divide that separates how I approach Chinese painting and how the students I have met from Chinese universities approach Chinese painting.

I have experienced a similar lack of understanding when confronted by art historians who have been trained to analyze artistic objects in ways that are irrelevant to Chinese art objects. The quandary that Chinese art historians face is made all the more difficult for this reason, which Elkins brings forward: "It is not unjust to say the history of Chinese art remains marginal in the everyday pedagogy and the professional structure of the discipline of art history. Chinese art is optional and often excluded from debates in visual theory, from entry-level historiography, and from students' course loads. It is virtually nonexistent in visual studies."⁵² Although Elkins was moved to reconsider the nature of art history when he looked into the mirror of Chinese painting, very few scholars of Euro-American art have been similarly moved.

Zhang Hongtu (b. 1943) made a series of paintings *Shitao–Van Gogh* in 1998 that illuminates the marginal position of Chinese art in museums and classrooms across this country (fig. 6.5). Given my training in Chinese painting, I suppose, I observe how Zhang has reworked Shitao in the manner of van Gogh: rather than use ink and vegetal dyes, he used oil paint to render the landscape; lightening and darkening the rock formations, Zhang created shadows and highlights, whereas Shitao was indifferent to modeling form as though it were lit from a specific direction. This aspect of Zhang's painting is most apparent in the way the light in the studio is reflected on the path and on the surface of overhanging rocks. I understand this picture to exemplify the Chinese practice of *fang*, or transformation. But, as Jennifer Purtle has suggested, Zhang Hongtu, a painter in exile, shuffled between van Gogh and Shitao, and weighed the deck of cards in favor of van Gogh.[53] Which painter dominates the picture? For most viewers, it would probably be van Gogh's *Starry Night*.

> *The woman was imposing and she knew it. "Have you ever seen a Chinese vase in an African art gallery?" Her interlocutors all shook their heads in unison. I looked outward, to the bright domes that lay beyond the small room where I stood, isolated, a view to which I had become attached. I thought to myself: Have you ever seen a Chinese vase in a Chinese art gallery? History may always be under construction, but what is history in a global era that remains exclusive?*

Is it possible to imagine a global art history that does not favor Euro-American traditions and methods of understanding? Is it possible to write a truly global art history without possessing expertise in countless different fields of inquiry? Do the questions asked today about global art demand collaboration of a sort not ordinarily seen in the practice of the humanities?

180 Chinese Calligraphy and Painting Studies

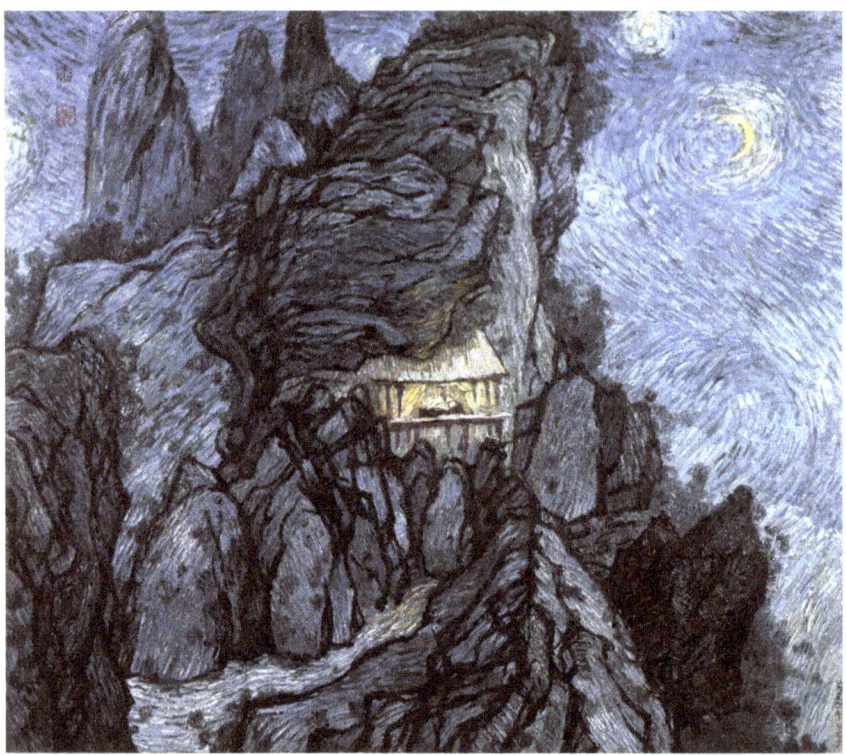

6.5. Zhang Hongtu, *Shitao–Van Gogh*, 1998. James Elkins, *Chinese Landscape Painting as Western Art History*, fig. A, p. x

Coda

I still think of her, often. I still see the large brown eyes; the waves of white hair that broke around her face; her anger. I can still see the slender, long fingers. I showed her a small geode; its tiny crystals glittered in the light that came through the high windows. A miniature paradise, just as I had learned to see. She held the stone as gently as if it were a bird: "You are ready." Did it embrace you, too, in the end, weary as you were? She told me to bury myself in my work. But it is so full of sorrow. Bury. Me.

Why write a memoir? Paraphrasing Joan Didion, I write to learn what I am thinking. My friend may still consider that what I have written here is too heavily documented and far too polemical. But I have made connections that I never expected to make. Recently, I became familiar with Lauren Berlant's notion of "cruel optimism." How well she represents what I did not expect to bring out in my partial memoir: "In other words, all attachments are optimistic. That does not mean that they all *feel* optimistic: one might dread returning to a scene of hunger or longing or the slapstick reiteration of a lover's or parent's typical misrecognition. But the surrender to the return to the scene where the object hovers in its potentialities is the operation of optimism as an affective turn."[54] Unexpectedly, I have depended on a single verb—to dare—which I have repeated throughout these pages, to contain my optimism. Having articulated my vision, dare I allow the fault lines to be just there, either still or in tumult, but simply there?

Notes

1   Haun Saussy, *Great Walls of Discourse and Other Adventures in Cultural China* (Cambridge, Mass.: Harvard University Asia Center, 2001), 3.
2   I have in mind works that range from Alice Kaplan's intimate *French Lessons: A Memoir* (Chicago: University of Chicago Press, 1993) to Kathleen Stewart's polemical *Ordinary Affects* (Durham, NC: Duke University Press, 2007).
3   I borrow the word "outlier" from Lynne Cooke, "Boundary Trouble: Navigating Margin and Mainstream," in *Outliers and American Vanguard Art*, ed. Lynne Cooke et al. (Washington, D.C.: National Gallery of Art, 2018), 3–29. Cooke defines today's outlier as a "mobile individual who has gained recognition by means at variance with expected channels and protocols" (p. 4).
4   Virginia Woolf, *To the Lighthouse* (New York: Harcourt, Brace and World, 1927; repr. 1955), 29. Eric Hayot interprets the connection between modernism and an appeal to China in *The Hypothetical Mandarin: Sympathy, Modernity, and Chinese Pain* (Oxford: Oxford University Press, 2006), 172–206.
5   Barbara Maria Stafford, *Good Looking: Essays on the Virtue of Images* (Cambridge, Mass.: MIT Press, 1996), 11. I became acquainted with Stafford at the University of Chicago during the early 1990s. She showed me kindness in a place that was otherwise full of malice.
6   Jennifer L. Roberts, "The Power of Patience: Teaching Students the

Value of Deceleration and Immersive Attention," *Harvard Magazine* (November–December 2013). https://harvardmagazine.com/2013/11/the-power-of-patience (accessed 23 January 2019).
7   Ibid.
8   Jennifer L. Roberts, *Transporting Images: The Movement of Images in Early America* (Berkeley: University of California Press, 2014), 23–29. Documentary evidence suggests that at times seventeenth-century Chinese paintings moved from painter to recipient through the post.
9   Ibid., 26–27.
10 For good reason Michael Baxandall argued that art-historical description represents what has been thought about the object under discussion rather than what has been seen by the eye, in *Patterns of Intention: On the Historical Explanation of Paintings* (New Haven: Yale University Press, 1985), 4–5.
11 See, for example, James Cahill, "The Case Against *Riverbank*: An Indictment in Fourteen Counts," in *Issues of Authenticity in Chinese Painting*, ed. Judith G. Smith and Wen C. Fong (New York: The Metropolitan Museum of Art, 1999), 13–64. Cahill contends that *Riverbank*, which is dated by some scholars to the tenth century, is a forgery produced by Zhang Daqian (1899–1983). Sadly, the controversy was perpetuated in the obituaries published in *The New York Times* of both key players, Cahill and Fong.
12 Robert E. Innis, "The Making of the Literary Symbol: Taking Note of Langer," *Semiotica* 165 (2007): 91–106. doi:10.1515/SEM.2007.034 (accessed 18 February 2019).
13 The description of *Early Spring* is from Cahill, *Chinese Painting* (Geneva: Skira, 1960), 35.
14 Mieke Bal, *Reading Rembrandt: Beyond the Word-Image Opposition* (Cambridge: Cambridge University Press, 1991), 1–4.
15 Ibid., 4. Bal does not consider her observation of the nail hole to be an act of good looking. Dedicated to the study of signs, Bal instead refers to her interaction with the painting as an act of reading. She promotes "visual textuality" as a method of analysis that evinces the instability of the verbal narratives that painters render visible (p. 19).
16 My interpretation of Chen's *Elegant Gathering* was published as "Between Representations: The Historical and the Visionary in Chen Hongshou's *Yaji*," *Art Bulletin* 84, no. 2 (June 2002): 315–33. I recognize other scholars who had written about the painting, p. 330, note 7. More recent scholarship about the painting is acknowledged by Patricia Berger, "Living in a World of Regret: Buddhist Paintings," in *Repentant Monk: Illusion and Disillusion in the Art of Chen Hongshou*, ed. Julia M. White (Oakland: University of California Press, 2017), 55,

note 11. Having been asked more than once, I want to clarify for the record that the curator did not invite me to participate in this exhibition.

17 Burkus-Chasson, "Between Representations," 318–21. By contrast, Shi-yee Liu and Julia M. White, citing James Cahill, who borrowed the idea from a seminar paper I wrote in 1978, claim that Chen depicted the members of a poetry society that was established in Beijing in 1598, in "*An Elegant Gathering*," in *Repentant Monk*, catalogue no. 16, p. 123. This proposition has gained widespread acceptance; I regret having initiated its establishment.

18 My interest in historical ways of seeing began with "'Clouds and Mists That Emanate and Sink Away': Shitao's *Waterfall on Mount Lu* and Practices of Observation in the Seventeenth-Century," *Art History* 19 (June 1996): 168–90. Jennifer Purtle has delved further into this subject, focusing in particular on optical devices, in "Scopic Frames: Devices for Seeing China, c. 1640," *Art History* 33, no. 1 (February 2010): 64–73. Purtle expands on this topic in "Double Take: Chinese Optics and Their Media in Postglobal Perspective," *Ars Orientalis* 48 (2018): 71–117. See also Kristina Kleutghen, "Peepboxes, Society, and Visuality in Early Modern China," *Art History* 38, no. 4 (September 2015): 762–77.

19 See, for example, Tamara Heimarck Bentley, *The Figurative Works of Chen Hongshou (1599–1652): Authentic Voices, Expanding Markets* (Farnham, UK: Ashgate, 2012), 161–65. Liu and White adhere to Bentley's bias, in "*An Elegant Gathering*," in *Repentant Monk*, catalogue no. 16, p. 123.

20 Berger, "Living in a World of Regret," in *Repentant Monk*, 47–55.

21 Berger concurs with the interpretative approach of Hsing-li Ts'ai, "Ch'en Hung-shou's *Elegant Gathering*: A Late-Ming Pictorial Manifesto of Pure Land Buddhism" (Ph.D. diss., University of Kansas, 1997), a tribute to her long-time associate Marsha Haufler, who supervised the dissertation.

22 Ibid., 51–52, 53–54.

23 Chün-fang Yü, *Kuan-yin: The Chinese Transformation of Avalokiteśvara* (New York: Columbia University Press, 2001), 88.

24 Cahill, "Xieyi in the Zhe School? Some Thoughts on the Huai'an Tomb Paintings," *Archives of Asian Art* 62 (2012): 7–24. http://www.jstor.org/stable/43677801 (accessed 24 March 2018).

25 Ibid., 20. In this context, Cahill indirectly rejects the conclusions of a paper that I delivered in May 1989 at the Cleveland Museum of Art. My paper was subsequently published as "Elegant or Common? Chen Hongshou's Birthday Presentation Pictures and His Professional

Status," *Art Bulletin* 76, no. 2 (1994): 279–300. Cahill's opposition still puzzles me, for I looked into birthday presentation pictures that were produced in the seventeenth century, hundreds of years after the Huai'an paintings were produced. Moreover, I was concerned primarily with identifying the rituals that governed the exchange of paintings in the late Ming period, notably the rituals evidenced in contemporary letter-writing manuals. "Elegant" members of the society may have established these rituals, but "common" elements of the same society appropriated them for their own use. Social boundaries had blurred in late Ming China. I was not concerned with correlating the stylistic features of Chen's painting with his social status. In my view, his work is eclectic; there is no clear-cut correlation between his elite status and how he chose to paint. Then again, many scholars, including Cahill, consider Chen to have been a "professional." Or a "specialist," as his colleague and former student Howard Rogers prefers.

26 Cahill, "Xieyi in the Zhe School?" 20.
27 In particular, I refer to Stephen Greenblatt, *Renaissance Self-Fashioning: From More to Shakespeare* (Chicago: University of Chicago Press, 1980).
28 For a similar critique of cultural analysis, see John Neubauer, "Cultural Analysis and the Ghost of 'Geistesgeschichte'," in *The Practice of Cultural Analysis: Exposing Interdisciplinary Interpretation*, ed. Mieke Bal, 287–302 (Stanford: Stanford University Press, 1999).
29 For example, see John A. Pope, "Sinology or Art History: Notes on Method in the Study of Chinese Art," *Harvard Journal of Asiatic Studies* 10, nos. 3–4 (1947): 388–417, doi:10.2307/2718222 (accessed 28 February 2019).
30 Jennifer Purtle, "Even Exchange: Craig Clunas' Elegant Debts and What Art History and Sinology Offer Each Other," *Ming Studies* 54 (Fall 2006): 107–14.
31 Craig Clunas, *Elegant Debts: The Social Art of Wen Zhengming* (Honolulu: University of Hawai'i Press, 2004), 159–60.
32 For the transformative history of Guan Yu, see Prasenjit Duara, "Superscribing Symbols: The Myth of Guandi, Chinese God of War," *Journal of Asian Studies* 47, no. 4 (Nov. 1988): 778–95, in addition to the work of the Japanese sinologists on which Duara relied, notably that of Inoue Ichii.
33 Ju-hsi Chou, with contributions by Anita Chung, *Silent Poetry: Chinese Paintings from the Collection of the Cleveland Museum of Art* (Cleveland: Cleveland Museum of Art, 2015), 308–13. I have slightly emended the translation.

34 Clunas, *Pictures and Visuality in Early Modern China* (Princeton: Princeton University Press, 1997), 148.
35 Ibid., 9.
36 Martha Kingsbury and Debra Pincus, "Art History Co-Chairs Program Statement," *CAA News: Newsletter of the College Art Association* 16, no. 3 (May–June 1991), 3, http://www.collegeart.org/pdf/caa-news-print-archive/caa-news-05-91.pdf (accessed 18 March 2019).
37 James Elkins, *Chinese Landscape Painting as Western Art History* (Hong Kong: Hong Kong University Press, 2010), 144.
38 Ibid., 134.
39 Ibid., 145.
40 Dorothy Ko, *The Social Life of Inkstones: Artisans and Scholars in Early Qing China* (Seattle: University of Washington Press, 2017).
41 Ibid., 11.
42 Ibid., 190.
43 Ibid., 198–200.
44 See, for example, note 25, above.
45 Ko, *Social Life of Inkstones*, 25.
46 Ibid., 27–28.
47 Ibid., 116–23.
48 Ko argues that the highly successful craft market in eighteenth-century Suzhou depended on the "establishment of a recognizable style across media" (ibid., 124). It is unclear to me how this pertains to craftsmen who had previously worked at court.
49 Ibid., 21.
50 For definitions of *disegno* and a striking example from the hand of Leonardo da Vinci, see https://www.nationalgallery.org.uk/paintings/glossary/disegno; https://www.metmuseum.org/art/collection/search/341703.
51 Ko, *Social Life of Inkstones*, 124.
52 Elkins, *Chinese Landscape Painting as Western Art History*, 19.
53 Purtle, "Foreword: Whose Hobbyhorse?" in Elkins, *Chinese Landscape Painting as Western Art History*, x–xii.
54 Lauren Berlant, "Cruel Optimism," in *The Affect Theory Reader*, ed. Melissa Gregg and Gregory J. Seigworth (Durham, NC: Duke University Press, 2010), 93.

Chapter 7

Michael Sullivan and His Study of Modern and Contemporary Chinese Painting

Jerome Silbergeld

The 2013–14 academic year was a winnowing time in the field of East Asian art history, claiming a host of preeminent senior scholars who had redefined and guided East Asian art studies throughout much of the post–World War II era. Among them were Michael Sullivan (1916–2013, Stanford University and Oxford), James Cahill (1926–2014, Freer Gallery of Art and University of California at Berkeley), and Anne de Coursey Clapp (1928–2013, Wellesley College) in Chinese art history, and John Rosenfield (1924–2013, Harvard University) and Donald McCallum (1939–2013, UCLA) in Japanese art history. Ill health removed still others from continuing service, most notably Wen Fong (Princeton University). Theirs was the generation that shifted the dominant locus of research and publication from museums to the college classrooms, who made intensive language training and usage a professional necessity, and who assured that even those working in the museums would have a rigorous scholarly background in order to publish scholarly research at the highest levels in their fields.

Among these scholars, Michael Sullivan will be remembered best for his pioneering role in the study of modern and contemporary Chinese painting. Before Sullivan's efforts took effect, late Qing period and twentieth-century Chinese painting was considered either too derivative of earlier Chinese painting to deserve serious attention or too belated and derivative of Western painting to be seriously considered as Chinese. He wrote the first major book on the subject, *Chinese Art in the Twentieth Century*, in 1959, long before the subject became popular, and he followed that with a half-century of increasingly sophisticated and informative publications that help to chart the growth of the discipline, among them: *The Meeting of Eastern and Western Art, from the Sixteenth Century to the Present* (1973, revised and expanded 1989); *Art and Artists of Twentieth-Century China* (1996); *Modern Chinese Artists: A Biographical Dictionary* (2006).[1]

Despite this distinction, Sullivan was not a specialist in the subject—he never taught a course on it[2]—and he should be remembered as well for a remarkable breadth of interests and knowledge unmatched in later generations of Asian art scholars. It was this breadth that made possible his authorship of the most popular of all Chinese art history textbooks, *An Introduction to Chinese Art*, 1960, revised in five successive editions as *The Arts of China*. This was the first general survey to bring the general reader fully up to date, which he did with this passage introducing the last two centuries:

> It is the general custom for books on Chinese art to end with the pious abdication of [the emperor] Qianlong in 1796, as though from that moment until today nothing of the least significance had occurred. If we glance at the decorative arts, there is indeed enough depressing evidence to support such a view. The porcelain, lacquer, carved jade and other crafts of the late nineteenth and the first half of the twentieth century are derivative and uninspired. Although a chiefly foreign demand has kept the quality of the workmanship at a high level, these things betray a consistent refusal to recognize the fact that China has been undergoing a hundred years of revolution. Even more depressing are the decorative arts produced since the People's Government came to power in 1950; for though the techniques have been maintained, and even improved, the designs are generally a pastiche borrowed indiscriminately from every epoch in Chinese history. The position in regard to painting, however, is rather different. For painting is a private art, and cannot but reflect in a highly personal way the response of the individual to the world around him. Indeed, the painting of the last fifty years provides us with a vivid illustration

of the conflicting forces that have been at work in shaping modern China.³

In this one hears the voice of the critic alongside that of the historian, more unabashedly judgmental than that of the generation of writers who followed. It also implies a preference for the medium of painting, unlike his British colleagues, who tended to prefer and collect ceramics and other "objects"; this derived from Sullivan's experience in China and suited him well for the years of teaching and publication in the United States that lay ahead.

When Michael Sullivan came to China for the first time, in 1940, he brought with him a British background—born in Toronto of a Canadian father and American mother but reared in England from the age of three; a Cambridge education—a degree in architecture completed in the previous year, with strong interests in archaeology and European art history as well; and a skill in driving vehicles. His interest in things Chinese was kindled by a friendship with fellow architecture student Wang Dahong, who many years later designed the Sun Yat-sen Memorial in Taipei and whose fast-moving Voisin automobile Sullivan had raced at one hundred miles per hour in 1937. It was the war itself that brought Sullivan to China. Chongqing was already under air assault by the Japanese and Sullivan was soon behind the steering wheel of an International Red Cross British Relief Unit truck, his driving skills tested by terrain that was challenging enough without bombs falling and unexploded ordnance lying all around. In 1942, he met and shortly afterward married a young bacteriologist from Amoy, Wu Huan (Khoan), who became his partner in scholarship throughout the remainder of their long and devoted life together.

In wartime China, Sullivan put his artistic interests to good use. His first publication, in 1945, was on Tibetan art in the West China Union University Museum.⁴ He participated with Zheng Dekun in 1942 excavating the tenth-century tomb of the Former Shu Kingdom emperor Wang Jian, near Chengdu, and this became the subject of his first article on Chinese art (1946).⁵ In Sichuan, Sullivan also taught Renaissance art history to Chu-tsing Li, who later taught that subject at the University of Iowa before his decades as a Chinese art specialist, most notably the arts of the Yuan dynasty and the twentieth century, at the University of Kansas.

Throughout the war years, Michael Sullivan personally befriended many of the artists and intellectuals who had retreated west to Sichuan—some individually, many together with their transplanted academies—just ahead of Japanese troops and airplanes, including Liu Haisu, Wu Zuoren, Liu Kaichu, Xiao Ding, Zhang Anzhi, Hua Tianyu, Xu Beihong, and his personal favorite, Pang Xunqin, all of whom he thanked individually for making his *Chinese Art in the Twentieth Century* possible, as well as Zhang Daqian, Guan Shanyue, Lin Fengmian, Zhao Wuji, Pan Yuliang, Huang Yongyu, Ding Cong, the sculptor Liu Kaiqu, and others. Sullivan's four favorite artists were represented by color plates in that publication: Huang Binhong, Pang Xunqin, Zhao Wuji (Zao Wuki, who emigrated to Paris in 1948 and whose work shows an appreciation of artists ranging from Cezanne to Matisse and Klee), and Zeng Youhe (who moved to Honolulu in 1949 as Betty Ecke, the young wife of Chinese art scholar and curator Gustav Ecke). This firsthand experience shaped Sullivan's approach to his contemporary subject: not as an abstract or remote object of study but—as it had been with ancient authorities on the subject—by means of personal friendships, intimate observation, and strong emotions tempered by discriminating standards of quality. Returning to China after a long hiatus, in 1973, 1975, 1979, and many times afterward, Sullivan renewed these friendships and continually extended his in-person studies. His contemporary studies were more like first-person anthropological reporting than secondary text-based research.

When Sullivan returned to academic studies in England in 1947, it was at first to pursue European art at the Courtauld Institute, but he soon transferred to the University of London's School of Oriental and African Studies (SOAS) to study classical Chinese (MA, 1950), and within another two years he had obtained his doctoral degree from Harvard—the first dissertation on Chinese painting in the English language. It was to early landscapes that he turned for his dissertation topic (in close consultation with curator Laurence Sickman of Kansas City's Nelson Gallery of Art), later published as *The Birth of Landscape Painting in China* (1962) and further extended as *Chinese Landscape Painting*, volume 2, *The Sui and T'ang Dynasties* (1980).[6] Six years of teaching and curating at the Malaya University of Singapore, 1954–60, gave Sullivan an in-depth knowledge of

Southeast Asian arts, Chinese trade wares, and Buddhist arts, and it was there that he wrote his first two books, already mentioned above. After six years as a lecturer in Oriental art at the School of Oriental and African Studies of London University, 1960–1966, Sullivan settled into a professorship at Stanford University's young art history department, and he held it from 1966 to 1985. Two tours back to England as Slade Professor at Oxford, 1973–74 and 1983–84, and a return to Oxford's St. Catherine's College as a fellow by special election, 1979–89, where he continued to take graduate students, rounded out Sullivan's teaching career.

The absence of previous writings on modern Chinese art, and even the paucity of available visual materials, left Michael Sullivan in a peculiar professional situation: without the benefit of museum holdings and published illustrations, like Chinese collectors of the pre-photographic past who could only write about what they saw and only see what they and friends had painted themselves or collected, Sullivan could write only about the limited number of painters he had met or come to know personally. As with writers from China's past, this tended to collapse or compress the distinction between art history and art criticism. One sees this in his writing on individual artists, however highly regarded, or on individual works, however famous—for example, in his comment on Xu Beihong's canonical *Yugong Moving the Mountain*: "Though a technical *tour de force*, it is one of the most unpleasant works to come out of modern China."[7] Nor did he hesitate to apply this critical brush more broadly, as when writing of Cantonese painting and the leading role it had taken during the 1920s and 1930s in modernizing Chinese painting by imitating the earlier marriage of East Asian and Euro-American techniques of Japan's Nihonga tradition:

> In the case of the *Lingnan pai* ("Cantonese school"), it seems often that feeling is lacking altogether, being replaced by a purely technical and theoretical attitude of mind. The significance of the failure of this school to create a new art lies partly in this very synthetic basis, and partly in the nature of the foreign art which was assimilated. When certain Chinese traditional painters deserted the principles and the whole outlook that were theirs by inheritance for a for-

eign attitude and approach to nature which they but partly understood, the results were likely to be disastrous. How much more was this the case when that alien aesthetic had already passed through the hands of Japanese artists. Japan has notoriously fastened with enthusiasm on many of the more superficial (and even discreditable) aspects of Western culture, and she has equally failed, with a few outstanding exceptions, to take to herself the true spirit of Western art.[8]

Thus, one of the most striking and perhaps surprising impressions that comes from a re-reading of Sullivan's major texts, despite his personal enthusiasm and deep professional dedication to the subject, and his intention to counter the lack of interest and respect given to it by his contemporary peers and colleagues, is the overall negative assessment he gives to the period. His overall view, in other words, is not all that different from that of others, with his enthusiasm reserved for the small number of artists who have risen above the ordinariness of their times, and perhaps for the notion that every period deserves its own historical accounting.

While his critical praise was bestowed on artists of "true creativity," they were few in number, and the object of Sullivan's negative criticism lay in what he saw as an elevation in the baseline level of conventionality under the Manchus, understood as an outgrowth of advanced antiquarianism. As he wrote in *Chinese Art in the Twentieth Century*,

> The last century of the Manchu Dynasty saw many feeble attempts to copy European Art and the further degeneration of the *wenren hua* [literati painting] into mere ink-play, while the stylistic moulds became fully and rigidly fixed, supported by an inevitable antiquarianism…. The existence of these handbooks [what Sullivan calls "pattern-books, or technical handbooks," like the *Mustard Seed Garden Painting Manual* and the *Ten Bamboo Studio Painting Manual*] is significant, for not only do they demonstrate that the forms of traditional painting had become completely conventionalized, but they reveal also the inherent weakness of a tradition that could be learned by a kind of cumulative process.

For so long as the artist was possessed of true creativity, the language of symbolic forms was, to him, merely a means to a higher end, no sooner mastered than taken for granted. But inevitably the accumulation of "type forms" that could be learned out of a book equipped the mediocre artist with precisely the same range of expression as his more gifted brother possessed. The degeneration of the last centuries is seen not in the creation of less beautiful pictures, but in the empty repetition of a set of pictorial formulae that had once been pregnant with vitality and meaning.[9]

This is, after all, a fairly standard account of the era, derived from fairly normal standards. It does not describe, let alone explain, why one era produces greater change than any other, or why this era in particular tolerated the lack of it. It does not define creativity nor observe that all culture is based on cumulative learning. It does not speculate on patterns of historical distortion whereby a more complete and less selective record of earlier eras than that which now survives might yield a similar impression of rampant conventionalism. As for critical standards, moreover, Sullivan rewarded artistic individualism much as his Western contemporaries did, but he was dissatisfied with the kind of beautiful but repetitious craftsmanship like that often found in arts governed by ritual, religion, and tribe; in reality, given its exceptional respect for traditional lineage through imitation and copywork, both in youthful study and adult practice, Chinese painting—tribal, ritualistic—may best fit somewhere in between. Moreover, once the practice of poetry, calligraphy, and belatedly (in the Song dynasty) painting were appended to the scholarly means of success and social status in China, it was perhaps inevitable that painting would become a platform for the aspirations and pretensions of an ever-expanding population of those seeking to discover and display whatever such talents they had, making it a more laborious task as time went on to critically sift and sort out works of "quality" from the increasing expanse of mediocrity. Finally, Sullivan at that time—and perhaps one cannot expect this of any writing at that time—does not account for the role of the Manchus, everywhere building local support for their sprawling multi-ethnic empire by appropriating, sanitizing, authorizing, regularizing the tamest, most conservative modes of traditional culture, rooting out all those born of or prone to dissent. In painting, that which the Manchus favored at court and eventually practiced themselves was borrowed directly from the scholars' own country-club tradition, labeled the "Southern school" in the decades just prior to the Manchus' arrival, and referred to by Sullivan as the "academic" tradition in its nineteenth- and early twentieth-century phase:

> The extreme "right wing" consists of the adherents to the academic and antiquarian traditions which have been handed down through generations of court painters and others in touch with palace circles.... The [royal Manchu] Pu family were perhaps a special case, for if the majority of traditional painters were merely conservative in outlook these survivors of the Manchu imperial house were utterly remote from the life around them.... Every Chinese painter has studied the great painters of the past, and on occasion, as a tribute to a particular favourite, painted deliberately in his style.... But in this decadent age few of these academic painters could do anything else, clinging instead to the belief common in traditional Chinese thinking that perfection is not something still to be striven for, but rather something that has been attained in some earlier epoch; hence [by that mode of thinking] it should be our ideal to recapture this lost greatness by a complete absorption in the achievements of the past. For this reason, the academic tradition, if it survives at all, is likely to do so in a semi-petrified state, for by its very nature it is unable to find a place for itself in twentieth-century China, except as a relic of a bygone age.[10]

Dividing the early twentieth century's artists into three groups (plus the few who fit into no grouping at all), then, in addition to Beijing's "academic" school of professional and royal painters and the already excoriated Cantonese ("Lingnan") painters, Sullivan's third group was that of the scholars of the court bureaucracy, or "literati"—whose style had previously been appropriated by the court to form the "academic" school early in the dynasty, which therefore, he admits, made it difficult to tell them apart.[11] One looks here, at last, for the author's favor, only to be disappointed and to run into yet another brand of conventionalization:

> The painting of the *wenren*, or *literati*,…represents, in a very general way, a revolt on the part of the scholar class against the extreme conventionalization of academic art. It is both freer in technique and more personal in expression, and as a result is both more alive and more susceptible to changing conditions…. The number of literary painters in China is enormous, for the term may be said to include any educated person who paints for pleasure…. This has led to the spread—one might even say dilution—of art in traditional China among a large proportion of the educated class…preventing that specialization of talent which alone can produce a great art. But that is a highly debatable point….[12]

And further:

> To the modern *wenren*, technique too often is an end in itself. One looks in vain for a deeper content. The influence of the West on modern traditional painting has added a new vigour and a certain superficial element of realism; to this extent there has been a revival in the traditional school. But the artist is too often absorbed in the delights of the brush for its own sake. Through a long tradition of technical mastery the forms that he creates are assured a certain degree of abstract beauty and vitality, but through constant repetition they have, by losing touch with the world of outward experience, become the words and phrases of a dead language.[13]

Sullivan's *Chinese Art in the Twentieth Century* covered the first fifty-five years of the century in a mere eighty-three pages (to which he appended a "Biographical Index" listing some 261 artists).[14] Within this timeframe, then, these three groups—Cantonese artists; court and professional painters, mostly from Beijing; and literati artists, mostly centered in the Yangzhou-Nanjing-Suzhou-

Hangzhou region—plus those few artists who stood out from the conventionalized, many as ungrouped individuals, and occupied much of his discussion, formed the basis of the author's organization. Each group came with its own burden of conventionality: whether it was derived from the pictorial realism offered by Western models, or China's own art-historical past, or an infatuation with traditional Chinese brushwork, the average twentieth century Chinese artist seemed to be doomed by some uncanny capacity for studying things to death and reducing them to dry scholasticism, to mechanical repetition—the bane of genuine artistry.

Everything in *Chinese Art of the Twentieth Century* seemed to be happening pretty much at the same time. It was only with the last chapter of his next publication, *An Introduction to Chinese Art*, that Sullivan provided readers with a historical structure by which to gauge the diachronic development of those years, as described here:

> Artists and writers became involved in bitter controversies regarding their responsibility to society, the Bohemians proclaiming a doctrine of art for art's sake, the Realists urging a closer identity with the people. Finally, all doubts about the place of the artist in modern China were resolved by the Japanese attack on Peking in July 1937. Three years of steady retreat brought the painters and intellectuals close to *the real China*, and the later work of Pang Xunqin, of the Realists such as Xiao Ding, and of the best of the wood-engravers is full of a sense of discovery—not only of their own people, but also of their own land; for they were driven by the war far into the interior, to come face to face for the first time with the beauty of the western provinces, as yet untouched by the cosmopolitan culture of the treaty ports. But, as the war dragged on, artists with a social conscience became increasingly disturbed by decay and corruption on the home front. Some joined the woodcut movement which had been founded by the great writer Lu Xun in the nineteen-twenties and was now being promoted by the Communists at Yan'an for political ends; others turned in protest to political cartooning or to an elaborate and indirect form of social symbolism.[15]

Art itself could not unify a badly fractured China. Only the Japanese military invasion could force the people together, physically and spiritually, and only the experience of togetherness in China's geographical interior could reveal their common heritage and offer a solution. The operant phrase, italicized above, is "the real China," meaning the Chinese hinterlands and especially Sichuan—the place that Sullivan himself knew best and, romantically no doubt, saw as older, truer, and more essential than the commercialized, Westernized eastern seaboard. But soon afterward, once Japan was out of the way and China's interior was abandoned, the Chinese people divided once again, in art as they did in their civil war.

Whereas to the historian of Western culture modernity has represented an era of explosive growth in material, military, and cultural matters, to the China historian it has meant seeking the root causes of decline. And just as the Chinese themselves divided over whether to seek solutions in Westernization or some hidden virtues of their own past, China historians have been obligated to examine just what it was that separated and linked these two great cultural spheres. Having experienced China's trauma firsthand, and having already broadly surveyed its art history, it is hardly surprising that Michael Sullivan turned his serious attention to this examination and traced it backward in time to its earliest origins. In 1970, he completed a detailed and ground-breaking study, "Some Possible Sources of European Influence on Late Ming and Early Ch'ing Painting," presented to an unprecedented international symposium of China art historians.[16] In this, he laid open new possibilities that his California colleague James Cahill would come to utilize so well and convincingly in his own works.[17] Cahill later wrote in his influential book *The Compelling Image,* "The impact of European pictures on late Ming painting remains controversial. Besides Yoshiho Yonezawa in Japan, who suggested it tentatively many years ago, and Michael Sullivan, who took the important step of identifying the European engravings that were in China and accessible to artists by the beginning of the seventeenth century, hardly anyone seems willing to recognize it at all, at least publicly."[18]

This research was dramatically expanded to produce Sullivan's *Meeting of Eastern and Western Art* (1973 and 1989), which even now remains the foremost overview of the subject. From what has already been quoted here of his earlier writings, it is unsurprising that he should have approached this subject with the realization that Westernization offered no quick fix for the troubles that ailed latter-day China and its artistic culture.

Exploring the topic from the arrival of the Jesuits in the late sixteenth century onward, with a richness in detail not found in his earlier books, Sullivan found himself obliged, in some significant sense, to raise the topic only to dismiss it: "While foreign forms and techniques in the arts might be borrowed to fulfill a particular role, there was, at least in China, a tendency for them to be kept firmly in their place. The 'foreign realism' in the art of the early Qing dynasty was confined largely to the Nanking painters and professional artists; the scholars in general ignored it."[19]

Nor was this pattern of rejection new in China's history. While well aware from his own landscape studies of the many ways in which pre-Tang and Tang cultures were enriched by Chinese engagements with South and Western Asia, Sullivan wrote,

> Buddhist art had brought with it to China a number of foreign techniques such as shading, chiaroscuro, "relief painting" and some peculiar drapery conventions which were assiduously applied by Chinese painters to the figures in the Buddhist banner and wall painting, but these techniques were, as far as we know, very little used, if at all, by scholarly masters such as Yan Liben [of the Tang] and Li Longmian [of the Song]. The Chinese evidently felt that foreign techniques were appropriate only to foreign subject matter. In fact, these techniques were gradually forgotten as Buddhism lost its hold over China. The Japanese, as we would expect, have not taken so uncompromising a view.[20]

Recognizing the limitations of the topic perhaps protected the author from making too much of it, as so many others both before and since have done. Throughout his study, already alert to the superficiality of many Chinese cross-cultural perceptions, Sullivan resisted superficial resemblances between arts of the East and West that merited no appreciation and deserved no analysis; for example: "There is nothing to suggest that Pollock was directly influenced by Oriental art. That Action Painting and the practices of the early Chinese Expressionists have much in common, although it brings East and West together, is pure coincidence."[21] But Sullivan found through this study a meaning deeper than the mere dismissal of East-West relationships as a historical indicator of nothing more to offer than superficial and sterile misapprehensions, as one might by now anticipate—a meaning consistent with the views expressed earlier in his writings, namely that if Chinese art were to find any purchase in Western art it would come only when a true understanding had been achieved, nothing less. He concluded with a note that in writing,

> I have not once used the word "synthesis" in this book—not, at least, with this larger meaning—for the notion of synthesis implies something final and therefore static. To the Chinese view, it is not the synthesis of *yang* and *yin* but the eternal, dynamic interaction of these opposite but complementary forces that is life-giving. So also should we regard the interaction between East and West as a process in which the great civilisations, while preserving their own character, will stimulate and enrich each other. Such a condition for the meeting of Eastern and Western art seems to offer far more creative possibilities than a synthesis, which would be sterile if it were consciously pursued.[22]

This may sound more editorial than art historical, more prescriptive than descriptive, and even unduly optimistic for the period—especially given Sullivan's typical reserve when it came to the Chinese ability to absorb the requirements of creativity and initiative into its formula for modernization. But a comment at the outset of this volume provides his rationale for optimism, and in most regards this has proven quite prescient:

> Just as important as Abstract Expressionism in breaking down barriers between Eastern and Western art has been the rejection of the idea of the avant-garde. As long as it was thought that the cutting edge of modern art could be identified and localised in New York, Paris or Tokyo, it

was natural to see the latest movement as something that the less advanced countries must somehow catch up with if they were to be taken seriously by the critics and art historians. But by the 1980s the idea of progress in art had been virtually abandoned. Today, in America, Europe and Japan an enormous variety of styles and techniques in art, and view of what art is, happily coexist; in Kandinsky's phrase, everything is permitted.[23]

Presumably no one at that time could have predicted the economic success of Chinese painting in the late 1990s and early twenty-first century. By 1987, Chinese artists I knew were using me to hustle works with risky themes out of their country. But Michael Sullivan was right about how the audience for art was opening up to non-elite media and messages. Most of the successful Chinese artists today, whatever one may think of their aesthetics, have unhitched their fate from agendas dictated by national pride or stilled their self-satisfied identification with the avant-garde and, rather, have tagged their success to a careful reading of (pardon the apparent contradiction) the wealthy masses, that is, a conglomeration of foreign sympathies and confusion and the need of big Chinese money to be wisely invested in something—*anything*—leave it to the artists and foreign taste to figure out what. How long can this last? Perhaps, back in 1989, Sullivan already had an answer:

> Today the nature of [East-West] interaction is changing, as ideas, forms, and techniques in the arts move with lightning speed across the world. In rapid succession they are borrowed, absorbed, made use of, adapted, distorted, forgotten, but they cannot be shut out for long.... [An] effect of this rapid flow of art from culture to culture, which we are now coming to take for granted, is that what would once have been thought of by the art historian as an exotic or fascinating event—such as, for instance, the influence of Pozzo's perspectives in eighteenth-century Chinese painting, or of Hiroshige on the Impressionists—is no longer surprising or even historically very important. When Japanese erotic prints become the starting point for paintings by Balthus or

for a series of drawings by Picasso, that their inspiration is Japanese seems hardly worth mentioning. It happens too easily, and too often. The age of mutual discovery, of wonder and revelation, is almost over.[24]

Almost, perhaps, but not yet; Western interest in things Chinese has had a long run. After China, under Deng Xiaoping's new leadership, finally turned down the heat on class warfare, set revolutionary Maoism aside, and "opened up" to the West, they sent their first exhibition of contemporary—post-Cultural Revolution—painting to America late in 1983. Over a two-year period it traveled from San Francisco to Birmingham, New York City, Ithaca, Denver, Indianapolis, Kansas City, and Minneapolis. Michael Sullivan, who had traveled repeatedly to China under a British passport in the 1970s, was ready for it and the changes it heralded, as a consultant to the exhibition and essayist for the catalogue. In it he wrote about the potential of traditional Chinese painting (*guohua*) for a modern resurgence, again in pessimistic terms, naming the one artist in the show whom he and the exhibition organizer had both liked best:

> Tied to a repertoire of traditional rural landscapes, birds, flowers, bamboo, and certain edifying or at least agreeable and charming figure subjects, it simply did not touch on many things that might be the province of art. What about the types of landscape, for instance, for which there were no conventions in the repertory, such as deserts, and the wild places where no scholar ever trod; the shape and character of the city, the canals, roofs and white damp-stained walls of Suzhou; the life of the common people in all its complexity, from the humorous to the tragic? But to break free from the pictorial conventions without violating the language was not easy.... For the language of the Chinese brush by its very nature tempts the artist to conventionalize. Why does a truck in a traditional landscape look out of place, a steamboat absurd? Is it that the manuals contain no stereotypes for trucks and steamboats? Or is it rather because both the style and technique of *guohua* seem to belong to a timeless past, to the world of art itself, rather than to the

world of present-day visual experience. If this is so, it provides a further explanation of why so many younger painters are turning away from *guohua*, declaring that they find it "too abstract" .... Today one paints "in the manner of" [the old masters] only for study purposes, and there are few paintings in this exhibition in which the stylistic debt to an old master is obvious, none in which it is declared in the inscription. Young painters know little of art history. Who is to say, for instance, whether Li Huasheng's apparent flouting of conventions is due to a deliberate defiance of them, or merely to ignorance of them? Perhaps, except for the very strongest creative personalities, such ignorance is the best road to freedom.[25]

Published in 1996, Sullivan's *Art and Artists of Twentieth-Century China* massively revised his outdated (but still unique) *Chinese Art in the Twentieth Century*. In covering an additional four decades, and all the decades in far greater detail than in the earlier volume, with far better historical perspective, the original 83 pages became 280; the original 81 illustrations (4 in color) became 274 (94 in color). Now included were nearly double the length of the previously covered years, plus new chapters on Taiwan, Hong Kong, and expatriate artists and art. Reviewers waxed favorable and unfavorable, found mistakes (a reviewer's internal delight) and overlooked others, but that is not our concern here—our attention is focused on the author's perspectives and perceptions, like this which comes toward the very end; he wrote that, looking back over the whole twentieth century from the near-end of it, one can see

> the birth of the idea, shocking in ethnocentric China, that art was a world language that obliterates all frontiers; the introduction of the concept of art as a social activity and an instrument of reform and revolution; the undermining of the Chinese belief in fine art as the prerogative of an elite; the struggle to understand, absorb, and adapt a plethora of traditions and styles that had evolved historically in the West but were imported into China more or less simultaneously; the crisis in personal identity felt by artists torn

between East and West; and, not least, the existence from the middle of the century, of a cultural tyranny that made the free exploitation of these ideas, forms, and institutions virtually impossible.

Can it be said that, by the early 1990s, artists had met and solved these problems? That they had engaged with them all, and found many solutions, must be obvious from some of the illustrations in this book. But late in the century, just when Western art seemed to have been successfully absorbed and traditional art reborn, there came from the West the wholly new question of the nature of art itself. Conceptual art, performance art, multimedia presentations of an infinite variety arrived to make some Chinese artists question the validity of all that had been achieved since 1900.[26]

In comparing Sullivan's two texts on twentieth-century Chinese painting, written nearly forty years apart, it is evident that while his knowledge and perspective were greatly broadened, his taste had remained remarkably stable. Friends of many artists, Michael and Khoan Sullivan slowly built their own collection of modern Chinese art.

Some of it was purchased but most of it gifted by the artists, in the oldest of Chinese traditions. Gifting took the control of quality and the nuanced expression of taste out of the collector's hand, except inasmuch as the collector chose his artist friends. But regardless of that, the contents of his private collection became a critical statement, as much as anything he might put into words and publish—and eventually, as the gifts were transferred as his own gift to Oxford University's Ashmolean Museum, it *was* published: one of the largest collections of modern Chinese art in the world (not including those few massive, and massively expensive, collections quickly built of the latest, biggest "hits" by the best-known contemporary artists, strictly limited to the mid-1980s and after). In recognizing (above) the decline of the avant-garde and the modern elite, and with the concomitant devolution of artistic judgment to a more pluralistic array of critics, Michael Sullivan might well have predicted the response to his own taste. When his collection traveled for display in 2007 to Seattle,[27] this was the published response of one local journalist: "Even before this exhibit's 2001 debut [at the Ashmolean], art in China exploded far beyond the confines of the Sullivans' idea of it. Not only does Chinese art engage the global stage, it dominates it. Increasingly, artists whom the Sullivans favor have been pushed to the background…. [This] show is the equivalent of warm milk at bedtime. What could SAM [the Seattle Art Museum] have been thinking?"[28]

Seattle's other leading newspaper critic called it "an odd and wildly uneven show…a haphazard array…that throws together academic and self-taught artists in an awkward mix."

> The artworks [in this exhibition] are billed as "modern," but that title seems to allude only to the fact that the work dates from the 20th century, with a sprinkle of additions from the past few years. It's a strange conglomerate of styles, from traditional to avant garde, that didn't lead me to any meaningful conclusions about Chinese art of the past century, except that it was in some ways influenced by Western trends…. With so much contemporary Chinese art making big waves in the international art scene, it seems a shame that the Seattle Art Museum didn't seek out a show for the SAAM [Seattle Asian Art Museum] that's more timely and relevant…. As an unedited survey, [this exhibition] no doubt holds scholarly interest. But for a museum striving to serve a broader public, it doesn't add up to the wow factor.[29]

By this, the enthusiastic acceptance of modern Chinese art into the public's critical embrace was made evident and Sullivan might at last rejoice at this long-belated event, except that the range of "modernity" now included only the most recent decade or so and excluded most of the twentieth century. Whatever was meant by this "wow factor," the "awkward mix," and the "strange conglomerate of styles" that these local critics complained about and dismissed is exactly what had defined the twentieth century in China, in art as in other matters.

Now that the Warholian contemporary in Chinese art had to be addressed along with the modern, Sullivan spoke to an academic audience about this in 2009:

I could give you a long list of contemporary Chinese works that I consider merely trash and others that I admire…. That, you will say, is just my opinion; I am an old fuddy-duddy who doesn't belong in this [twenty-first] century at all. But in the absence today of any fixed criteria, all one has to rely on is one's memory, experience, and gut feeling—the last especially—which tell one that a work has integrity.

If I don't belong in this century, I certainly belong in the last one, but perhaps because pendulums have a habit of swinging, I belong in the next one too….

All this sounds naive. The problems and issues that face contemporary art are many and complex, and it may sound absurd to cut through them with simplistic statements of this sort…. Kandinsky put it very simply: "Art," he said, "is the living face, not of the mind, but of feeling and only feeling. For anyone who cannot feel, art is dark and silent." In other words, if we can't trust our own feelings, our own aesthetic conscience, we have no business to be involved with art at all.[30]

Notes

An earlier version of this article was published in *Journal of Art Historiography* 10 (June 2014), n.p.

1   *Chinese Art in the Twentieth Century* (London and Berkeley: Faber and Faber and University of California Press, 1959); *The Meeting of Eastern and Western Art, from the Sixteenth Century to the Present* (Berkeley: University of California Press, 1973; revised and expanded edition, 1989); *Art and Artists of Twentieth-Century China* (Berkeley: University of California Press, 1996); *Modern Chinese Artists: A Biographical Dictionary* (Berkeley: University of California Press, 2006). All publications cited herein were authored by Michael Sullivan unless specified otherwise. Except in titles, Chinese transliterations originally in Wade-Giles have been converted into Pinyin.
2   Nonetheless, three of Sullivan's Stanford University Ph.D. students completed the first dissertations on twentieth-century topics: Mayching Gao, "China's Response to the West in Art, 1989–1937"

(1972); Shirley Sun, "Lu Hsün and the Chinese Woodcut Movement, 1929–1936" (1974); James Soong, "A Visual Experience in Nineteenth-century China: Jen Po-nien (1840–1895) and the Shanghai School of Painting" (1977).
3   *An Introduction to Chinese Art* (London: Faber and Faber, 1959; repr. Berkeley: University of California Press, 1960), 204.
4   *An Introduction to Tibetan Culture* (Chengdu: West China Union University Museum, 1945).
5   "The Excavation of a T'ang Imperial Tomb," *The Illustrated London News*, April 20, 1946, 429.
6   *The Birth of Landscape Painting in China* (Berkeley: University of California Press, 1962); *Chinese Landscape Painting*, vol. 2, *The Sui and T'ang Dynasties* (Berkeley: University of California Press, 1980).
7   *Chinese Painting in the Twentieth Century*, 50.
8   Ibid., 45.
9   Ibid., 36.
10 Ibid., 37–38.
11 Ibid., 36.
12 Ibid., 39.
13 Ibid., 44.
14 This list was expanded to include more than eight hundred artists in *Art and Artists of the Twentieth Century*, and that total was more than doubled in his *Modern Chinese Artists: A Biographical Dictionary*.
15 *Introduction to Chinese Art*, 206–7. My emphasis.
16 In *Proceedings of the International Symposium on Chinese Painting* (Taipei: National Palace Museum, 1970), 593–634.
17 James Cahill, "Wu Pin and His Landscape Painting," in *Proceedings of the International Symposium*, 635–720 and especially 654–55; James Cahill, *The Compelling Image: Nature and Style in Seventeenth-Century Chinese Painting* (Cambridge, Mass., and London: The Belknap Press of Harvard University Press, 1982), especially chapter 1, "Chang Hung and the Limits of Presentation," 1–35 and figures 1.20, 1.22.
18 Cahill, *Compelling Image*, 70.
19 *Meeting of Eastern and Western Art* (2nd edition), 273.
20 Ibid.
21 Ibid., 252.
22 Ibid., 282.
23 Ibid., 4–5.
24 Ibid., 283.
25 Lucy Lim, with James Cahill and Michael Sullivan, *Contemporary Chinese Painting: An Exhibition from the People's Republic of China* (San Francisco: The Chinese Culture Foundation of San Francisco, 1983), 29–30.

26 *Art and Artists of Twentieth-Century China*, 281.
27 See *Modern Chinese Art: The Khoan and Michael Sullivan Collection* (Oxford: Ashmolean Museum, 2001); for the symposium that accompanied the exhibition of these works in Seattle, organized by Josh Yiu, see *Writing Modern Chinese Art: Historiographic Explorations* (Seattle: Seattle Art Museum, 2009).
28 Regina Hackett, *The Seattle Post-Intelligencer*, March 2, 2007.
29 Sheila Farr, *The Seattle Times*, March 16, 2007.
30 These are from Sullivan's oral remarks delivered as an introduction to the Princeton symposium "Articulations," March 7, 2009, which accompanied the opening of the *Outside In: Chinese × American × Contemporary Art* exhibition; published as "The Best" in *Articulations: Undefining Chinese Contemporary Art,* ed. Jerome Silbergeld and Dora C. Y. Ching (Princeton: P. Y. and Kinmay W. Tang Center for East Asian Art and Princeton University Press, 2009), 24–31. On Sullivan's best contemporary art list, as named there, were Zhou Chunya's *Green Dog*, Xu Bing's *Book from the Sky*, the earliest grinning men of Yue Minjun, Wang Huaiqing's *Night Entertainments of Han Xizai* ("beside which," wrote Sullivan, "Wang Qingsong's photomontage parody of the same work is a meretricious travesty"), and sculptor Ju Ming's bronze *taiji* figures. He also had the highest regard for the contemporary painter Liu Dan.

Chapter 8

Beyond the Seas: A Sojourn in Chinese Calligraphy and Painting

Jason C. Kuo

> A student of cultural history is the last person who can believe he is self-made or the sole begetter of his most original idea.
> —Jacques Barzun

I came to the study of Chinese calligraphy and painting through an interest in the relationship between poetry and painting in general. I aspired to be a poet when I was quite young; I had a poem published when I was about fifteen; the poem was about the assassination of John F. Kennedy. I joined some local literary clubs while I was in high school and then, in college, I published a few poems in the college's literary magazine. Of my early work, only one poem is extant.[1]

During my senior year in the Department of Foreign Languages and Literatures at the National Taiwan University (NTU), Professor Wai-lim Yip (1937), from the University of California in San Diego, offered a seminar in literary criticism. He is not only a scholar of Ezra Pound and of the comparative study of poetics, but is also a poet himself.[2] For his seminar, I wrote a paper on how the misunderstanding of written Chinese characters on the part of Ernest Fenollosa and Ezra Pound played a role in the development of modern American poetry, especially the Imagists. Professor Yip himself was very interested in Chinese landscape poetry and landscape painting, perhaps not primarily from the viewpoint of art history but from the viewpoint of aesthetics, but I think it was by taking that course in literary criticism that I realized that there was a field of Chinese painting within the field of art history. Professor Yip received his MFA in creative writing at the International Writers Workshop at the University of Iowa and his Ph.D. in comparative literature at Princeton University and was familiar with the academic study of Chinese art in the United States. It was also Professor Yip who gave me his personal copy of Osvald Sirén's *The Chinese on the Art of Painting*; I still have the book.³

After I graduated from college, I was admitted into the MA program in Foreign Languages and Literatures at NTU and hoped to continue my work in literary criticism and comparative literature, with some vague ideas of pursuing further the subject of the relationship between poetry and painting. So, in a way, my first encounter with Chinese and calligraphy and painting was through an interest in poetics. Yip also got me involved in a performance art project that he put together with other poets and composers in Taipei during my senior year; he asked me to shout back from a spot in the audience at the performance on stage, thereby breaking the traditional division between the performer and the audience. I remember vividly even today that the music accompanying the performance was made on some cooking pots and pans, not on regular musical instruments. That was one of my first experiences with contemporary art. I guess it was also through Yip that I have maintained a strong interest in contemporary art. And that is also perhaps why I have never lost interest in other media in Chinese art (such as architecture and ceramics).

My later work in modern and contemporary art (for example, my essays and exhibition catalogs on contemporary artists such as Chen Chi-kwan [1921–2007], Gao Xingjian [1940–], Chuang Che [1934–], Lo Ch'ing [1948–], and Yu P'eng [1955–2014]) can be traced back to 1971, when I studied with Yip. I think his book *Yü tang-tai i-shu-chia te tui-hua: Chung-kuo hsien-tai-hua te sheng-ch'eng* [Dialogues with Contemporary Artists: The Growth of Chinese Modern Painting]⁴ should have been consulted and cited by more scholars working in modern and contemporary Chinese painting; I think it has been virtually neglected, either intentionally or unintentionally, by American scholars.

During my senior year, I would sit in on the classes on classical Chinese poetry given by the poet-scholar Yeh Chia-ying (1924-), who was then on the faculty at the University of British Columbia and a visiting professor at the National Taiwan University. Her classes on the poetry of the T'ang dynasty and on the *tz'u* poetry of Su Shih (1037–1101) and Hsin Ch'i-chi (1140–1207) of the Sung dynasty opened my eyes not only to the world of classical poetry but also to the deep cultural meaning of later Chinese poetry. My impression was that she knew how to use judiciously the methods of New Criticism as well as other Western critical approaches in her study of classical Chinese poetry. I think my interest in relating poetry (and verbal texts in general) to painting in my study of post-Sung painting and my work on Chinese seal-engraving and calligraphy couplet scrolls have grown, to a large extent, out of my exposure to classical Chinese poetry at NTU. I was also fortunate to live with several students who majored in Chinese literature, history, and philosophy. Several of my roommates later became professors of Chinese literature and history at NTU and the National Tsing Hua University. My association with them, along with my own study of classical Chinese poetry, has played a role in my research and teaching on the relationship between words and images in Chinese painting.

About two months into my graduate study in the Graduate Institute of Foreign Languages and Literatures at NTU, a brand-new graduate program in Chinese art history was created within the Graduate Institute of History at NTU; it was cosponsored by the National Palace Museum, with generous support from the Asia Foundation. (This program later became the Graduate Institute of Art History at NTU.) After taking a very competitive entrance examination, I was admitted into the program; there were five students in my class. We all felt fortunate to be in the program. For one thing, in addition to the scholarship given by the Ministry of Education to every graduate student at that time, we received an extra stipend. At the National Palace Museum, we enjoyed many privileges of its staff; we could ride free of charge in the museum's staff buses; we could eat in the museum's restaurant with the same discount as the staff. I think Dr. Chiang Fu-ts'ung, Director of the National Palace Museum, regarded us as future staff members of the museum. In fact, three of my classmates did end up working for the museum.

Although we were exposed to all the media (bronzes, jades, ceramics, lacquer, calligraphy, and painting) represented by the fabulous collection of the National Palace Museum and we had opportunities to study with most of the senior curators there (such as Na Chih-liang in jades, Tan Tan-jiung in bronzes, and Wu Yu-chang in ceramics), I was personally attracted to the teaching and scholarship of two people: Li Lin-ts'an (1913–1999) and Chiang Chao-shen (1925–1996). Both served, during different periods, as Curator of Calligraphy and Painting and Deputy Director of the National Palace. One of the most enjoyable and useful aspects of my training in the program was the constant exposure to original works of art from the National Palace Museum. In addition to looking at the works in the regular exhibitions, we were able to have special study sessions on important works from storage that my teachers would select for us in order to teach the fundamentals of connoisseurship. For example, we would spend a whole afternoon comparing, side by side, the two versions (the original dated 1350 and the copy made in the 17th century) of Huang Kung-wang's handscroll *Dwelling in the Fu-ch'un Mountains*.

Two other teachers, who at that time were on visiting appointments in the Chinese art history program at NTU, also had strong links with the National Palace Museum. Chuang Shen, at that time a faculty member at Hong Kong University, gave us a good introduction to the historiography of Chinese art and archaeology; his father, Chuang Yen (1899–1980) began to work for the Palace Museum as a young man and later served in the National Palace Museum in the capacity as both Curator of Calligraphy and Painting and Deputy Director. From his father and from his graduate work at Princeton, Chuang Shen had an encyclopedic knowledge of the field of Chinese art, which he was eager to transmit to us. During the second year of my graduate program, Fu Shen (1937–), who was on a research fellowship from Princeton, gave a most illuminating course in connoisseurship; he had been a member of the Department of Calligraphy and Painting at the National Palace Museum before going on to Princeton for his graduate work. Trained as a calligrapher-painter in the Fine Arts Department of the National

Taiwan Normal University, Fu Shen was particularly knowledgeable in authenticating calligraphy and painting and taught at Yale before becoming the Curator of Chinese Art at the Freer and Sackler Galleries in Washington, D.C.

It was Chiang Chao-shen, however, who was most influential in my later development as an art historian. Chiang Chao-shen was not only a scholar but also a calligrapher, painter, and poet. I eventually took some lessons in calligraphy, painting, and classical poetry from him in addition to a two-year course on connoisseurship, and this experience had a strong impact on my decision to go on to doctoral work in Chinese painting. In fact, it was through Chiang Chao-shen that I got to know Richard Edwards, who had been working with Chiang Chao-shen on a major project on the Wu School of painting, and who encouraged me to go to Ann Arbor, where I was to study from 1975 to 1980.

When I returned to Taiwan in 1980, after I completed my doctoral studies, I had two job offers; one was to work in the Department of Calligraphy and Painting at the National Palace Museum, the other was to teach in the program in Chinese art history at NTU. I chose to teach and turn down the museum job and I think Chiang Chao-shen was deeply disappointed. As I mentioned above, some of my teachers in Taiwan were trained and mostly self-taught in the Chinese tradition (e.g., Li Lin-ts'an and Chiang Chao-shen), while others had been exposed to American training (both Chuang Shen and Fu Shen were trained at Princeton), so in a way, from the very beginning of my training in art history, I was able to benefit from both traditions. Actually both Li Lin-ts'an and Chiang Chao-shen had extensive experience working or interacting with American scholars during their travels to the United States. They also often had the opportunity to discuss scholarly matters with American scholars who visited the National Palace Museum from time to time. Richard Edwards was trained mostly at Harvard and Princeton but had the opportunity to work with Chinese scholars working in the United States. So the situation was quite fluid, not absolute. But if I want to make some differentiation, I would say that my training in Taiwan, especially under Li Lin-ts'an and Chiang Chao-shen, was quite broad and went beyond mere research in a specific topic. They were more interested in developing in me a foundation for a long-term scholarly way of life. That was why, I think, Chiang Chao-shen taught me how to read the poetry of Tu Fu (712–770), and to copy again and again the calligraphy of Ou-yang Hsun (557–641). The purpose of studying T'ang dynasty poetry, with its rich literary and historical allusions, was to make me a better-educated person, not a professional specialist in classical poetry. Although I may not be able to look at a Ming painting in the same way as the Ming dynasty scholar would, at least I could get as close as possible. My essay on Shih-t'ao's painting can be cited as an example of how my training in Taiwan, including my early interest in landscape poetry as an undergraduate, has impacted my scholarship.[5]

In addition to art history and connoisseurship, I studied classical Chinese poetry and the practice of calligraphy and painting under Chiang Chao-shen. I practiced calligraphy by copying the classic example of the *Chiu-ch'eng-kung li-ch'uan-ming* (632) by Ou-yang Hsun, which also formed one of the foundations of Chiang Chao-shen's own lifelong pursuit in the art of calligraphy and painting.

Under the influence of Chiang Chao-shen, I have maintained a strong interest in research in calligraphy and seal engraving, aspects of Chinese calligraphy and painting often given perfunctory treatment by Western art historians (even though they apologize for their neglect). My interest in this area led me to organize the exhibition and write the catalog *Word as Image: The Art of Chinese Seal Engraving*, at the China Institute in New York in 1992. In a way, I also feel that people trained exclusively in the United States might have missed some of the subtle cultural underpinnings of certain works of art, unless they have tried very hard to cultivate a sensitivity to the complex web of meanings associated with a work of art done in the remote past in a foreign culture. But I think most U.S.-trained scholars have been doing their best to grapple with this distance in culture.

Of all the art historians in Taiwan, Chiang Chao-shen taught me the most. For example, my work on Wang Yuan-ch'i (1642–1715), Hung-jen (1610-1664), and Huang Pin-hung (1865–1955) has been inspired by Chiang's attention to the importance of the aesthetics of *pi-mo* ("brush-ink"); in this sense, he gave me the foundation for the study of Chinese painting as far as its value as art is concerned. He was not interested in any grand scheme of the history of Chinese painting. Wang Yuan-ch'i is perhaps the most creative among the Orthodox masters of the early Ch'ing dynasty, especially his powerful use of brushwork and his construction of dynamic space in his late landscape paintings; my work on Wang Yuan-ch'i was published not only in *The National Palace Museum Quarterly*, but also as a volume in the museum's monograph series, in part due to Chiang's support. From time to time I heard him mention Hung-jen and Huang Pin-hung; in many ways he was calling my attention to the artists from his home town, She-hsien of Anhui (Hung-jen was born in She-hsien and Huang Pin-hung's ancestral home was also in She-hsien). But I believe that he also thought highly of them as artists. I was eventually to write my dissertation on Hung-jen, and later I organized the first international exhibition on the paintings of Huang Pin-hung, held at the Williams College Museum of Art and the Taipei Fine Arts Museum. And in 1984, I was able to visit She-hsien. I would never have expected that my scholarship was to have so much connection with Chiang Chao-shen. The most important thing he taught me was how to look at Chinese painting *as painting* first and then to consider the related texts. His command of textual material, which he utilized with thorough visual analysis, as seen in his work on T'ang Yin, is really hard to match by American-trained art historians.

During my two-year stint in the Nationalist army, I kept in touch with my teachers at the National Palace Museum. One day, I came by to see Chiang Chao-shen and he introduced me to Richard Edwards (1916–2016), Professor of the History of Art at the University of Michigan. Edwards kindly reserved a graduate assistant's position for me at Michigan for almost two years. As soon as I finished my military service obligation, I left Taiwan for the University of Michigan, Ann Arbor in time to begin my graduate study in the fall of 1975. I still remember vividly how he picked me up at the airport in Detroit in his beat-up old Saab sedan and drove me to his house to stay for a few days before I found my own place.

As a graduate student at Michigan, I was forced to be more analytical, especially in the formal analysis of painting in particular and of works of art in general. In this regard, I was fortunate to study with Rudolf Arnheim, well known for his writings on the visual perception of art, who had arrived from Harvard University to assume his Visiting Professorship at Michigan one year before I arrived; he had published, as early as 1932, *Film als Kunst,* one of the earliest theoretical treatises on film (English translation published in 1933 in London).[6] His emigration in 1933 from Berlin to Rome, then to London in 1938, soon after the Italian Fascists adopted the racism of the German Nazis, and then to the U.S. in 1940, exemplifies the exiles of so many European scholars and intellectuals in the turbulent years of the twentieth century. My own work in relating film studies to art history can be traced back, at least in part, to my study with Arnheim.

On the other hand, my study in Indian art with Walter Spink (born in 1928), who studied under Benjamin Rowland at Harvard, opened my eyes to other areas of Asian art that I could not have had the opportunity to study in Taiwan. Spink has a strong humanistic approach to art history and often tries to compare Asian art with Western art in terms of fundamental outlooks on life, as can be seen in his little book *The Axis of Eros* (Penguin Books, 1973) and his exhibition catalog *Krishnamandala* (University of Michigan Museum of Art, 1971). So, while paying attention to formal analyses, I have been keenly aware of the cultural, religious, or spiritual significance of an art object.

Also, while I was studying there, Michigan had a strong and broad program in Asian art; there were two professors in Chinese art, one in Japanese art, two in South and South East Asian art, and one in Islamic art. I was even able to take a course in Chinese ceramics, using the University of Michigan Museum of Art's collection. This experience, in addition to my earlier work on ceramics at the National Palace Museum, enabled me to organize two exhibitions of Chinese ceramics (one in 1992 at the Baltimore Museum of Art [with Frances Klapthor] and the other in 1994 at the Art Gallery of the University of Maryland) and to introduce a fair amount of material on ceramics in my undergraduate courses in Asian art.

Graduate students in Asian art at Michigan were required to take at least one course in Western art; at the same time students in Western art were required to take one course in so-called non-Western art. I still think it is a good policy, because many entry-level positions in art history today, especially in small schools, often would favor those people who, in addition to their specialty in Western art, have some experience, however limited, in non-Western art. In any case, I took a course in Mannerism and a museum research course. The combination of a broad training in Asian art and some exposure to Western art was indeed a wonderfully broad education for me. Later I was able to participate in teaching surveys of Western art both at NTU and at Williams College. Of course my undergraduate education in Western literature also helped build a background in the cultural history of the Western tradition. But the opportunity to see many works of art, both Asian and Western, during my frequent field trips to museums in the United States and abroad also gave me a broad perspective in art, both Chinese and non-Chinese, as embodiment of culture.

I would write differently for a Chinese audience than I do for an American audience. An example is the large number of reviews (including exhibition reviews published in the two major newspapers *Lien-ho-pao* and *Chung-kuo shih-pao* and the two major art magazines *I-shu-chia* and *Hsiung-shih mei-shu*) and essays written for a Chinese audience; some of these writings have been collected in the following books: *Lung t'ien-ti yü hsing-nei* [Trapping Heaven and Earth in the Cage of Form] (1986), *Ts'o wan-wu yü pi-yuan* [Embodying Myriad of Things at the Tip of Brush] (1994), and *I-shu-shih yü i-shu p'i-p'ing te tan-suo* [Rethinking Art History and Art Criticism] (1996). I have also edited and written the introductions to several anthologies, such as *Mei-kang yü tsao-hsing* [Sense of Beauty and Creation of Form] (1982), *Tang-tai Taiwan hui-hua wen-hsüan, 1945–1990* [Essays on Contemporary Painting in Taiwan, 1945–1990] (1991), and *Taiwan shih-chüeh wen-hua, 1975–1995* [Visual Culture in Taiwan, 1975–1995] (1995). I think I write more like a public intellectual than an academic when I write for a Taiwan audience; the first anthology, *Mei-kang yü tsao-hsing* [Sense of Beauty and Creation of Form], is now in its thirteenth printing and has been also reprinted in mainland China by two major academic publishers and can therefore reach a much larger audience.[7] In short, when I write for a Chinese audience, I write more or less as a public intellectual.

Very few American scholars in Chinese painting can write as a public intellectual to an American audience. When I write for an

American audience, it is mostly for fellow art historians, and I work more or less within the constraints of academic writing, with its own conventions and politics. When I write, however, for the journals of the National Palace Museum, for instance *The National Palace Museum Bulletin* and *The National Palace Museum Research Quarterly*, I am writing for audiences both in Taiwan and the United States, for I know that people in the field, no matter where they work, are going to read it. Interestingly, I have also discovered that my Chinese writings have been cited by Western scholars, indicating that, in this age of increasing global communication, one's audience is not limited by geography. I think my backgrounds in both Taiwan and the United States have enabled me to pay attention to art in Taiwan, during both the Japanese occupation and the Postwar period.

Through a series of seminars at Michigan, Edwards gradually guided me not only in the way of looking at paintings but also of how to express what I saw in words. Like Chiang Chao-shen, Edwards did not have any particular theory, and he insisted that we scrutinize paintings themselves first, and then use whatever available written texts to help understand the paintings. This insistence on the primacy of the art objects was to have a strong impact on my scholarship later on. I often enjoyed looking at paintings together with him, in his home, in private collections, and in museums, both in the United States and abroad. I especially enjoyed looking at paintings with him during several of our trips to Japan, where he was well received by many scholars. Being a student of his often made it easier to gain access to private collections in the United States and Japan. But above all, it was his attention to the details in a work of art and his insistence on looking at paintings closely (before being distracted by external textual material) that really left a lasting impression on my own work.

I should perhaps add that it was at Edwards's modest house, during many of the dinner parties he and his wife Vee often gave, that I first became familiar with the oeuvre of modern painters such as Chen Chi-kwan and Chuang Che; he would often display their paintings from his personal collection. In addition, during my graduate student years, and when I returned to Ann Arbor from 1982 to 1985 to work with him on a special exhibition project on the art of the late Sung dynasties (planned to be shown at the Detroit Institute of Arts but never completed due to financial troubles at the museum), I often visited Chuang Che's home, located in a former farm house in Ann Arbor, to see his paintings. To a large extent, my work on art in Taiwan, as seen in the book *Art and Cultural Politics in Postwar Taiwan*, can be traced back to my years working with Edwards.

During my first year as a graduate student in Taiwan (1973–74), I had the opportunity to study the Buddhist and Taoist temples in Lukang with Nelson I. Wu (1919–2002) of Washington University during his research trip to Taiwan. His flair for language (his Chinese novel *Wei-yang-ko* [Tender Is the Night], about the life and love stories of college students in China during World War II, was a best-seller for many decades) and his eloquence were most impressive to me. I think his approach to art history is primarily cultural, as can be seen in his book *Chinese and Indian Architecture*.[8] From him I developed an interest in architecture and gardens, and I have been able to spend more time than others might on these aspects in my courses in Chinese art.

While a graduate student at Michigan, I had the opportunity to visit the Cleveland Museum of Art many times and to look at paintings together with Wai-kam Ho (1924–2004) whenever he was around. His extensive knowledge and experience, not only in Chinese art but also in various aspects of Chinese cultural history, made me aware of the importance of studying Chinese art objects as concrete embodiments of Chinese culture, including China's ongoing relationships with her neighbors through the ages. At the same time, Ho's extensive use of textual evidence exemplified to me the importance of integrating words and images in the study of Chinese painting. His essay "Tung Ch'i-ch'ang's New Orthodoxy and the Southern School of Theory" (in *Artists and Traditions: Uses of the Past in Chinese Culture*, edited by Christian F. Murck, 1976) is a tour de force that, in my opinion, very few Chinese painting scholars working in the West can match, mainly because of his command of primary sources in classical Chinese.[9] I was also very encouraged one day when, after I told him that I was organizing an exhibition on Huang Pin-hung at the Williams College Museum of Art, he told me that he believed that Huang Pin-hung was perhaps the most important early twentieth-century painter. On another occasion, I

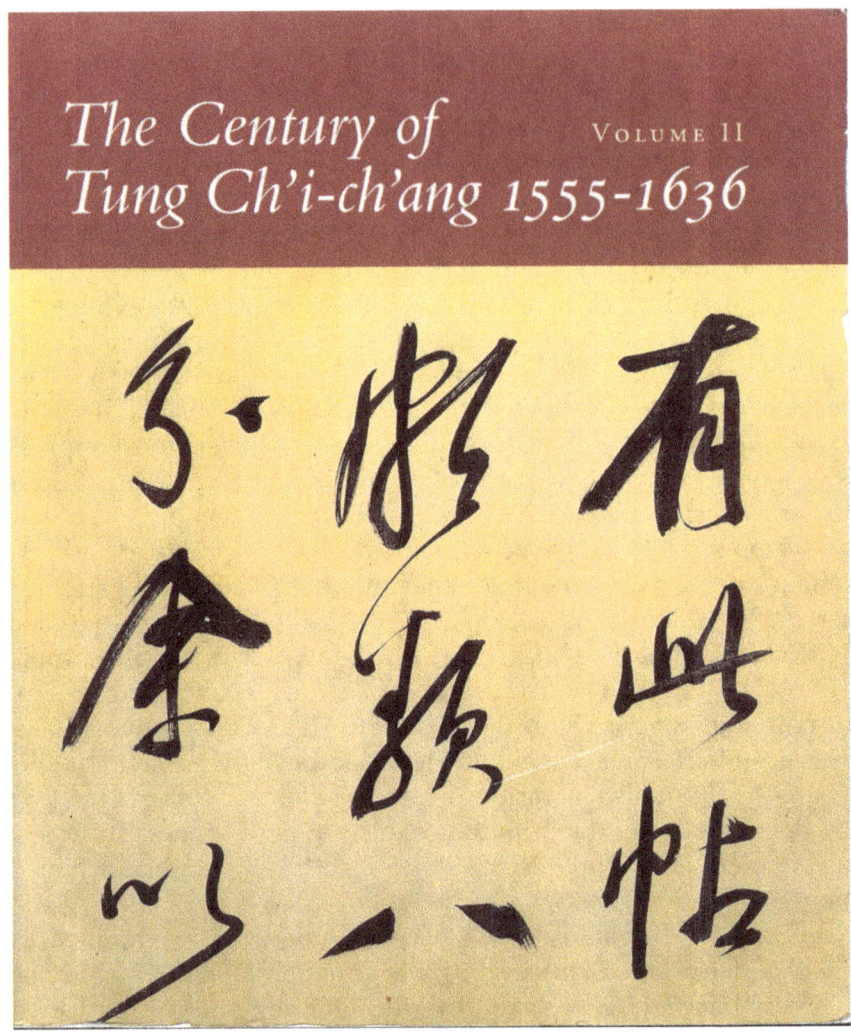

8.1. Cover of volume 2 of *The Century of Tung Ch'i-ch'ang, 1555–1636*, edited by Wai-kam Ho, with Judith G. Smith, 2 vols. (Kansas City, Mo.: Nelson-Atkins Museum of Art in association with the University of Washington Press, 1992).

was pleasantly surprised to discover that Ho was also interested in modern Chinese poets such as Feng Chih (1905–1993) and Tai Wang-shu (1905–1950), whom I had been reading since my college years. Even though I never studied with Ho formally, I learned much from him when we were looking at paintings together. From him I also learned that to rely on pure visual analysis of an art object or to impose any preexisting or external framework on an art object would likely lead to a misunderstanding or even distortion of history. When Ho organized the major exhibition on Tung Ch'i-ch'ang, he invited me to contribute thirteen entries to the catalog *The Century of Tung Ch'i-ch'ang* (The Nelson-Atkins Museum of Art, 1992) which later (in 1993) won the prestigious Shimada award (established by the Freer and Sackler Galleries and the Metropolitan Center for Far Eastern Art Studies in Kyoto). Wai-kam Ho's generosity and encouragement have been important to me. (fig. 8.1)

Wang Fangyu (1913–1997) is another scholar who has had an impact on my work. I first got to know him when we both presented papers at an international conference organized by the National Museum of History in Taipei in 1989; my topic was on contemporary art criticism and his was on contemporary calligraphy. I had, of course, read most of his writings on Pa-ta shan-jen and was very much impressed by his erudition and scholarship in the area of late Ming and early Ch'ing painting. After I moved from Williams College to the University of Maryland in 1990, I began to organize an exhibition of Chinese seal engravings at the China House Gallery of the China Institute in New York. Wang was most helpful and generous in taking me to see private collectors in the New York area (including Dr. Paul Singer) and to make his own collection available to me for study and exhibition purposes. He also gave a talk at the symposium organized in conjunction with the exhibition *Word as Image: The Art of Chinese Seal Engraving* (1992).[10] Wang continued to encourage me to study seal engravings and to teach the subject. His judicious use of stylistic features and documentary sources in his study of Pa-ta shan-jen has been most inspiring to me.

Wang Fangyu died in 1997. In 1998, in memory of him and his wife Sum Wai, a group of friends and I established the Wang Fangyu Endowment for Calligraphy Education at the University of Maryland in order to enhance the scholarship to which he had devoted so much of his energy. I also contributed to the catalog accompanying the exhibition *A Literati Life in the Twentieth Century: Wang Fangyu, Scholar, Artist, Connoisseur* organized by Christopher H. Luce and held at the China House Gallery in 1999. As a tribute to his work, I coedited with Peter Sturman (at the University of California, Santa Barbara) a catalog to accompany an international traveling exhibition of Chinese calligraphy couplets organized by the Art Museum of the Chinese University of Hong Kong.[11]

During my last year of my doctoral dissertation writing, which was on the paintings of Hung-jen, I was invited by James Cahill (1926–2014) to be a research associate (with funding from the National Endowment for the Arts) at the University Art Museum in Berkeley, and to participate in his seminar and exhibition project on the Anhui School. I spent the spring of 1980 working with Cahill and his graduate students on the exhibition *Shadows of Mt. Huang*. The exhibition was held at the University Art Museum, Berkeley; the Detroit Institute of Art; the University of Texas, Austin; and the Art Museum of Princeton University, in 1981 and 1982. Cahill's attention to the social contexts of art certainly was to make me aware of different approaches among U.S. art historians in the field. Another art historian who has had an impact on my development as a scholar-teacher is Chu-tsing Li (1920–2014) of the University of Kansas. I first got to know him through reading his monographs and articles, including his book *The Autumn Colors on the Ch'iao and Hua Mountains: A Landscape by Chao Meng-fu* (1965), as a graduate student in Taiwan. In 1980, he invited me to give a paper on Hui-chou merchants as art patrons in the late sixteenth and early seventeenth century at a workshop titled "Artists and Patrons: Some Social and Economic Aspects of Chinese Painting," which he co-organized with James Cahill and Wai-kam Ho at the Nelson-Atkins Museum of Art in Kansas City. The paper was subsequently translated into Chinese and published in China in 1987, even before its publication in English in the conference volume in 1989.[12]

Li's support not only encouraged me to continue to pay attention to the social and economic aspects of Chinese art, but also helped me develop my research agenda in modern and contemporary Chinese art, including art in Taiwan. In 1989, as I mentioned, I organized an exhibition on the paintings of Huang Pin-hung at the

Williams College Museum of Art; the show eventually traveled to the Taipei Fine Arts Museum; it was, as far as I know, the first international traveling exhibition on the art of Huang Pin-hung. During the preparation of the exhibition and the accompanying catalog, he showed me strong support.

In 1990 I presented a paper on the art of Chen Chi-kwan at the international conference "China: Modernity and Art" held at the Taipei Fine Arts Museum; Li also gave a paper at that conference. When the Taipei Fine Arts Museum held a retrospective of Chen Chi-kwan's work in 1991, I was invited by the museum to revise my paper from 1990 and publish it in the catalog, with an essay by Li, on Chen Chi-kwan's artistic development.[13] In the summer of 1991, I participated in the National Endowment for the Humanities (NEH)'s Summer Institute for College and University Faculty on "Modern Chinese Art and Culture" that he organized at the University of Kansas. This intensive summer program not only helped my ongoing research in modern Chinese art but also encouraged me to begin to offer courses in modern Chinese art.

Sometime between 1982 and 1985, when I was a Stoddard Fellow in the Department of Asian Art at the Detroit Institute of Art, I sat in on a course on modern Chinese art given by Ellen Johnston Laing, who was then a visiting professor at the University of Michigan. I think that course encouraged me to further develop my expertise in modern Chinese art, and I am grateful to her for her pioneering efforts, both inside and outside the classroom, in developing modern Chinese art as a subfield.

As to scholars in mainland China and Hong Kong who influenced me, I would mention Wang Shih-ch'ing in Peking and Jao Tsung-i (1917–2018) in Hong Kong. I was very much impressed by the erudition of Wang Shih-ch'ing, whose compilation (with Wang Ts'ung) of sources on Hung-jen was indispensable to my work on Hung-jen and the Anhui School.[14] His command of source materials of the late Ming and early Ch'ing dynasties is without peer.

I first got to know Jao Tsung-i when he gave a talk on the relationship between poetry and painting at the National Taiwan University, when I was still a graduate student there. His work on the late Ming and early Ch'ing dynasties, as well as on Tun-huang caves, was characterized by an equal attention to text and image.

Similar to Chiang Chao-shen, Jao Tsung-i is equally versed in poetry, calligraphy, and painting, and both can be considered two of the last literati artists in modern China. Even though I never studied with Jao Tsung-i, his contributions have been inspiring to me. In 1992, he wrote a piece of graceful calligraphy as the frontispiece for my edited book *Heirs to a Great Tradition: Modern Chinese Paintings from the Tsien-hsiang-chai Collection*.[15]

Even though I have never studied with Hsieh Chih-liu (1910–1997) and Hsü Pang-ta (1911–2012), their writings on the connoisseurship of Chinese calligraphy and painting have served as excellent examples for me. I am a firm believer in the primacy of the art object. Having said that, I also believe that every art object has to be understood in some kind of context. Therefore, I am constantly in search of a way to help me understand an art object in its context; and that is where methodology, by which I mean a study of one's methods, or the metaphysical or philosophical premises of one's methods, whether it is connoisseurship or social art history, comes into play. I do not believe in an absolute, universal method or art theory, or, to use a more current term, simply "theory." I am in agreement with the literary scholar Jonathan Culler when he says, "One of the most dismaying features of theory today is that it is endless. It is not something that you could ever master, not a particular group of texts you could learn so as to 'know theory.'" Nowadays, it seems that if you do not do "theory" you will be considered outdated. I think the danger lies in the possibility of the field being taken over by "theory" without proper attention given to connoisseurship. It is possible for some people to know all the theories in the world (even though, as Culler has observed, "It will depend on who 'you are' and who you want to be"),[16] but not to distinguish a forgery from a genuine painting; worse, they may use a forgery to illustrate their theories. That would be the worst case.

Scholars in the field of Chinese painting in this country, sooner or later, will have to consider the following questions: What are the possible implications of recent developments in, for instance, semiotics and poststructuralist and postmodernist theories for the practice of Chinese art history in general, and that of Chinese painting history in particular? To what extent do we think these theories can help us better understand Chinese painting? To what extent do we think, as scholars working at the beginning of the third decade of the twenty-first century, that we can untangle the meaning of Chinese painting that was done, for instance, in the Northern Sung dynasty?

My approach in research certainly has had a strong impact on my teaching. My approach to teaching can be characterized as contextual, experiential, and critical, and of course I try to infuse my research into my teaching whenever appropriate, for I believe that one teaches best when one teaches what one knows best.

I have always tried to demonstrate to my students how the visual arts embody religious and cultural ideals as well as give expression to social practices. Since different societies and cultures define art in diverse ways, I believe it is important to look at the institutional contexts in which works of art are produced (such as the class basis for Chinese literati painting as well as the distinction between public and private art, and between male and female style in Japan). In my courses, I often begin with an introduction to the environmental and geographical backgrounds of art history.

My concern with a contextual approach to art, however, is matched by my belief that students should respect and experience the concrete art objects themselves. Whenever possible, I have either demonstrated the actual processes of making art (e.g., Chinese calligraphy and painting) or brought in actual works of art to class and asked students to handle them. I have also taken students on field trips to museums in New York, Boston, and Taipei. The interest and enthusiasm of students taking my honors course on Chinese poetry, calligraphy, and painting convinced me that it is important to keep in mind the specificity and concreteness of the work of art.

I have often assigned students to write papers on art objects in nearby museums. To give them the opportunity to work with art objects, I have been able to place students as interns at the Freer and Sackler Galleries in Washington, D.C., as well as at the National Palace Museum in Taipei. I plan to continue to make good use of the excellent art collections in the Washington–Baltimore area.

Furthermore, as I believe that the visual arts cannot be separated from other imaginative and creative activities, I have often encouraged students to take part in relevant programs such as demonstrations of Chinese opera, Japanese *kabuki* (a highly-stylized traditional play with singing and dancing), and Indian music. I have asked students to relate Japanese *emaki-mono* (narrative handscrolls) to Kurosawa's films. I have brought the Chinese film series at the Sackler Gallery to the attention of my students. My goal has been to emphasize an experiential approach to teaching and learning.

Contextualism and attention to concrete works of art, however, are not sufficient. I think it is also important to expose students to the how and the why of art history as an academic discipline and intellectual pursuit. In my introductory courses such as "Art of Asia," I have often begun with a brief discussion of the historiography of Asian art in the West. It has proved most effective to let students know where they have come from before I take them to new territory. In more advanced courses (such as "Chinese Art," "Chinese Painting," and graduate seminars), I would call students' attention to the intellectual backgrounds of individual art historians (e.g., Max Loehr's formalistic approaches and their origins in Henrich Wölfflin, in Kwang-chih Chang's anthropological emphasis in ancient Chinese archaeology, and in James Cahill's increasing semiotic and deconstructionist concerns in his recent writings). Just as I have often reflected on the methodological and historiographical issues in my field of research, I have also often reflected on my teaching.

Although there is a certain core knowledge of art history that I would like students to grasp, I think the most important goal in my teaching is to encourage students to learn how to think critically and how to continue learning on their own, later in life.

To achieve this goal, I have directed a number of independent projects, including an honors paper on the Chinese literati artist Ch'iao Chung-ch'ang and an on-site project in Tokyo on contemporary Japanese architecture. I also try to help students in my lecture courses become independent lifelong learners.

As a lifelong learner myself, I have participated in a year-long faculty discussion group on teaching at Williams College. In the fall of 1991, at the University of Maryland, I participated in a group discussion on teaching as part of the Lilly Teaching Fellowship program. I have also attended several teaching seminars. All of these activities have been quite useful. Above all, I have learned much from my students through observing them in class, reading their examinations and papers, and responding to their suggestions. I shall continue to learn from them. The development of my honors course "Chinese Poetry, Calligraphy and Painting: Visual and Verbal Representation" in 1992 was the result of my participation in a Summer Seminar for College Teachers on "Visual and Verbal Representation" organized by W. J. T. Mitchell, funded by the NEH and sponsored by the University of Chicago in 1988. In order to develop a new course in modern Chinese art, I participated in a Summer Institute for College and University Faculty titled "Modern Chinese Art and Culture," organized by Chu-tsing Li in 1991 (it was funded by the NEH and sponsored by the Kress Foundation Department of Art History and the Spencer Museum of Art at the University of Kansas in Lawrence).

I would like to conclude my reflections on teaching Chinese art in American universities by quoting Vincent Scully, an excellent teacher and art historian at Yale whose teaching has been my model: "Teaching is a combination of Apollo and Dionysus. When you plan, it must be very intellectual, Apollonian, thorough, logical. I only teach things I know very well. The challenge is to balance clarity with the complexity of reality. The aesthetic reaction is constantly leaping out of the logical boxes you set for yourself. Then when you deliver the lecture, you must hope that the emotional, intuitive, Dionysian elements take over and the lecture takes on a rhythm of its own."[17]

Turning now to the new generation of art historians who began their studies in the People's Republic of China and then did their graduate work and continued their work here, I can only speak about Wu Hung and Gao Minglu, because I am more familiar with their work and less knowledgeable about the work of others. They exemplify a new generation of scholars that have a native Chinese cultural background and have experienced the social and political turbulence of the Cultural Revolution, and who later became versed in theoretical approaches in the West through their graduate work and professional experience.

Wu Hung has made judicious use of selected Western theoretical approaches in his work, both in premodern and contemporary Chinese art. The difference between his work and that of the generation who came from China to this country a half century ago (I have in mind people like Wang Fangyu, Chu-tsing Li, Wai-kam Ho, Wen Fong, and Nelson I. Wu) is clear. The previous generation not only had a solid grounding in the Chinese cultural tradition but also had experience in Western art and culture, but as a whole they were less inclined to make use of current theoretical or interpretative tools developed in the West. They have mostly preferred to work within the Chinese cultural tradition. Of course their contribution to the field has been indispensable. In many ways, I am more sympathetic with Wu Hung's approaches. For instance, in my book *Art and Cultural Politics in Postwar Taiwan*, I attempted to incorporate postcolonial theories and postmodern thoughts whenever appropriate.[18] Gao Minglu's work on Chinese contemporary art, in particular the exhibition *Inside Out: New Chinese Art* (1998) with an accompanying catalog, will have a lot of impact on the development of contemporary Chinese art as a subfield in this country.

One major problem with the current curriculum in art history is that many colleges and universities teach only Western art. Survey courses on "art history" often either omit non-Western art entirely or treat non-Western art as afterthoughts or appendices. Some widely used textbooks (such as H. W. Janson's *History of Art*, 4th ed., 1991) do not mention Chinese art; others (such as Frederick Hartt's *Art: A History of Painting, Sculpture, Architecture*, 3rd ed., 1989; *Gardner's Art Through the Ages*, 9th ed., 1991, by Horst de la Croix and others) have responded to the cry for cultural diversity by adding brief chapters on Chinese art to traditional Western art history, rather than balancing and integrating the text as a whole. Hartt places Chinese art at the very end of his book, while discussion on Chinese art in *Gardner's Art through the Ages* follows Gothic Art and precedes the Renaissance.

No wonder non-Western art in general and Chinese art in particular are still either misunderstood or little understood by many experts on Western art, let alone our undergraduate students. Chinese art is still perceived by many in the West as embodiment of the "Gorgeous Orient," despite the tremendous contributions made in the past five decades by many scholars and museum curators in the West to the study, exhibition, and publication of Chinese art.

Western misconceptions about Chinese art have a long history.

During the eighteenth century, chinoiserie, a decorative style in which pseudo-Chinese motifs were mixed with those of India and Japan, was highly popular in Europe. The tendency to lump the arts of all Asian cultures together was continued even among many scholars of Asian art active in the West in the first half of the twentieth century under the strong influence of Ananda K. Coomaraswamy, who maintained that "Asia is One," thereby ignoring the distinctive features of Chinese art as compared with Indian art and Japanese art. They also, perhaps unintentionally, reinforced the centuries-old Western image of Asian art as strange and exotic. Another form of distortion of Chinese art was made by scholars such as Ernest Fenollosa, who saw Chinese art through Japanese eyes and dismissed Chinese painting since the mid-13th century as "formless and woolly" and as "the deification of the dead bones of formalism."

Until recently, many Western scholars disparaged Chinese painting because it did not utilize oils, Western perspective, and chiaroscuro. The reason was simple. As late as the 1950s and 1960s, even historians of Asian art active in the West were for the most part trained first in Western art. No wonder many of them accepted as a truth that the linear progress of Italian art from the fourteenth century to the seventeenth was paradigmatic of all artistic developments.

Even though the monographic approach in later Chinese painting (especially from the Yuan dynasty on) will likely continue for some time to come, because there is still a large body of textual and visual material to be collected, authenticated, and presented in the form of traditional monographs on single artists or a group of artists, a more interpretative approach will become common in the near future. I also believe that the idea of visual culture, as opposed to the elitist idea of the primacy of the literati tradition (whether pre-Tung Ch'i-ch'ang or post-Tung Ch'i-ch'ang) will become more popular. In fact, in the edited volume *Visual Culture in Shanghai, 1850s–1930s*,[19] which grew out of a U.S.–China cooperative research project on art in Shanghai that I organized and directed under the auspices of the Henry Luce Foundation from 1993 to 1999, I tried to look at an important aspect of modern Chinese art. In this volume, through commissioning a number of essays from historians and literary historians in addition to art historians, I tried to present a multifarious visual culture, in a variety of media, in Shanghai in order to dramatize the complexity of modernity in China. In another edited volume, *Calendar-Posters: History, Art, and Culture* (Taipei: SMC Publishing, in press), I also tried to argue, through my editor's introduction and the commissioned essays, that the mass-produced calendar-posters from the 1930s and 1940s in fact embody Chinese modernity better than traditional Chinese painting.

At the risk of oversimplification, however, I still think that we should pay more attention to the connoisseurship of calligraphy and painting. As John Walsh, Director of the Getty Center, aptly put it in his convocation speech at the 1999 annual meeting of the College Art Association, one of the most important challenges facing art historians and museum professionals today is that graduate schools have produced art historians with serious weaknesses, particularly a lack of direct firsthand experience with original works of art. As Walsh convincingly argued, this situation could be attributed to a major shift in the field of art history since the 1960s toward contextual and theoretical questions about art and its functions. Although we have gained a broader understanding of art and its history because of this shift in our teaching and study, we have also neglected the works of art themselves to the extent that it is entirely possible for graduate students to get advanced degrees without working with original works, for contextual and theoretical approaches to art history often ignore original works of art. Indeed, in the book *The Art of Art History: A Critical Anthology*, edited by Donald Preziosi (Oxford University Press, 1998), which is hailed by Norman Bryson of Harvard University as "definitely the best introduction to art history currently available," there is very little, if any, attention to connoisseurship. Walsh called for closer cooperation between art history programs and museums in rectifying this deficiency in our education of both future art historians and museum professionals.

In this country, graduate programs in Chinese art in general and in Chinese calligraphy and painting in particular have not escaped this general problem. In fact, many of our advanced graduate students and recent recipients of Ph.D.s in Chinese art have received very little, if any, formal training in connoisseurship. Many of them could not decipher the calligraphy written in cursive and seal scripts in the inscriptions or colophons that accompany Chinese paintings, or legends of seals used by calligraphers, painters, and collectors that are found on almost every piece of Chinese painting. Thus, in many cases, they could not even identify important information about the works of art, let alone make a sound judgment about their quality or authenticity. As to the nature of brushwork in Chinese calligraphy and painting, because these students rarely possess experience in creating calligraphy and painting with the pliant brush employed by Chinese calligraphers and painters, they often fail to see patterns in the ways that Chinese calligraphers and painters make decisions, and fail to connect these patterns to the art of the past. It is no surprise that connoisseurship in Chinese calligraphy and painting is often avoided not only by art history graduate students but even by the faculty. To construct art history from art works unproven as to their authorship and dates of production results in a "history" without foundation and of little value. If we base our construction of art history on works of calligraphy and painting and on the inscriptions, colophons, and seal impressions that accompany them, we must first make sure of their authorship and identity. For these reasons, I organized three iterations of the Summer Institute for Chinese Calligraphy and Painting Connoisseurship with the support of the Henry Luce Foundation (they were held at the University of Maryland with museum sessions in the Freer and Sackler Galleries in Washington, D.C., in 2001 and 2003 and at the National Taiwan Normal University with museum sessions in the National Palace Museum in Taipei in 2002).

As we enter the third decade of the twenty-first century, the study of modern and contemporary Chinese art will become more important. In contrast to extensive literature on premodern Asian art, there has been very little, if any, serious scholarly study of modern and contemporary Asian art as a whole by mainstream art historians working in Europe and North America. Introductory college texts either ignore it completely or denigrate it (e.g., Sherman E. Lee's *History of Far Eastern Art* [5th edition], where we read that, for example, "Rajput painting deteriorated sadly by the middle of the nineteenth century"; that "China in the nineteenth century…was not a fountainhead of great painting"; and that there was a "sad decline of Japanese art in the late nineteenth and early twentieth century").[20] Since scholars of Asian art have in general ignored the subject, there is no surprise then to find that most surveys of art history published in the United States (e.g., H. W. Janson and Anthony F. Janson, *History of Art*) have not devoted any space to modern and contemporary Asian art.[21] The only exceptions are Hugh Honour and John Fleming, *The Visual Arts: A History*, where contemporary Chinese art is noted briefly, and Marilyn Stokstad and others, *Art History*, where modern art in India, China, and Japan is covered in about three pages in contrast to three long chapters devoted to modern and contemporary art in Europe and North America.[22] I am really encouraged that scholars in the United States are paying more attention to Chinese art of the twentieth century. I hope that eventually their research, publications, and exhibitions will find their ways into major college textbooks.

Notes

An early version of this essay was published as my responses to a series of questions posed by Jerome Silbergeld and included in Jason C. Kuo, ed., *Discovering Chinese Painting: Dialogues with American Art Historians* (Dubuque, Iowa: Kendall/Hunt Publishing, 2000), 167–88 (second edition as *Discovering Chinese Painting: Dialogues with Art Historians*: 2006, 227–48). Interested readers may refer to the earlier publications for the original questions posed by Silbergeld, to whom I am most grateful for his probing questions and subsequent suggestions.

1. *T'o-fang wen-hsueh* 1 (February 1969), 53.
2. Wai-lim Yip, *Ezra Pound's* Cathay (Princeton: Princeton University Press, 1969). Examples of his poetry can be found under "Ye Weilian" in Michelle Mi-Hsi Yeh and N. G. D. Malmqvist, eds., *Frontier Taiwan: An Anthology of Modern Chinese Poetry* (New York: Columbia University Press, 2001), 231–38.
3. New York: Schocken Books, 1963.
4. Taipei: Tung-ta Publishing, 1987.
5. Jason Kuo, "Word and Image in 'Watching the Waterfall at Mt. Lu' by Shih-t'ao," *The National Palace Museum Bulletin* 28, no. 5 (November–December 1993): 1–16.
6. Berlin: Ernst Rowohlt Verlag, 1932. The first English version was

published as *Film*, translated from the German by L. M. Sieveking and Ian F. D. Morrow, with a preface by Paul Rotha (London: Faber and Faber, 1933); an adaptation of *Film* was publish as *Film as Art* (Berkeley: University of California Press, 1957). Most of his film essays and criticism, written between 1925 and 1940, were collected and republished in Germany as Rudolf Arnheim, *Kritiken und Aufsätze zum Film* (München: C. Hanser, 1977) and translated into English (by Brenda Benthien) as Rudolf Arnheim, *Film Essays and Criticism* (Madison: University of Wisconsin Press, 1997), where readers can find a very useful "Complete Bibliography of Writings on Film by Rudolf Arnheim" compiled by Helmut H. Diederichs (pp. 233–48). Arnheim's relevance to contemporary cinema and media studies can be seen in Nathan Holmes, "Rudolf Arnheim: Cinema and Partial Illusion," in *Thinking in the Dark: Cinema, Theory, Practice*, ed. Murray Pomerance and R. Baron Palmer (New Brunswick: Rutgers University Press, 2016), 101–12.
7   Most recently, it was re-typeset in simplified characters and retitled as *Chung-kuo yi-shu chih te-chih* by Huang-shan shu-she in Ho-fei in 2012.
8   In the series The Great Ages of World Architecture, New York: George Braziller, 1963.
9   Princeton: Art Museum, Princeton University, 1976, 113–29.
10 New York: China House Gallery, China Institute in America, 1992.
11 *Double Beauty: Qing Dynasty Couplets from the Lechangzai Xuan Collection*, co-edited with Peter Sturman (Hong Kong: Art Museum, Chinese University of Hong Kong, 2003).The exhibition was held at the Art Museum, the Chinese University of Hong Kong; the Honolulu Academy of Fine Arts; and the Santa Barbara Museum of Art.
12 "Hui-chou Merchants as Art Patrons in the Late Sixteenth and Early Seventeenth Centuries," in *Artists and Patrons: Some Social and Economic Aspects of Chinese Painting*, ed. Chu-tsing Li, with James Cahill and Wai-kam Ho (Lawrence, KS: Kress Foundation Department of Art History, University of Kansas; Nelson-Atkins Museum of Art, 1989), 177–88.
13 Taipei: Fine Arts Museum, 1991, pp. 38–94.
14 *Chien-chiang chih-liao-chi* (Ho-fei: Anhui jen-min ch'u-pan-she, 1964); a revised edition was published in 1984.
15 College Park, Md.: Department of Art History and Archaeology, University of Maryland; distributed by the University of Washington Press, Seattle and London, 1992.
16 Jonathan Culler, *Literary Theory: A Very Short Introduction* (Oxford: Oxford University Press, 1997), 15–16.
17 Quoted in Donald K. Jarvis, *Junior Faculty Development: A Handbook* (New York: The Modern Language Association of America, 1991), 67.

18 Bethesda, CDL Press; distributed by the University of Washington Press, Seattle and London, 2000; revised ed. published by SMC Publishing, Taipei, 2001.
19 Washington, DC: New Academia Publishing, 2007.
20 New York: Harry N. Abrams, 1994, pp. 262, 505, 549.
21 Revised, fifth ed., New York: Harry N. Abrams, 1997.
22 Honour and Fleming: fifth ed. (Upper Saddle River, NJ: Prentice Hall, 2000); Stokstad et al.: revised ed. (New York, Harry N. Abrams, 1999).

About the Editor

Jason C. Kuo is Professor of Art History and Archaeology, University of Maryland, College Park. He has taught at the National Taiwan University, Williams College, and Yale University. He was a Fellow at the Freer Gallery, a Stoddard Fellow at the Detroit Institute of Arts, and an Andrew W. Mellon Fellow at the Metropolitan Museum of Art, and he has received grants from the J. D. Rockefeller III Fund, the National Endowment for the Humanities, and the Henry Luce Foundation.

He is the author of *Wang Yuanqi de shanshuihua yishu* [Wang Yuanqi's Art of Landscape Painting] (1981), *Long tiandi yu xingnei* [Trapping Heaven and Earth in the Cage of Form] (1986), *The Austere Landscape: The Paintings of Hung-jen* (1992), *Yishushi yu yishu piping de tanshuo* [Rethinking Art History and Art Criticism] (1996), *Art and Cultural Politics in Postwar Taiwan* (2000), *Yishushi yu yishu piping de shijian* [Practicing Art History and Art Criticism] (2002), *Transforming Traditions in Modern Chinese Painting: Huang Pin-hung's Late Work* (2004), *Chinese Ink Painting Now* (2010), *The Inner Landscape: The Paintings of Gao Xingjian* (2013), and *The Poet's Brush: Chinese Ink Paintings by Lo Ch'ing* (2016).

He has curated exhibitions such as *Innovation within Tradition: The Painting of Huang Pin-hung* (1989), *Word as Image: The Art of Chinese Seal Engraving* (1992), *Born of Earth and Fire: Chinese Ceramics from the Scheinman Collection* (1992), *Heirs to a Great Tradition: Modern Chinese Paintings from the Tsien-hsiang-chai Collection* (1993), *The Helen D. Ling Collection of Chinese Ceramics* (1995), *Double Beauty: Qing Dynasty Couplets from the Lechangzai Xuan Collection* (with Peter Sturman) (2003), *The Inner Landscape: The Films and Paintings of Gao Xingjian* (2013), and *Lo Ch'ing: A Contemporary Chinese Poet-Painter* (2018). His edited books include *Contemporary Chinese Art and Film: Theory Applied and Resisted* (2013). He currently serves on the International Advisory Board of the *Journal of Contemporary Chinese Art* and the Editorial Board of the book series Philosophy of Film, published by Brill.

About the Authors

Anne Burkus-Chasson (Ph.D., University of California, Berkeley, 1987) writes about seventeenth-century Chinese paintings and woodblock-printed books. Her articles, several of which have been translated into Chinese, have appeared in the *Art Bulletin*, *Art History*, and the *Journal of Chinese Literature and Culture*. Her book, *Through a Forest of Chancellors: Fugitive Histories in Liu Yuan's Lingyan ge, an Illustrated Book from Seventeenth-Century Suzhou*, was published by the Harvard University Asia Center, Harvard University Press, in 2010. In 2017–18, she was Senior Fellow at the Center for Advanced Study in the Visual Arts, National Gallery of Art, Washington, DC. She is currently writing a book tentatively entitled *Chen Hongshou (1598–1652) and the Illustrated Book*.

Arnold Chang was born in 1954 in New York City. He studied art history with Professor James Cahill, and holds a master's degree from the University of California, Berkeley, and a bachelor's degree from the University of Colorado. He studied painting and connoisseurship with C.C Wang for twenty-five years. Chang has taught Chinese art at Columbia University, Connecticut College, and Arizona State University; has organized several exhibitions; and is the author of a book and numerous exhibition catalogues and articles on Chinese painting. Chang served for many years as Vice President and Director of Chinese Paintings at Sotheby's, and was formerly a painting specialist at Kaikodo Gallery in New York. Chang's own landscape paintings have been exhibited internationally and are in the permanent collections of many museums, including the Metropolitan Museum of Art, the British Museum, the Asian Art Museum SF, and LACMA.

Noelle Giuffrida is assistant professor of Asian art at Ball State University and assistant curator of Asian art at the David Owsley Museum of Art. Her research focuses on Chinese art, particularly the history of collecting and exhibiting premodern works in the

United States after World War II and the visual culture of Daoism in imperial China. Her teaching and curatorial experience extend broadly both temporally—from Neolithic to contemporary—and cross-culturally—from China, Korea, and Japan, to South and Southeast Asia. Giuffrida's first book, *Separating Sheep from Goats: Sherman E. Lee's Collecting of Chinese Art in Postwar America* (Berkeley: University of California Press, 2018), excavates an international society of collectors, dealers, curators, and scholars who comprised the art world of the 1930s through the 1980s. Her Daoist-related publications include articles and book chapters on imagery and narratives associated with the Daoist god Zhenwu (the Perfected Warrior) and the patriarchs Zhang Daoling, Xu Xun, and Lü Dongbin.

Stephen J. Goldberg is Professor of Art History at Hamilton College, Clinton, New York. He received his Ph.D. in the history of Asian art from the University of Michigan with a specialization in the history and aesthetics of Chinese painting and calligraphy. Publishing widely in books, periodicals, and exhibition catalogs, he pursues issues concerning identity, subjectivity, and voice in traditional and contemporary Chinese painting, and the aesthetic reception of Chinese calligraphy. His most recent publication is *André Kneib and the Art of Chinese Calligraphy* (Paris: Mare and Martin, 2018), which has also been translated into French and Chinese.

Jerome Silbergeld is the P. Y. and Kinmay W. Tang Professor of Chinese Art History at Princeton University, emeritus, and was the director of Princeton's Tang Center for East Asian Art. He is the author of *Chinese Painting Style: Media, Methods, and Principles of Form*; *China into Film: Frames of Reference in Contemporary Chinese Cinema*; *Contradictions: Artistic Life, the Socialist State, and the Chinese Painter Li Huasheng* (with Gong Jisui); *Body in Question: Image and Illusion in Two Chinese Films by Director Jiang Wen*. His recent books include *Persistence—Transformation: Text as Image in the Art of Xu Bing* and *ARTiculations: Undefining Chinese Contemporary Art* (both coedited with Dora C. Y. Ching and published by P. Y. and Kinmay W. Tang Center for East Asian Art, Princeton University). He is Visiting Professor of Chinese Art History, Department of the History of Art and Architecture, University of Oregon.

Nancy S. Steinhardt is Professor of East Asian Art and Curator of Chinese Art at the University of Pennsylvania. She has broad research interests in the art and architecture of China and China's border regions, particularly in the interaction between Chinese art and the art of peoples to the North, Northeast, and Northwest. She is author or coauthor of *Chinese Imperial City Planning*; *Liao Architecture*, *Chinese Architecture and the Beaux-Arts*; *Chinese Architecture in an Age of Turmoil*; *China's Early Mosques*; and *Chinese Architecture: A History*. Steinhardt is a member of the board of directors of the Society of Architectural Historians.

Xiaoqing Zhu (Ph.D., University of Maryland, College Park) is Professor in Humanities and Art History at Central Pennsylvania Community College and was Visiting Professor of Art History at Gettysburg College (2018–2019). Her writings on modern Chinese art have appeared in anthologies and exhibition catalogs such as *Chinese Artists in Paris* (Paris: Musée Cernuschi, 2011).